The
Story of Luton

James Dyer & John G. Dony

with a Foreword by
The Rt Hon The Lord Hill of Luton

White Crescent Press Ltd

Luton

ISBN 0 900804 11 4

In Memory

of

Charles Freeman

©

1st Edition 1964

2nd Edition, revised 1966

3rd Edition, extensively revised 1975

Printed and Published by White Crescent Press Ltd, Luton

The text is set in 12pt 'Monotype' Bembo   H1423

The Story of Luton

Preface

IT IS TEN YEARS since the First Edition of this brief history of Luton was published. This co-incided with the securing by the town of county borough status which was lost in 1974 by a re-organisation of local government. The first nine chapters of the First Edition were the responsibility of James Dyer and remain here with comparatively little change. The dates he has given in Chapters 2 and 3 for the period before the Norman Conquest are based on those given in the *Anglo-Saxon Chronicle*. There are, however, four slightly different versions of this and whilst what appear to be the best authenticated dates have been chosen, they do not always agree with those used by ealier workers.

The remainder of the First Edition was contributed jointly by John G. Dony and Frank Stygall, the latter being mainly respon-sible for a sound analysis of the various factors governing the industrial structure of Luton in 1964. Much of this forms an essential part of the revision which now becomes necessary after the passage of ten years. With Mr Stygall no longer resident in Luton the last seven chapters have become the full responsibility of John G. Dony who has been able to give a more complex account of the churches, educational developments and the struc-ture of the hat industry than was previously possible.

The Preface to the First Edition acknowledged the advice and assistance of many people to whom we give our continued thanks. We wish now to thank in addition the present staffs of Luton Museum and Art Gallery and Luton Public Library, and also Mr David H. Kennett and Mr Terence P. Smith for their valued comments. We express once more our indebtedness to previous local historians and above all to William Austin for his comprehensive *History of Luton*. We are again conscious that in a work of this kind, notwithstanding our care, there may be errors. These we trust are few compared with omissions which many of our readers may regret. What has been achieved here will we trust be of use to the town's school children and their teachers, as well as of interest to a wider public.

JOHN G. DONY
JAMES DYER

Maps

Contents

Illustrations in the Art Section

The Trade Token illustrated on the title page was issued by
Richard Hopkins of the Red Lion Inn, in 1666

A collection of 145 pictures of OLD LUTON is available from the
same publishers or from booksellers

Sources of Illustrations

Art plates A to P between pages 80 and 81

The publishers acknowledge their obligation to the organisations and photographers for illustrations which appear in this book.

Birmingham Museum and Art Gallery   I▲
Parker Library, Corpus Christi College, Cambridge   E▲
Cecil Higgins Art Gallery, Bedford   K▲
County Records Office, Bedford (Collection of Mrs Casebourne)   J▲

Rev. H. E. Frankham   F▲
The late A. C. Jordan, Esq, (Dyer Collection)   M, P▼
Luton Museum and Art Gallery   A, C▲, D, E▼, H▼, I▼, N
The Luton News   B, J▼, L▼
Eric G. Meadows, Esq   F▼, G, H▲
Walter R. Rainbow   C▼
Skefko Ball Bearing Co Ltd   O▼
Vauxhall Motors Ltd   O▼, P▲

ENGLISH-METRIC EQUIVALENTS

LENGTH

Inch	= 25.4 millimetres	Centimetre	= 0.393 in	
Foot	= 30.48 centimetres	Metre	= 1.093 yd	= 0.049 chain
Yard	= 0.9144 metre	Kilometre	= 0.621 mile	= 4.97 furlongs
Mile	= 1.609 kilometres		= 1093.6 yd	

AREA

sq inch	= 6.45 sq cm	sq cm	= 0.155 sq in	
sq yard	= 0.8361 sq m	Centiare (1 sq m)	= 1.196 sq yd	
Acre	= 0.404 hectare	Hectare (10,000 sq m)	= 2.471 acres	
sq mile	= 2.589 sq km	sq km	= 0.386 sq mile	

Change in the Monetary System

In 1971 a decimal system of currency was introduced replacing one of a long standing in which there were twelve pence (12d) in a shilling and twenty shillings (20s) in a pound (£1). For obvious reasons prices in the past must be related to the old system as with prices having risen in the course of time little useful purpose is served in trying to give their equivalents in the decimal system.

xi

Some Books to Read

A complete list of books and articles dealing with various aspects of Luton's past history can be found in *A Bedfordshire Bibliography*, L. R. Conisbee (1962) and its Supplements (1967 and 1971). The works mentioned here are the major sources only.

The History of Luton, Frederick Davis (1855) and its second edition, *Luton, Past and Present* (1874) are interesting, but contain much that is unreliable. William Austin's two volume *History of Luton* (1928) still remains the standard work, but, as it was published posthumously, the second volume, dealing with the more recent events, lacks a theme and an interpretation.

The prehistory of the Luton neighbourhood received much attention from Worthington G. Smith and the reader is especially referred to his *Man the Primeval Savage* (1894) and his paper in *Archaeologia*, Vol. 67 (1916) in which he discusses his discoveries at Round Green.

Luton Church: Historical and Descriptive Henry Cobbe (1899) is a sound, but somewhat tedious, work. There are a number of books dealing with various aspects of the hat industry, and for further information the reader is referred to *A History of the Straw Hat Industry*, John G. Dony (1942) and *Luton and the Straw Hat Industry*, C. E. Freeman (1953), both of which contain bibliographies. The *Report on Luton*, F. Grundy and R. Titmuss (1945) contains a great deal of information on the town in the immediate post-war period. Education has been covered by John G. Dony's *A History of Education in Luton* (1970).

Many works dealing with the county contain much relating to Luton, and the most useful of these are the three volumes of the *Victoria County History of Bedfordshire* (1908) and Joyce Godber's *History of Bedfordshire* (1969). Luton's buildings are considered in Nikolaus Pevsner's *Bedfordshire, Huntingdon and Peterborough* (1968) in his Buildings of England series. A number of volumes of the *Transactions of the Bedfordshire Historical Record Society* are devoted to Luton and the immediate neighbourhood, and articles of archaeological and historical interest have appeared in the *Bedfordshire Archaeological Journal*. Equally informative articles appear from time to time in *The Bedfordshire Magazine*.

Foreword *By* THE RIGHT HON LORD HILL OF LUTON

I HAVE KNOWN Luton well for some thirty years and, even in that time, the changes in its size, its character and its people have been dramatic. But thirty years is but a snapshot of time in a history which may well have begun a quarter of a million years ago! The mind may boggle but the archaeologists have some evidence for such an assertion. Beyond doubt, some hunters of fish or fowl, renouncing the wandering life, settled beside the springs of the River Lea at Leagrave about three thousand years B.C., some of their descendants moving on a thousand years later to where the Runfold Estate now stands.

Then, another thousand years on, the men of Luton stood sturdily to an army of invading Danes and defeated them.

To hurry on over the centuries, in 1066, an army of William the Conqueror invaded Luton sacking Biscot on the way and, in the fourteenth century, Luton's Parish Church of St. Mary – its greatest monument of the past – was built. Such items of Luton's longer history are but a tiny selection of the historical facts assembled with such skill and clarity in this remarkable book.

The recent history of Luton is no less fascinating. The origins and ups and downs of the hat industry, the influence of the churches, the arrival of the railway, the growth of education and the evolution of local government, the assault of the temperance movement on drink (one pub for every 77 inhabitants in 1871), the birth of Luton Town Football Club in 1885 (professional players received five shillings a match!) – these are but few of the pieces in the fretwork of Luton's history in the nineteenth century. And, of course, the story is told of the twentieth century revolution which turned Luton into a large and predominantly engineering town and brought thousands of men and women from all over the country.

It is in the setting of the past that some of the problems of the present and the future can be more clearly seen. It is especially good when one can look back with the help of two such extra-ordinarily well informed guides and delightful writers as James Dyer and John Dony in this fascinating edition of *The Story of Luton*.

HILL OF LUTON

Census	Population	Census	Population
1821	2,986	1901	36,404
1831	3,961	1911	49,978
1841	5,827	1921	61,342
1851	10,648	1931	70,486
1861	15,329	1951	110,381
1871	17,317	1961	131,505
1881	23,960	1971	161,178
1891	30,053		

The Mayors of Luton

1 The Beginnings of Luton

LUTON lies at the northern end of a river gap in the Chiltern Hills, thirty miles north of London. One of its earliest names, Lygetun, means 'the enclosure by the river Lea', and it was as a riverside settlement that Luton first entered the pages of history. Today excessive drainage has so reduced the size of the river, that it no longer plays any effective part in the town's function. From its banks houses have spread in all directions, especially on to the wide, alluvial, fan-shaped plain which sweeps from Warden Hill on the east to Blows Downs on the west. Between these points the town is $3\frac{1}{2}$ miles wide, whilst from Vauxhall in the south, to Sundon Park in the north a distance of $4\frac{1}{2}$ miles is covered. Within this span, an area of about 12 square miles is devoted to houses, shops, schools, factories, streets and parks.

One hundred years ago, the buildings and streets of our town covered less than a square mile. The reasons for this sudden phenomenal growth will become clear in the later chapters of this book. For centuries, until this growth spurt, Luton had been first a small farming community and then a tiny market town; in the seventeenth and eighteenth centuries it can be described as a town in decay and then, early in the nineteenth century, the development of the straw hat industry changed Luton into a pleasant but dirty factory town, the chief centre of hat manufacture in the south-east Midlands. In the twentieth century the decline of the hat industry has been balanced by the introduction of new industries, primarily in the engineering fields.

THE POSITION OF LUTON

We have said that Luton is situated on an undulating, fan-shaped wedge of gravel at the northern end of the Lea gap through the Chilterns. The town lies in a natural amphitheatre open only towards Sundon in the north-west and Luton Hoo in the south.

Chalk hills rise steeply to the north, east and south. The main railway line from London to Leicester and the north passes north-westwards through the town from the Lea valley.

The valley through which the river Lea runs is a mile wide and 200 ft deep south of Luton near Luton Hoo. Clearly such a valley could not have been cut by so tiny a river as the present river Lea. No detailed study has yet been written about the formation of the valley, but the general sequence would seem to have been as follows.

Thousands of years ago in geological times, the chalk hills continued further north into Bedfordshire. From some point many miles north of Luton a much longer river Lea flowed south-wards, cutting a deep river valley across the country past the place where Luton now stands. With the coming of the Ice Ages the head-waters of this river were cut off and the water ceased to flow. When the Ice Age glaciers began to melt, water poured through the river gap, modifying it to some extent, but for the most part its shape had already been determined. The ice sheets removed most of the higher chalk land leaving only a few out-lying spurs such as Galley Hill and Warden Hill. The new river Lea that ran southwards following the old course, was a much reduced version of its former self, what geomorphologists – people who study how the land has been shaped – would call a 'misfit'.

OLD STONE AGE MAN

The first traces of human occupation also belong to this early period. On the hills to the east of the town at Round Green and Mixes Hill, flint implements of the Palaeolithic period have been found in their thousands. These Old Stone Age tools were not found lying on the modern ground surface, but at depths of from 12 to 25 ft under the brick earth in old clay pits dug at the end of the last century to obtain material for making bricks.

A London architect named Worthington Smith moved to Dunstable in 1884 where he was able to follow his hobby of collecting ancient remains. He became interested in prehistoric flint implements when he found them buried deep down in clay pits in London and at Caddington, and he later traced similar flints in the Luton pits. He was able to show that men of the

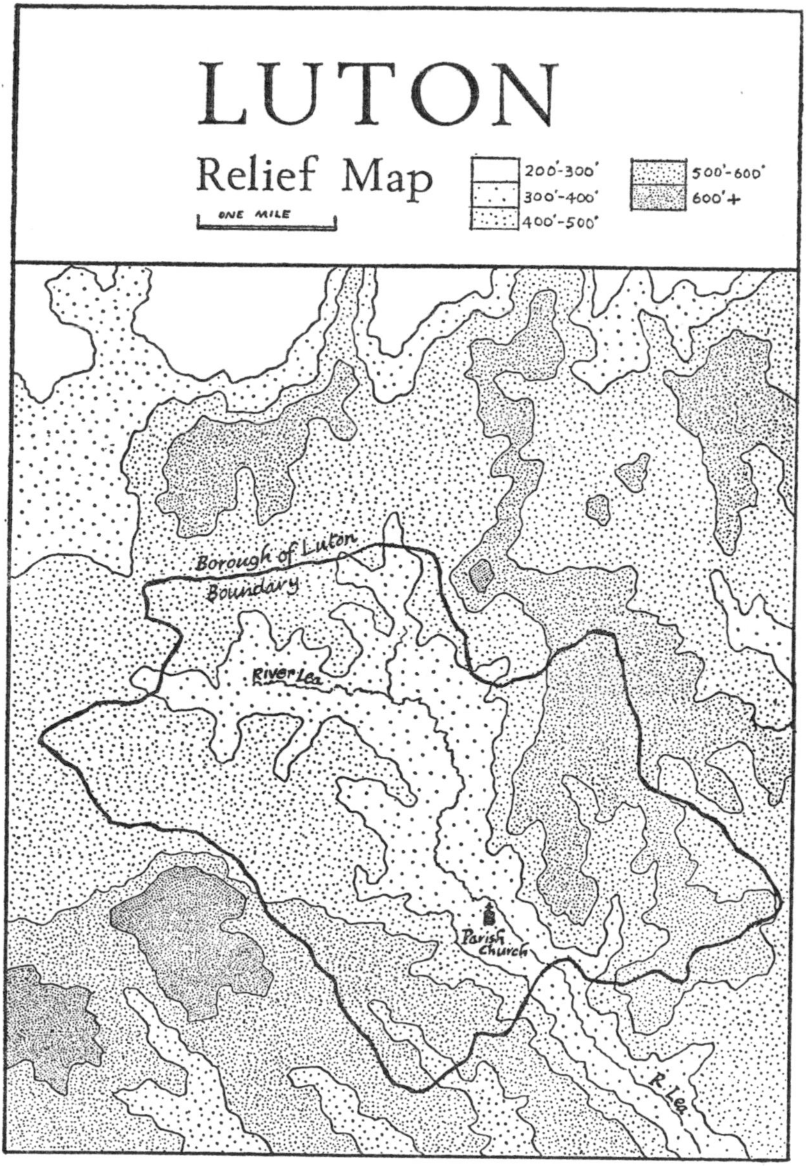

LUTON

Relief Map

ONE MILE

200'–300'	500'–600'
300'–400'	600'+
400'–500'	

Borough of Luton Boundary

River Lea

Parish Church

R. Lea

middle Acheulean period (about 250,000 BC) had camped beside lakes on the hills above the old river Lea. Here the men hunted wild animals like the bear and mammoth whenever they came to drink at the lakeside. Sometimes they built dead-fall traps; but more often they simply threw their wooden spears or stone axes at the beasts.

With the coming of the last Ice Age, great quantities of clay and flints were pushed southwards across the Midlands until the ice sheets stopped, exhausted, across southern Bedfordshire. Much of the material in front of the ice was pushed over the chalk hills to the south, depositing a contorted mass of clay and flints 12 ft or more deep over the lakeside settlements of the Acheulean men. It was this glacial debris that the brick workers of the last century dug away to reveal the Stone Age tools beneath.

One of the most important Palaeolithic finds was also one of the most frustrating. In one of the Mixes Hill clay pits, under the western end of what is today Sunningdale road, at a depth of 22 ft, was the complete skeleton of a man about 5 ft 6 in in height. The man lay on his right-hand side together with flint implements and animal bones. The bones were terribly soft and Worthington Smith, who found them late one evening, left them until the next day to dry out. When he arrived at the clay pit, having walked from Dunstable, he found to his horror that the workmen had smashed up the burial and thrown the pieces away. Had he been able to remove them, Smith would have found one of the earliest skeletons ever uncovered in Britain, about 250,000 years old.

Although we can show that man lived in the Luton area so long ago, we cannot really claim that at the time he played any part in the development of our town. It was not until the Ice Age had reshaped the hills and river valley that the Luton district bore the slightest resemblance to its present land form.

For thousands of years England was covered with forest, lake and swamp. Only as the climate slowly grew warmer did animals such as the deer move from the sunny areas of southern Europe back into Britain. In those days our country was still joined to the Continent.

If we can imagine the Luton area of 10,000 years ago, we must visualise hills covered with oak and ash forests which extended down to the banks of the river Lea. The river was wide and marshy and bordered by bushes and clumps of reeds and rushes. An extensive area of marsh lay around the springs of the river at Leagrave, where it remained until draining began at the beginning of the present century. One legacy of the Ice Age was a low ridge of gravel called a moraine, which ran roughly from south-west to north-east across the northern end of the Luton gap between Leagrave and Warden Hill.

We call the period when the ice had retreated, and Britain was covered by forests and marshes, the Mesolithic or Middle Stone

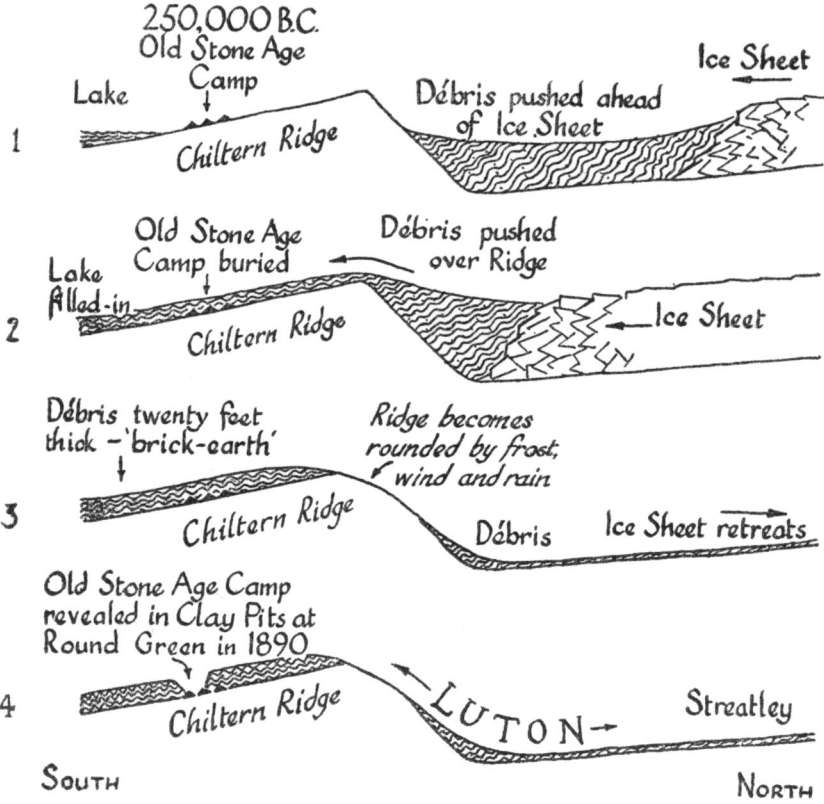

These diagrams show how the Old Stone Age Camp at Round Green was buried beneath 20 ft of brick-earth during the last Ice Age.

Age. Mesolithic men inhabited the Leagrave area, possibly living in hollows scooped in the river gravels, sheltered with branches and skins. Again it is the flint tools that he left behind him which have been preserved to show us where he lived. A pick-like Mesolithic tool was found in excavations beside Leagrave Marsh a few years ago and was possibly used to dig out roots, which supplemented a diet of berries, fish and meat.

New Stone Age Man

About 3,400 BC the Neolithic or New Stone Age men moved into Britain from France and the mouth of the Rhine, bringing with them the first pottery, cattle and seed corn. By that time the English Channel had formed, so we can imagine that the journey, probably on rafts, was a rather hazardous one. These early farmers must have built themselves wooden houses, though few traces have remained. We know more about them from the long barrows in which they buried their more important dead. In our part of the country such barrows were made by covering a small wooden hut containing the dead man or woman with a long mould of chalk. The old Biscot Windmill seems to have stood on one such barrow, and another lay beside the Icknield Way at the foot of Galley Hill, but both have been destroyed. The remains of one can be seen on the county boundary east of Pegsdon, whilst a good example lies on the Heath at Royston in Hertfordshire. Sometimes Neolithic burials were made in round burial mounds. A barrow on Galley Hill excavated in 1961 covered a shallow grave in which lay the dismembered remains of a young man, together with scraps of Neolithic pottery. In Roman times a second person had been buried over the first, scattering some of the earlier bones. Whether the first young man had died a natural death and had then been dismembered, or whether he had been the victim of some form of sacrifice, we shall never know.

From East Anglia to Wiltshire ran the trackway known as the Icknield Way. This track was certainly in use in Neolithic times and passed right across the area that was later to become Luton, by following the slightly higher well-drained gravel moraine already mentioned. We should not visualise the early Icknield Way as a roadway, or even a bridle way. It is most likely to have been a belt of relatively open countryside along which travellers passed at will, avoiding muddy patches and fallen trees, and so causing their path to meander about. Outside the Borough boundary to the north of the Icknield Way near Barton Hill Farm, stood a rough Neolithic building within an encircling bank and chalk-dug ditch. The building was made of wood, 12 ft long and $5\frac{1}{2}$ ft wide. Outside it, but inside the surrounding ditch, were two burials. One was of an old woman, the other of a boy of about 16. The boy had a shale bead under his chin and a joint of meat at his side – perhaps a last present from his grief-stricken mother. The building might have been a temple, or 'mortuary chapel', where the dead were stored until there were enough bodies to warrant all the labour of constructing a burial mound. There was evidence to show that processions or dances may have taken place around the graves.

These first Neolithic farmers are known as the Windmill Hill folk. This name comes from one of their earthworks found on Windmill Hill near Avebury in Wiltshire. The earthwork consisted of three concentric banks of earth, the material for them being quarried from a series of interrupted or causewayed ditches. Such earthworks were once thought of as camps, but this view is not often held nowadays, mainly because there were few signs of permanent occupation inside them. Instead they seem to have been communal meeting places in which the special business of the farmers was carried out. Perhaps it was here that laws were made and upheld, and tribal ceremonies, initiations, and religious observances, connected with seed-sowing and the harvest were carried out. After the important tribal business was over trading seems to have taken place, rather like the fairs of the Middle Ages, where people could buy or sell pots or flint implements, cattle or sheep. Such an earthwork is known at Maiden Bower near Dunstable, and another may have existed at Streatley, although it has not yet been excavated.

THE FIRST SETTLEMENT AT LEAGRAVE

Around the marshes of the river Lea at Leagrave, Mesolithic hunters and fishermen came into contact with the Windmill Hill folk. The hunters seem to have realised that a permanent way of life had many advantages. If you keep cattle and grow corn you no longer need to spend all your time hunting and collecting

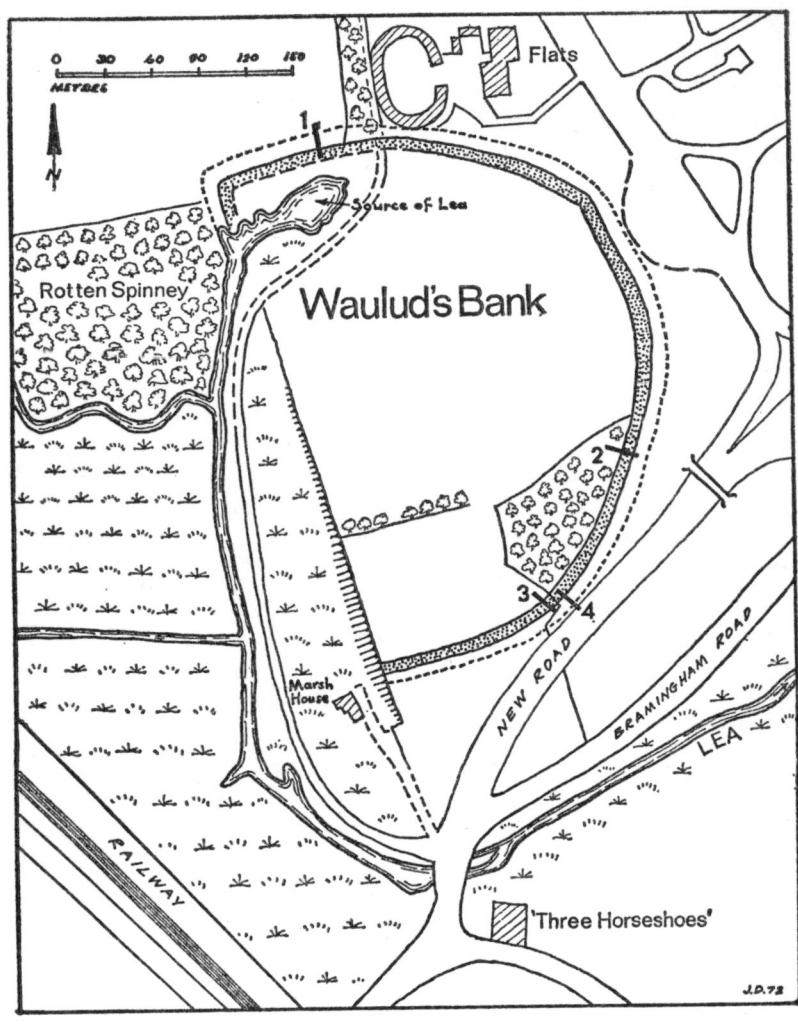

Waulud's Bank showing position of excavations in 1954 and 1972.

berries or roots; although a certain amount of fishing and fowling provided a valuable addition to the diet. So it was that people who for centuries had lived a wandering life following herds of wild animals and birds as they moved about in search of fresh grazing grounds, decided to settle beside the springs of the river Lea some

3,000 years BC. They chose to live at the foot of a low gravel hill in what today is Sundon Park Recreation Ground. Here a small circular hut was found, 3 m in diameter, with wattle and daub walls. The ground inside the hut had been slightly hollowed out to make leg-room. The building must have been very flimsy and may have been only a temporary summer shelter.

Above the hut and round the hill a strong bank of gravel, clay and chalk was made, the material dug from a deep, wide ditch, reinforced with stout wooden posts and faced with turves. The plan of this bank and ditch formed the curving side of a letter D, the straight side being made by the river and its broad marshes beyond to the west. The earthwork can still be seen today, although it is very mutilated. It is called Waulud's Bank and curves from the Marsh Farm Community Centre at Leagrave round to the multi-storey flats on the Marsh Farm Estate, and on into the recreation ground. In 1954 and 1972 excavations were carried out on the site which showed that the ditch had been 2.4 m deep and 6 m wide. Inside it had been a bank, composed of chalk rubble and faced with vertical timbers and a stack of turves. A search on the northern side has failed to reveal an entrance into the enclosure. It is believed that Waulud's Bank belongs to a group of large earthworks each more than 180 m across called henge monuments. Very often such places have one or more circular wooden buildings inside. These henges were almost certainly ceremonial centres, used, like the causewayed enclosures before them, for tribal administration and religious observances. The circular buildings may have been communal meeting halls in which the elders addressed the tribe and made important decisions about its future. Since the river Lea forms one side of the henge monument, and water is often close to other similar sites, we may suppose that it had some part to play in whatever business took place there. The interior of Waulud's Bank has not been excavated so we do not know if any wooden buildings existed there. In other parts of Britain henge monuments often replaced the earlier causewayed enclosures, and our Leagrave site may have taken the place of the Neolithic Maiden Bower earthwork at Dunstable.

Many hundreds of flint arrowheads and skin scrapers have been found in the vicinity of Waulud's Bank, showing that the extensive marshes around the springs of the river Lea were a centre of hunting and leather working – a fusion of the Mesolithic and Neolithic ways of life.

The site chosen for Waulud's Bank was an ideal one, with the Icknield Way running along the gravel ridge to the south, and bringing visitors from east and west. Almost certainly a small settlement would have grown up nearby, that might be considered the first of a long series that have grown into the present town of Luton.

We do not know how long people used Waulud's Bank, but by the Bronze Age it had probably fallen out of use. It is possible that by that time most local people were living in small farmsteads, perhaps comprising family units, built on the hills around the river Lea. One such farmstead seems to have existed on the slopes of Warden Hill. It was once possible to see the depressions of hut foundations, but the golf course has obliterated these. Ditches probably marking the boundaries of this farmstead were excavated in 1958 on the northern edge of the Borough. Another farm was found on the western side of the town just beyond Dunstable, on Blows Downs. Here huts and storage pits were found during the last century, and again in 1929.

At Barton Hill Farm, a new temple was constructed in the Bronze Age with a mortuary chapel of turf within a circular ditch and bank.

THE IRON AGE

If our evidence for settlement in the Bronze Age is slender, by the Iron Age we have a mass of information indicating quite a large population. When the Iron Age began (c 700 BC) the Icknield Way had become a trackway of major importance. It was constantly in use by traders selling bronze and iron, pottery and clothing, who moved across the country from the south of England to East Anglia and the continent.

Here and there were farmholdings – large huts with stockyards, enclosed by palisades and sometimes ditches. The farmers seemed to have formed an alliance for their mutual protection by fortifying suitable hilltops in their areas and retreating into these fortifications, or hillforts as they are called, whenever danger threatened. Thus half a dozen farms might be responsible for the construction of one hillfort, and the fort in its turn would provide a place of refuge for farmers in an area of about nine square miles. All along the Icknield Way groups of farmers built their forts, and then separated their territory from their neighbours by constructing massive earthen dykes, with single gates in them to allow travellers on the Icknield Way to pass through. Perhaps tolls were extracted from the travellers at each barrier. At all events they impeded traffic to such an extent that sudden attack or cattle rustling would have been almost impossible. One of these Iron Age dykes lies on the edge of the Borough boundary and partly under the gardens of Turnpike Drive, from where it runs towards the northern end of Warden Hill. It is known as Drays Ditches, and consisted of three 'V'-shaped ditches, each about 2 m deep and 4.5 m wide, separated from each other by massive palisades of posts and packed chalk. As erected, Drays Ditches would have proved a most formidable barrier. It was probably constructed by farmers living north of it, whose hillforts stood at Ravensburgh Castle above Hexton and on Sharpenhoe Clapper. Within the Borough boundary a settlement existed to the north of Waulud's Bank on the Sundon Park Estate, and many fragments of early Iron Age pottery were found and destroyed when the modern houses were constructed there. One of the barrows on Galley Hill seems to have been built during this period as well.

The late Iron Age was a period of continual invasion, and from about 100 BC Belgic tribes from Gaul spread into southern Britain, establishing a capital in Hertfordshire. It seems likely that their move into the Luton area was a relatively peaceful one, and the Belgae soon had a considerable influence in the area. They established themselves beside the Lea marshes at Leagrave and seem to have controlled the ford across the river at that point. In all probability a log causeway was laid across the marsh making this an important fording point on the Icknield Way. We can imagine a small trading post growing up beside the ford, some of its houses built on timber piles in the marsh. Large quantities of Belgic pottery and traces of timber causeway were found in the area of Willow Way during post-war building development. Iron Age coins have also been found in the vicinity of the ford. Two gold coins of the Belgic tribe from Gaul known as the Morini were found at Luton, one at Leagrave in 1870 and one at Stopsley in 1949. Also in 1870 a gold coin of the Belgic chieftain Tasciovanus was found near Willow Way, and in 1960 a schoolboy found a gold and a bronze coin of Cunobelinus in the same area. A mile east of the ford, in Rosslyn Crescent, a group of Belgic cremation urns was found in 1961. These may well be part of the cemetery connected with the Leagrave site. Earlier historians of Luton also describe finds of pottery and bones made during the construction of the New Bedford Road. These may belong to an extension of the cemetery eastwards. Reference to 'cooking places' in the old reports certainly suggest cremation burials.

2 The Romans and Saxons at Luton

Julius Caesar's visit to Britain in 55 BC can have had little effect on people in the Luton area. His second visit in 54 BC may well have been a different story. The local Belgic tribe, the Catuvellauni, had their headquarters somewhere in Hertfordshire. The most likely place is the great hillfort called Ravensburgh Castle, 6 km north-east of Luton near Hexton. The Belgic chieftain's name was Cassivellaunus, and Caesar tells us that his stronghold was protected by forests and marshes, and had been filled with a large number of men and cattle. Caesar marched to the place with his legions, and found that it was of great natural strength and excellently fortified. He attacked it on two sides, and the Catuvellauni, unable to resist the attack, rushed out of the fortress on another side leaving a large quantity of cattle behind, together with a few of their men. If we are correct in identifying Ravensburgh as Cassivellaunus's stronghold, then it is quite likely that Julius Caesar reached it by following the river Lea as far as Leagrave, and then following the Icknield Way east until he was in striking distance of Ravensburgh. This would mean that Caesar and his soldiers marched right through the present site of Luton.

After the Roman Conquest in AD 43, the local Iron Age pottery more and more reflects Roman shapes, and was clearly being mass produced at places like Suloniacae (Brockley Hill) in Middlesex for local markets. Potters and pedlars toured the countryside distributing their copies of Roman pots and metal-work. The great military roads constructed across Britain made their journeys easier, but smaller side roads were clearly necessary if every settlement was to be brought within the Roman sphere of influence. Our nearest major Roman road was the Watling Street. On Half Moon Hill south of the modern town of Dunstable was a posting station known as Durocobrivae – a sort of inn where horses could be changed and their riders get refreshment. It was at this point that the old Icknield Way branched eastwards towards Luton. It is apparent that this stretch of the Icknield Way was resurfaced by the Romans and used as a minor road, although it should not be thought that the whole of the Icknield Way was re-used by the Romans.

A ROMAN SETTLEMENT AT LUTON

During the second century AD the people living beside the marsh at Leagrave seem to have got tired of their old home. It must have been very damp, unpleasant and liable to flood, and people would have suffered even more from rheumatism in those days than they do today. Marshes in England were also breeding grounds for malaria until well into the nineteenth century. At all events the Romanised Lutonians appeared to move across the Lea and along the Icknield Way to the gravel hill to the north-east on which the Runfold Estate now stands. Here, as a schoolboy, W. H. Manning, the archaeologist, found traces of a timber-built settlement dating from the second to the early fourth centuries AD. The settlement was of no great size and seems to have been little more than a collection of wayside houses. The buildings had been constructed mainly of timber, with some wattle and daub, and it is not surprising that the place seems finally to have been destroyed by fire.

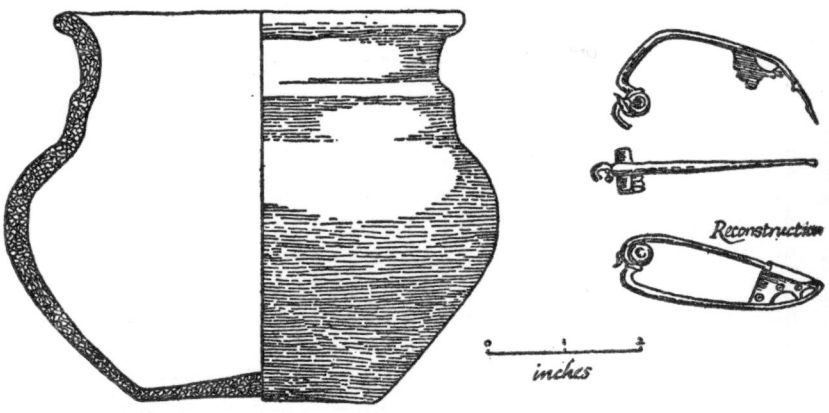

A Belgic pot and late Iron Age brooch from Marlin Road. About AD 50.

14

Just north of the town, in what today is Bramingham Road, there seems to have been a much more substantial Roman house. Whilst foundations for houses were being dug in 1928 the workmen found 'a lovely floor with a head in the centre in a different colour'. As no one was interested in it at the time, houses were built over it. It seems very likely that this floor was a Roman mosaic, and that a search of gardens in Bramingham Road near Ailsworth Road, might well reveal much more of the building.

There is only a little evidence to show that the Icknield Way ran further east than Luton as a Roman road. Parts of it were found under Turnpike Drive during excavations in 1971 and 1972. At one point it had cut deeply into the chalk, and there were many cart ruts, with Roman coins, and horse and ox-shoes bedded in them. Deep ruts on the side of Telegraph Hill near Hexton that are often claimed to be Roman, are almost certainly the result of coach transport during the seventeenth century, when a race track flourished on Lilley Hoo.

Somewhere in the area of Leagrave High Street the Icknield Way was probably joined by another minor Roman road coming from the Watling Street. Part of the road has long been known to run under the Corporation nurseries in Stockwood Park. It has been excavated in the grounds of Farley Junior School and seen in the foundations of flats at Whipperley Ring. It was quite close to this road near Luton Hoo in December 1862 that a pot containing several hundred coins of the mid-third century AD was found. Unfortunately most of the hoard was disposed of by the workmen who found it, but enough coins were traced to show that they ranged from Septimus Severus (193–211) to Claudius Gothicus (268–70). It is probable that the coins were buried soon after AD 270 perhaps as a result of local unrest.

SCATTERED FARMSTEADS

From chance references to Roman pottery being found along the banks of the Lea from Stockingstone Road to Barnfield College, it is likely that a series of farms was established in this area. In all probability some kind of track followed the Lea from Runfold Avenue towards Luton Hoo. A Roman building of some sort existed to the north of the Parish Church. Roman material has come from many parts of the town and in all cases is probably connected with isolated buildings. Pots in Luton Museum from Turners Knoll and Richmond Hill may indicate settlement in the Round Green area. The Richmond Hill pottery was not only domestic, for it included two cremation urns. There may have been another settlement on the hillslope above Elmwood Crescent.

Many hillsides around Luton are terraced with lynchets or cultivation strips. Particularly good specimens are to be seen adjoining the M1 on the Chaul End Downs, and on Bradgers Hill. Terraces in the People's Park have been damaged by landscaping. These cultivation terraces are the remains of an agricultural system which required the contour ploughing of hillslopes with a single furrow plough, often pulled by an ox. There is no evidence in the Luton area for the date of these terraces, which may have been constructed in the late Roman or Saxon period. It is assumed that they were ploughed when the land at the foot of the hill was already fully in use. An old trackway, which may well be contemporary, can be seen climbing diagonally up the middle of the Bradgers Hill series.

The Galley Hill Massacre
Towards the end of the Roman occupation of Britain an event of unprecedented horror took place on the edge of the Borough. Soon after AD 360 a number of men, women and children were slaughtered and their remains buried on the summit of Galley Hill, in the same burial mound that had contained the mutilated Neolithic burial. Excavations in 1961 revealed the grim spectacle of a man who lay with his arm round the waist of a young woman. She had been a cripple, and had lost her right leg during her lifetime. A young woman lay near by, her head and arm severed from her body by an oblique sword cut across her shoulder. Two young men shared the same shallow grave, one thrown on top of the other. Most poignant of all was the body of a woman flung face downwards above that of a man and beneath them both the trunk and limbs of an older man, whose head lay some distance away. Perhaps a wife had watched her father and husband brutally murdered, before she was treated in the same barbaric fashion. Who was responsible for this act and when did it take place? In the second half of the fourth century Roman power in Britain was on the decline. In the year 367 the Saxons,

Picts and Scots combined in a great assault upon the province. Hadrian's Wall and the forts in the north of England fell, and the barbarians stormed south, sacking towns and farms as far as London. It seems very likely that the people buried on Galley Hill were victims of this uprising.

We do not know if the Roman settlement at Runfold Avenue lasted until AD 367. Coins and pottery found there suggest that it had already been deserted, but signs of burning may be an indication that a few people had lingered on there and may have had their homes destroyed at this time.

THE COMING OF THE SAXONS

Order was eventually restored by Count Theodosius, but not for long. One petty native ruler after another controlled areas of varying extent, a few adventurers even taking troops to the Continent with thoughts of winning the Roman crown. At the same time, during the latter part of the fourth century, parties of Angles and Saxons were making their way into Britain and apparently living side by side with the Romanised Britons in their towns. A group of Saxons, from between the rivers Elbe and Weser in the old Saxon territory of Germany, was established at Luton by at least AD 475. The exact whereabouts of their settlement is not known, since their houses of wood have left no recognisable traces, but we can assume that it was somewhere on the ridge marked today by Alexandra Avenue. Our evidence for the settlement comes from the finding of an extensive Saxon cemetery at Luton in 1925. The cemetery is one of the earliest so far discovered in Britain and was found by workmen laying sewer pipes in Argyll Avenue. William Austin (author of the *History of Luton*) and Thomas Bagshawe (founder of the Luton Museum) were only able to carry out slight excavations which produced evidence of more than forty burials and at least three cremations. Many other burials were destroyed without record, and it is likely that the cemetery extended over a very large area, running along the west-facing hillslope from about a hundred yards north of St Andrew's Church to Biscot Mill. This would suggest that the Saxons, and probably the British too, occupied this part of Luton for a considerable time.

The finds from the cemetery included spears, a sword, the iron bosses from the centres of eight shields and thirty-two brooches of types used by men and women for securing their cloaks. One of the brooches is of a type which German archaeologists call *stuzarm-fibeln*, which means 'a short armed brooch'. This type is often found in the cemeteries between the rivers Elbe and Weser. It is one of the earliest Anglo-Saxon brooches in England. There are other early objects from the Luton cemetery including a cremation urn called a footed *buckelurne*. It was probably made about AD 450, and is so like those made in north-west Germany that it was almost certainly produced by the first generation of immigrants to Britain before they had time to forget what such urns looked like, and had begun to develop new styles.

Many of the women were buried with simple circular brooches, some of which can be dated to the early sixth century, though others are later. Two of these were buried with the largest brooch in the Argyll Avenue cemetery, a great square-headed brooch nearly 17 cm long, and thought to date late in the sixth century. The men were buried with their weapons. The presence of spears and shields in the graves tells us that the Saxons at Luton had not yet been converted to Christianity, but were still pagans, expecting to have to fight in the next world as they had done in this.

A Time of Unrest

Groups of Angles and Saxons had passed into Britain during the later years of the fifth century, along the Icknield Way from the Wash as far as Luton, and from there they followed an old trackway which lies on the northern edge of the Borough, called the Ede Way, through Chalton, Chalgrave and Eggington into Buckinghamshire and the valley of the Thames. From thence they established settlements and cemeteries in the middle Thames valley, notably at Dorchester-on-Thames. The Romans had withdrawn their forces from Britain in 410 leaving the native Romanised Britons to defend themselves against the barbarians of the north. One plan had been to invite more Saxons to settle in various parts of Britain in exchange for military aid against attack. As so often happens on these occasions, the country seeking help from outsiders was eventually attacked by those whose help it sought. The Saxon mercenaries rebelled against their employers about AD 450 and were supported by the many Saxons already living in Britain. A long period of warfare followed. Only under the reputed leadership of Arturus (King Arthur) did the British eventually succeed to a great victory at a place called Mons Badonicus. When this happened we are not sure, authorities differing on a date between AD 493 and 517. The later date would be better suited to our knowledge of the Luton settlements. After the battle of Mons Badonicus the Saxons in the Thames valley and Chiltern Hills were probably driven back into East Anglia. There they protected themselves by building such great dykes as the Fleam Dyke and the Devil's Dyke.

LYGEANBURGH

One of the oldest documents relating to Saxon Britain is known as the *Anglo Saxon Chronicle*. This is a group of several chronicles written at different times before the tenth century, some for King Alfred, which tell us a great deal about happenings during the later Saxon period. Some of the earlier entries in the *Chronicle* are very brief and often puzzling. We *do* learn that the earliest recorded name for any part of Luton was Lygeanburgh. This seems to have been the original name for that part of the town called Limbury, and so we may assume that our Saxon settlement at that time lay in Limbury parish.

In Hampshire about AD 500 the West Saxons under their leaders Cynric and Caewlin began a movement northwards from Southampton, which brought them gradually up into Wiltshire. All the time they were extending their territories. In 556 they fought the British, probably at Barbury Castle in Wiltshire, thus securing control of most of central southern England. This land of the West Saxons is still known today as Wessex. Caewlin then moved eastwards towards the Chilterns and in 571 his brother Cutha fought a battle at an unidentified place called *Biedcanforda*. As a result of this he gained for the West Saxons much of the south Midlands. We are told that he took Limbury, and also Aylesbury, Benson and Eynsham in Oxfordshire. Each of these is beside an early Anglo-Saxon cemetery. In the Luton cemetery, and elsewhere in Bedfordshire, we can see the dramatic results of that victory. New fashions in brooches connected with those in the upper Thames valley begin to appear, including the great square-headed brooch mentioned earlier.

Saxon Luton

Since no traces of the Saxon settlement at Luton have been found, we can only imagine what it was like. The cemetery at Argyll Avenue seems to have continued until the first years of the seventh century, but then like so many early Anglo-Saxon cemeteries it was replaced by another at a site not far away. The new Luton cemetery was at Biscot Mill, and traces of it have been found from time to time since 1923. The most important requirement of any town is water, and it seems likely that a new site was found beside the river Lea. As the Icknield Way was still the main road in the area, it is probable that the site chosen was fairly close to it, in the vicinity of the present Biscot Church.

We can imagine a great wooden hall for the chief man of the village, surrounded by sheds and cattle byres. Close by would have been vegetable gardens and orchards where beehives were kept. Adjoining the hall was a clearing for meetings, and around this stood the huts of the freemen, constructed of wood, daubed mud and thatch. The village would have been surrounded by a fence and probably a water-filled moat. Outside the village was the arable plough land, and the pasture or common land on which the villagers had the right to graze their animals. Beyond the fields was an area of cleared land known as the mark; this was prepared as a safety precaution so that strangers could be seen approaching. The woods beyond provided grazing for pigs and an abundant supply of firewood.

The Arrival of Christianity

By about AD 660 it is probable that the inhabitants of Lygean-burgh had become Christians. In AD 653 Paeda, under-king of the Middle Angles, had been baptised and sent four priests to instruct his people. One of these was the brother of St Chad, called Cedd, who, working from Leicester, seems to have converted many families and to have worked his way into Bedfordshire, certainly as far south as the Ouse, and probably down to the Chilterns. At the time of the death of Wulfhere in AD 675 we are told that heathenism had 'received its death blow and was entirely banished, and Christianity established in its stead'.

A small wooden church was probably built by Wulfhere inside the settlement at Biscot, but it is unlikely that its site will ever be found now, in view of the extensive building development throughout the Borough.

History is silent about the fortunes of the settlement at Biscot. We do not know who its chief men were, or how big it was. At an early date the church land became the property of a monastery whose abbot was called Alhmund. In 792 King Offa of Mercia gave this same land, about 500 acres, to the first Abbot of St Albans. A house for the Bishop of Mercia was built on the land at Biscot so that the Bishop had somewhere to stay should he want to visit that part of his large diocese. The name Bishopscote, meaning Bishop's House, still survives today in our name of Biscot.

VIKING RAIDERS

In 793 after dire portents of whirlwinds, lightning and a famine, the first Viking raiders attacked Lindisfarne. Spurred on by reports of rich treasure in English churches, and finding the Saxon kingdoms still quarrelling with one another, the Vikings raided the south and east coasts of England as they pleased. The Saxon armies were badly organised; there were no fleets of ships to oppose the Vikings; and the rivers which had provided the Saxons with a means of easy entry into Britain, now did the same for their enemies. During the following sixty years the Vikings raided south-eastern England at will and then in 867 launched a great and successful attack on Northumbria. This was followed by the conquest of the other Saxon kingdoms, until in 871 Wessex alone remained.

3 From Alfred to Cnut

IN 871 Alfred succeeded to the throne of Wessex. He came at a time when many people must have thought that English history was almost at an end. The Vikings, or Danes as they are generally called, were great soldiers and their earlier pirate groups were soon replaced by men disciplined and trained in the art of warfare. They had conquered the rest of England and in 876 it was the turn of Wessex. During that winter, whilst Alfred and his men were celebrating Christmas, the Danish army marched secretly into Wiltshire and overran eastern Wessex. Many of the inhabitants were driven abroad and Alfred and his small army had to seek refuge in 'woods and inaccessible places in marshes'. During the following spring Alfred gathered together soldiers from Wiltshire, Somerset and western Hampshire at a hide-out at Athelney in Somerset. Together they planned a secret raid on the Danish army. The attack in early May was a complete surprise and after a battle and siege lasting a fortnight the Danes surrendered and their king, Guthrum, and thirty of his chief followers were baptised.

THE DANELAW

For the next ten years Wessex was free from Danish attack and Alfred was able to build up the strength of Wessex. Attacks on the Kentish coast by new bands of Vikings were supported by Guthrum and in 886, in retaliation, Alfred captured London, at that time held by the Danes, and put it in charge of Ethelred, an aeldorman of the Mercians. After the battle a peace treaty was drawn up between Alfred and Guthrum which amongst other things decided on the boundary between Wessex and the Danes. It was of particular interest to the people of Luton and began: 'First concerning our boundaries: up the Thames, and then up the Lea, and along the Lea to its source, then in a straight line to Bedford, then up the Ouse to Watling Street.'

The treaty went on to forbid people to cross from one side of the frontier to the other, except for reasons of trade. All the Danish lands east of the boundary were known as the Danelaw.

As you can see, Luton was right on the boundary line, and

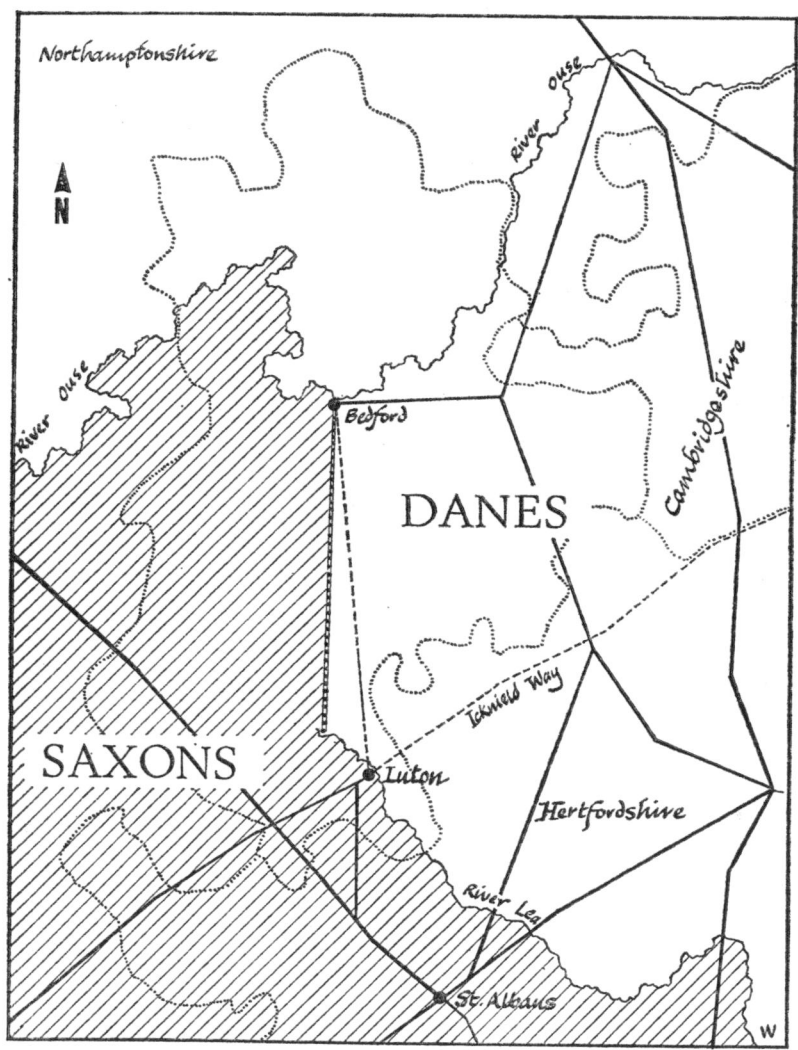

The Danelaw Boundary in Bedfordshire. The map also shows Roman roads.

became overnight a frontier town. All evidence suggests that the settlement at Biscot, together with newly formed nucleated farming settlements at Leagrave and on Park Square hill in the centre of the modern town, were on the Saxon side of the river, although much of their land may have been in Danish territory. The fact that small groups of farms should come together at about this time to form separate settlements, may well be a result of the need for greater protection against the Danes across the river. Even so, we must beware of seeing in the Danelaw a tenth century Berlin Wall. We can be fairly confident that the general relationship between folk on either side of the river was friendly enough, and continued as it had done for many years. It is unlikely that the Danes had a regular patrol along the frontier, and there must have been plenty of unofficial comings and goings.

The Lea, Ouse and Watling Street all formed well defined boundaries; but what of the gap between the source of the Lea and Bedford? It would be interesting to know exactly where the boundary ran. It may have passed from Leagrave marsh through Sharpenhoe, Pulloxhill, Flitton, Maulden and Houghton Conquest. Since the Saxons had no maps their line may not have been particularly straight, and the boundary might have bent further east to follow the line of the old road from Luton to Bedford. The A6 north of Barton might well have originated as a track running along the frontier. Alternatively we must remember that modern drainage has considerably reduced the amount of water in the river Lea, and although the source springs are now at Leagrave, the spring at Lewsey Farm or Houghton Regis may well have been considered the source in Danish times. In that case Toddington, Flitwick and Ampthill would be close to the boundary. The *Victoria County History* wrongly suggests that the road from Houghton Regis to Bedford was a Roman one, but this would have made an admirable boundary.

At the time of King Alfred's death in 899 Wessex included all England south of the Thames and Bristol Avon. In the west the allied kingdom of Mercia stretched from Cheshire to central Buckinghamshire, then down the Watling Street to London. This shows Danish encroachment in south Bedfordshire across the Lea, and puts Luton for a very short time inside the Danish frontier; but the Lutonians were very loyal Saxons as we shall see.

In 926 in a charter of King Æthelstan, land at Chalgrave belonging to the Danes was bought back by the Saxon thane Ealdred. The Danes held all the eastern part of England and established strong garrisons at Bedford, Cambridge, Northampton and Leicester.

The Men of Luton Defeat the Danes

Alfred was succeeded by his eldest son, Edward the Elder, and he, together with his sister Æthelflaed, 'The Lady of the Mercians', began to reconquer the Danelaw. Æthelflaed worked in the western Midlands, capturing Warwick and Derby; whilst in 912 Edward prepared for campaigns to the east and north and constructed fortresses at Hertford and at Maldon in Essex. The *Anglo-Saxon Chronicle* tells us that in the following year a party of Danes from Leicester and Northampton 'rode out against Luton. And then the people of the distrct became aware of it and fought against them and reduced them to full flight and rescued all that they had captured and also a great part of their horses and their weapons'.

In 1819 a large hoard of weapons was found in the fields close to Toddington, together with personal ornaments. Whilst some of the objects in the scanty descriptions appear to be of Saxon date and may have originated from a cemetery, others could be Danish. Unfortunately most of the material is lost. Perhaps these are some of the remains of the 913 skirmish. We are entitled to ask why the Danes should have chosen to attack the Luton settlement. Perhaps the answer lies in its position as a frontier town. Could the inhabitants have been overstepping their rights as laid down in the treaty of Alfred and Guthrum, perhaps even providing a base for guerilla warfare against Danish outposts in Bedfordshire? That such outposts existed, there is little doubt. One lay only eight miles north-west of Luton at Shillington, whilst another was situated south of Sandy. Such outposts were sited in marshy land and consisted of an artificial semi-circular island surrounded by a rampart and ditch and backing on to a river or navigable stream. Such sites could most easily be approached by water. Earthworks like these can be found in the homelands of the Danes at Hedeby in north-western Germany, and at Birka in Sweden. Earlier historians have spoken of a Danish settlement within the Iron Age fort called Ravensburgh Castle at Hexton, but there is no proof to support this suggestion at all.

The Manor of Luton

During, or shortly after, the Danish occupation the present town centre appears to have developed and a church, probably built of stone, was erected on land claimed by the King. This was in the neighbourhood of Park Square, and either on, or near to, the site of the present church. By 975 Luton was claimed as a royal vill (or township). It is not known whether there was an earlier settlement in the Park Square area, or why the later Saxon kings showed so great an interest in this district. The nearby manor of Houghton, was similarly claimed by the King, hence the suffix Regis, as was Leighton Buzzard.

To help the King rule his kingdom, a council of wise men called the Witenagemot was appointed. It was the parliament of the day and consisted of old men who had served their country loyally and wisely. Edward's successor, Athelstan, called a Witan at *Leowton* on 12 November 931. For many years it has been assumed that Leowton and Luton were the same place. Unfortunately, Sir Alan Mawer, one of the greatest authorities on place-names and their derivations, has been able to show quite conclusively that Leowton is the village now known as Lifton in Devon. In 931 Luton was known as Lygtun or Ligtun.

It is quite possible that King Athelstan visited Luton about this time to celebrate the consecration of the new church begun by Edward, which he had completed; and at the same time to confirm the grant to the church of five hides of land (about 600 acres) which we know it owned when the Domesday Book was compiled. By the east door of the parish church is a stone corbel which may have belonged to this early building.

The Danes Return

In 1013 King Sweyn Forkbeard landed in England and after a rapid campaign was accepted as king over most of the country. Unfortunately he died in the following year and it was not until 1016 that the Witan agreed to accept his son Cnut as king of England.

King Sweyn was a great military leader and he had prepared

his campaign of conquest for many years. He had made two previous expeditions to England, and had also systematised the training of the young men of his kingdom. He seems to have ordered the construction of a number of great military training forts in Denmark, known to the Danes as trelleborgs, after the most famous type-site in Zealand at Trelleborg. These camps were built with great mathematical precision and held up to 3,000 men. They contained boat-shaped long houses, and were surrounded by great circular ramparts and ditches, broken by four opposing entrances.

No forts of this type are known from England, but a study of earthworks near Shillington and Sandy suggest that Danish fortifications existed in our area, and may have been connected with the campaigns of Sweyn and Cnut.

4 The Norman Conquest and the Domesday Survey

BEFORE we look at the conquest in 1066 let us examine the social order in England during the reign of Edward the Confessor.

At the top was the King. To him the whole land belonged, and he could give or lease it to whom he pleased. Under him were the earls, bishops and sheriffs. It is interesting to notice that women seldom held any status in Anglo-Saxon society. The King's wife was his lady, but not his queen, and no title existed for an earl's wife. It was only after the Norman conquest, when the Norman equivalent to an earl appeared – the count – that the wives of earls assumed the title of their French counterparts – countess. Earls were appointed by the King and the title was not hereditary, although there was a tendency for a son to succeed his father. Each earl was responsible for the government of a shire or shires. Bedfordshire and Huntingdonshire seem to have been the responsibility of one earl. Together with the diocesan bishop the earl sat as joint president of the shire court and usually received a third part of the profits from the court. Since the earls were the main advisers to the King, it was often necessary for them to be away from their shires for long periods and so the *scir gerefa* or sheriff was appointed by the King to administer local finance and order. Many local lords within the shire were known as *thanes*; they lived on their own land and their duties included fighting the King's battles, defending his towns and maintaining his bridges. The mass of the country folk, although freemen, were in some way, either economic or personal, dependent on their lord, and either worked for him or paid a rent to him. The peasantry were of various rank and were known as *churls*. Amongst other things they were expected by law to serve in the *fyrd* or army. Cnut formed a personal army of bodyguards of these men, known as house-carls.

EDWIN AND MORCAR

Since Luton belonged directly to the King there was no earl responsible for the actions of the people of the manor. Instead a bailiff or steward represented the King in the local court and lived in the manor house. In the reign of Edward the Confessor, the only thane in the district whose name we know was Edwin, who owned Biscot, and could, if he wished, sell it without recourse to the King. One other person of importance was the priest, Morcar, who owned the income from the lands of Luton Church. The tenants and farmers of Luton were responsible for cultivating the land of the King and of Morcar and Edwin, as well as tending their own land. The poorer folk of the town, the cottagers, who owned little beside the roof over their heads and a tiny piece of land, hired themselves out to the richer tenants.

Domesday Book tells us that Morcar was one of the richer priests of his day. Not only did he own more than 600 acres of land in Luton, but a further 180 acres in Bedfordshire, together with about 75 acres of woodland and a watermill.

CONTENDERS FOR THE THRONE

The death of King Edward the Confessor on 6 January 1066 left three contenders for the English throne: Harold Hardrada of Norway, William of Normandy and Harold of Wessex. The throne had been promised to William fifteen years before, and Harold of Wessex had sworn on relics in Bayeux Cathedral to support this claim, but on the day after Edward's death Harold of Wessex was crowned king. In the few brief months of his reign Harold showed himself to be a courageous and determined leader. He ordered his army to guard the south coast of England in readiness for an attack from Normandy, but in September, when no attack had materialised and the ripened harvest was waiting in the fields, he disbanded his militia and allowed his men to return to their farms. Within a few days Harold Hardrada had sailed up the Humber and landed on the Yorkshire Ouse at Riccal. With great speed Harold of Wessex gathered his army together once more and marched on Hardrada's army at Stamford Bridge, east of

York. The attack was a surprise and after a day of bitter but decisive fighting, Hardrada was killed and King Harold was left victorious. Almost immediately he received news of a Norman landing in Sussex.

William had the whole of the church and the papal blessing behind his attack; after all Harold had broken his sacred oath. Nineteen days after the battle of Stamford Bridge the most famous battle in English history was fought with small armies, both about 3,000 strong, on Senlac Hill in Sussex – the Battle of Hastings. Stamford Bridge had been a great battle, but Hastings was a much slighter affair, although it was to be so decisive in shaping the future of our country. The battle lasted from dawn till dusk on 14 October 1066. As dusk began to fall Harold was killed and 'the French had possession of the place of slaughter'.

WILLIAM MARCHES THROUGH BEDFORDSHIRE

Unfortunately for William no one seemed to take his claim to the throne of England very seriously and getting tired of waiting for the English to surrender to him at Hastings, he began a long and circuitous route to London. Passing through Surrey, Hampshire and Berkshire, he crossed the Thames at Wallingford and then proceeded up the Chilterns to Thame. William harried the countryside as he went, his men living on anything that came within their reach, and behind them they left a trail of devastation. Before entering Bedfordshire William divided his army into two wings. One made for the royal manors of Leighton, Houghton Regis and Luton, whilst the other crossed the north of the county through Turvey and Stagsden to Potton and on into Cambridgeshire. Most of the south Bedfordshire villages were badly devastated but the royal manors hardly seem to have been troubled. Since these manors had belonged to Edward the Confessor they would now pass to William when he became King, and we can therefore assume that he gave protection to what he hoped would soon be his own. There can be little doubt that William visited all three of the royal manors as his army passed through Bedfordshire. The two wings of the army joined up again at Berkhamsted, and whilst William may have sheltered in the pre-Norman castle, his men camped in the park nearby.

By the time William reached Berkhamsted the Witan had

agreed to submit to him, and on Christmas Day he was anointed and crowned in Westminster Abbey.

Although Luton had escaped devastation, Biscot had not been so lucky and it was many years before it recovered from the attacks made upon it.

WILLIAM MAKES CHANGES AT LUTON

Once William was crowned, he appointed a Norman, Ivo Tallebosc as sheriff of the royal manors of Houghton and Luton. Ivo found that a number of little manors had grown up beside the royal manors, and appeared to have been gifts of land from King Edward to people in his service. In particular the manors of Biscot and Sewell caught Ivo's eye, and by 1086 he had added them to the royal manors of Luton and Houghton respectively.

William the Chamberlain, another Norman, took Morcar's place and held the church with all its lands 'in capite'. That means that he provided half the cost of keeping a fully armed soldier for forty days each year when the King went to war. The church had always been free of such service but now William the Chamberlain seems to have accepted it as one of the conditions of his holding office. As a chamberlain it was probably William's job to audit the accounts of the sheriff. As a clergyman he was responsible for the churches at Luton and Houghton Regis.

DOMESDAY BOOK

In 1086 the Domesday Book was compiled so that King William should have an exact record of the wealth of his tenants, and should know how much was being paid to the King's geld – or Danegeld – 'the one great tax levied over the whole of England'.

Contemporary writers tell us that 'The King sent his men all over England into every shire and caused them to find out how many hides [approximately 120 acres] of land it contained, and what land the King possessed therein, what cattle there were in each county, and how much tax or revenue he ought to receive every year from the shires. Also he caused them to write down how much land belonged to the archbishops, the bishops, the abbots and the earls, and what property everyone in England owned in land or cattle, and how much this was worth. So strictly did he cause the survey to be made that there was not a single hide or rood of land, nor was there ox, or cow or pig left, that was not set down in the accounts. Afterwards all these writings were brought to him.'

The commissioners who were sent out to collect the information were instructed to find,

'The name of the manor; who held it in King Edward's time; who holds it now; how many hides there are; how many ploughs belonging to the King and how many to the men; how many villeins, cottars, slaves, freemen and sokemen there are, how much woodland, meadow and pasture and how many mills and fisheries.'

To make sure that the survey was correct:

'Other investigators followed the first, in order to check the first survey and if necessary denounce its authors to the King if anything had been mis-represented.'

Five kinds of peasants are described in Domesday Book: freemen, sokemen, villeins, cottars and slaves. It is not easy to explain their exact differences, but broadly speaking the names describe a descending scale of freedom. Freemen and sokemen were bound to their lord by paying money rents. The villein was subject to labour services, possessed his share of the open fields of his village and had rights of pasturage and timber collecting. The cottar or cottager owned a smallholding and could be put to any kind of work decreed by the lord of the manor or his bailiff. The slave (serf) was the chattel – the possession – of his lord, and had no legal rights of his own.

LUTON IN DOMESDAY BOOK

The part of Domesday which relates to Bedfordshire begins with a description of the royal land. Much of it is written in technical language which needs a great deal of study. The following is a translation of the accounts of Luton, the church manor, Biscot and part of Luton manor that was in Streatley parish.

'Loitone. A royal manor of the king; is assessed at 30 hides. There is land for 4 score and 2 ploughs. On the king's private land are 4 ploughs. The villeins have 4 score all but 2. There are 4 score villeins and 47 boarders (cottars), and 6 mills yielding 100 shillings. Meadow sufficient for 4 plough teams, woodlands to feed 2,000 swine and from wood tax comes 10 shillings and eightpence. From the toll and the market come 100 shillings. In all it yields yearly 30 pounds of weighed money and half a day's provision in grain and honey and other customary dues purtaining to the king's "ferm". To the Queen 4 ounces of gold and a packhorse and other small dues 70 shillings and for customary payments for the dogs 6 pounds and 10 shillings. For the additional payment which Ivo Tallebosc imposed, 7 pounds weighed money and 40 shillings of white silver and one ounce of gold for the sheriff.

The church of this manor is held by William the king's chamberlain with 5 hides of land which belong to it. These 5 hides are part of the 30 hides of the manor. There is land in them for 6 ploughs. On the royal land is 1 plough, and the villeins have 5. There are 11 villeins, 4 cottars and 3 slaves, and 1 mill worth 10 shillings. The church yields 20 shillings yearly. There is woodland to feed 50 swine. In all it is and was worth 60 shillings. This church with its land Morcar the priest held in the time of King Edward.

Bissopescote [Biscot] was assessed at 5 hides in the time of King Edward. There is land for 5 ploughs. There are 2 ploughs on the royal land, and 10 villeins have 3 ploughs. There are three slaves and meadow sufficient for 4 plough teams. In all it is worth 40 shillings; when Ralph Tallebosc held it, it was worth the same amount. In the time of King Edward it was worth 60 shillings. This manor Edwin, a man of Ashger the staller, held and could do with it what he wished. Ralph Tallebosc added it to Loitone [Luton], the king's manor, for the sake of the additional payment which it gave him.

In Stradlei [Streatley] the bailiff of the hundred holds two-thirds of 1 virgate for the king's use, which now belong to the king's manor in Lintone [Luton] but did not belong thereto in the time of King Edward. Bondi the staller assigned them to this manor; Ralph Tallebosc found them there belonging. There is land for a half plough. It is and was worth 5 shillings, and in the time of King Edward 10 shillings. This land Ulmer a priest held and could give to whom he wished.'

From the survey we learn that there were 101 villeins in the present Borough, 51 cottars, and 6 slaves. These are of course the men only; women and children were not counted.

It is impossible to state the exact size of the lands referred to here, and in any case they were only estimations made for the purposes of taxation. It was, however, an exceedingly large manor, and there was none bigger in Bedfordshire. From details given of the neighbouring manors it must have covered about the same area as the present Borough with the parish of Hyde added. It had, even for its size, a large amount of woodland, but it would be a mistake to assume that there were 2,050 swine kept on the manor, and safer to assume that the commissioners estimated that the woodland was sufficiently large to feed that number.

In its wealth as well as its size Luton was, apart from Bedford for which few details were given, the most important town in the county. Leighton, the second in importance, had 88 villeins, 36 bordars and 2 serfs, whilst Shillington, the next in size, had 64 villeins, 12 bordars and 13 serfs. It was rare, by the way, to find serfs on royal manors. Only two other manors, namely Leighton and Arlesey, had markets, but no doubt Bedford had one too. Although about a 100 mills are listed in the Bedfordshire Domesday, no other manor has as many as the seven listed for Luton. Turvey and Tempsford (both on the river Ouse) and Stotfold had four each, and Leighton, Blunham and Southill had three. While the mills were a comparatively efficient means of grinding corn most peasants for many centuries to come were to grind their corn by hand.

Dunstable, it is interesting to note, was not mentioned in Domesday Book, although every village now in south Bedfordshire is. It was created by Henry I as a new town about 1119. If, in 1086, it was part of the manor of Houghton, it must have been a place of insignificant size.

We see in two places, at Biscot and Streatley, that the land worth £3 and 10s in the time of King Edward has decreased in value at the time of the survey to £2 and 5s. No doubt the result of the devastation caused by King William's soldiers in 1066.

What did the King get out of his manor each year?

Weighed money	£37	0	0
Mills	5	0	0

Market	5	0	0
White silver	2	0	0
Wood tax		10	8

£49 10 8

His Queen received £10 in money, of which £6 10s was for the upkeep of the royal dogs, and the remainder for her personal purse. In addition she received a packhorse and 4 oz of gold each year. The manor also provided a half day's ferm rent. The ferm was sufficient honey and grain to last half a day at the palace. The manor had held a market long before the Norman Conquest. It was held every Sunday and the stalls were set up round the church. From the market the King received a revenue of £5 a year. He received a further yearly rent of £5 from the water-mills.

THE LUTON WATER-MILLS

Both water-mills and windmills were to be found in mediaeval England, but only the former were in use before the later part of the twelfth century.

There were seven mills in use within the manor, one belonging to the church, the rest to the King. Here the lord profited from the needs of his tenants, since they had to grind corn to make bread. In many parts of the country, men were tempted to take their grain to cheaper rival mills in spite of manorial injunctions. In Luton this was scarcely possible since there were no other mills nearer than the Hiz and Ouzel valleys. Luton was a good corn growing area, and its large acreage of arable land must have kept the seven mills very busy.

Most of the water-mills at Luton had horizontal axles, and were of the type called 'overshot' wheels. In these mills, water, collected in large ponds upstream, passed over the top of the wheel, its weight causing the wheel to turn. The millstones were often brought from abroad, and this could be a very costly business.

It is possible to trace the seven mills, spaced out along the seven miles of the Lea valley from Leagrave to Hyde.

The site of the first mill may have been buried under the M1 motorway beside Leagrave Primary School, where there used to be two large ponds. On the other hand excavations at the springs of the Lea in Sundon Park Recreation Ground show that the ditch of the Waulud's Bank earthwork was considerably widened in Norman times, in all probability for a mill pond. The only disadvantage with this suggestion is that the mill was in Leagrave parish, but the springs are in Limbury.

The second mill was on the river Lea at Limbury Mead and stood close to where Neville Road crosses the river. The land to the west of the bridge was once the mill pond and covered about seven acres. The mill was in use in 1247 when the miller was stabbed to death by a robber, but had fallen into decay by the end of the fourteenth century.

The third mill, called the North Mill, was in Mill Street, under the railway embankment. It was probably the most important mill and was in use until 1859 when it was purchased and demolished by the Midland Railway Company.

The fourth, Church Mill, stood close to the eastern side of St Mary's Church opposite the Youth House.

The fifth mill was called the Brache Mill and stood in Osborne Road under the Vauxhall Styling Centre. It was in working order until about 1890.

Stapleford Mill, the sixth, has been absorbed into Luton Hoo Park. It probably stood close to the island in the Park Lake and was pulled down when the Earl of Bute made his enlargements.

The seventh, Hyde Mill, is the only Domesday mill still working. It stands on the county boundary at East Hyde.

It will not be out of place to mention at this point that another mill – the New Mill, was set up in the fifteenth century at New Mill End, but ceased to work about sixty years ago.

Eleventh Century Luton

By the end of the eleventh century we can see Luton as a small collection of wattle and daub houses with thatched roofs, clustering around the stone-built church at Park Square. The foundations of many of these buildings must have been destroyed during the construction of the College of Technology. It is interesting to notice that no castle was built at Luton during the Conqueror's reign. Since Luton was a royal manor and had suffered no destruction by the King, it is probable that the people of the town accepted him in a much more resigned manner than those people whose homes had been destroyed. We notice in Bedfordshire that it is often the worst devastated villages that have the remains of early motte-and-bailey castles.

Finally, we must remember that the people of Luton were still Saxons. Only 9.8 per cent of the population of England were Normans at the end of William's reign. The country may have been conquered, but it was not dominated by Normans. It was to remain Saxon for many centuries to come, and even today much of our language is still Saxon in origin.

5 From Henry I to King John, the Twelfth Century

KING HENRY I was a strong, capable and just ruler who inspired fear and respect from his subjects. Born in Yorkshire, he married Maud, the daughter of St Margaret of Scotland and King Malcolm. Like his father, Henry was a pious man, and liked to keep on good terms with the Church. Whenever possible he would endow religious houses.

In the year 1115 King Henry and Queen Maud spent Christmas at St Albans, where they witnessed the dedication of the new abbey by Robert, Bishop of Lincoln. As a present to mark the occasion King Henry gave the manor of Biscot to Abbot Richard. This was the same land that King Offa had given to the first abbot 323 years before.

EARL ROBERT

Five or six years later King Henry gave the manor of Luton to his illegitimate son, Robert, Earl of Gloucester. One of the first things Earl Robert did at Luton was to build a new church. We are told that he completely removed the old building and had the new one built, not on the old site, but on about 3 acres of his own land. We cannot be sure whether this church was on the site of the present church, or a few yards to the south. We do not know the architect of Earl Robert's church, but as William Austin pointed out, since St Albans Abbey had been completed in 1115, there would be plenty of builders and craftsmen available and it is possible that 'Robert, the master mason and builder' might have designed and superintended the work.

When the church was completed in 1137, two years after King Henry's death, Earl Robert granted it to a friend of his, Gilbert de Cymmay. This act caused trouble because the church had been held by William Chamberlain, son of William the Chamberlain who had received it from William the Conqueror. By moving the church onto his own land, Earl Robert considered that he could do with it what he pleased. For two years the ownership of the church was disputed. William Chamberlain claimed it as his and appealed to King Henry's successor, King Stephen, and he handed the matter on to a meeting of bishops at Oxford, where in 1139 they decided in favour of Gilbert de Cymmay.

King Henry had arranged that at his death he should be succeeded by his daughter Matilda. The barons had sworn allegiance to her; but they disapproved of her marriage to Count Geoffrey of Anjou. Geoffrey hoped to become King of England, but Henry seems to have tired of him, and refused to let him have any share in the government of the country. When in 1135 the old King died through overeating, he was at war with Geoffrey. Henry's nephew, Stephen, seized the country and for nineteen years held it by the skin of his teeth. Empress Matilda made a number of attempts to regain the country and each time she was supported by her half-brother, Robert, Earl of Gloucester.

In retaliation for Robert's support of Matilda, King Stephen deprived him of all his possessions in England, including the manor of Luton.

The Castle Builders

The barons, finding that Stephen was an easy-going, soft character, took advantage of his weaknesses and broke their oaths of allegiance to him. The *Anglo-Saxon Chronicle* for 1137 tells us that 'every great man built castles and held them against the King; and they filled the whole land with these castles. They sorely burdened the unhappy people of the country with castles; and when the castles were built, they filled them with devils and wicked men. . . . Never did a country endure greater misery . . . and men said openly that Christ and his angels slept.'

The Castle Street Castle

In order to retaliate against the barons Stephen hired soldiers from abroad – mercenaries – to come and support him. In 1139 the church and manor of Luton was given to just such a foreign mercenary – Robert de Waudari. On his arrival at Luton Waudari organised the erection of a castle. This castle probably consisted of a wooden house on a mound of earth known as a motte, which would have been surrounded by a deep dry ditch. Outside it was a defended yard or bailey, in which Waudari's men, animals and stores were kept. The memory of the castle has long been perpetuated in Castle Street, and the yard of the United Counties omnibus garage was once known as Castle Close. Excavations for *The Luton News* printing works in 1963 revealed the ditch surrounding the bailey of the castle. Its depth is unknown, but it was at least 3 m wide. The bailey was raised about 1 m above the surrounding land, and this rise is preserved in the change of ground floor level in the printing works. The ditch had been surrounded on its inner and outer edge by wooden posts which had supported a stockade. The motte of the castle was on the site of the bus garage and Castle Street seems to have followed the line of the ditch which separated the motte from the bailey. When the foundations of *The Luton News* building were dug the castle ditch was visible for a few days. No pottery was seen, although holes

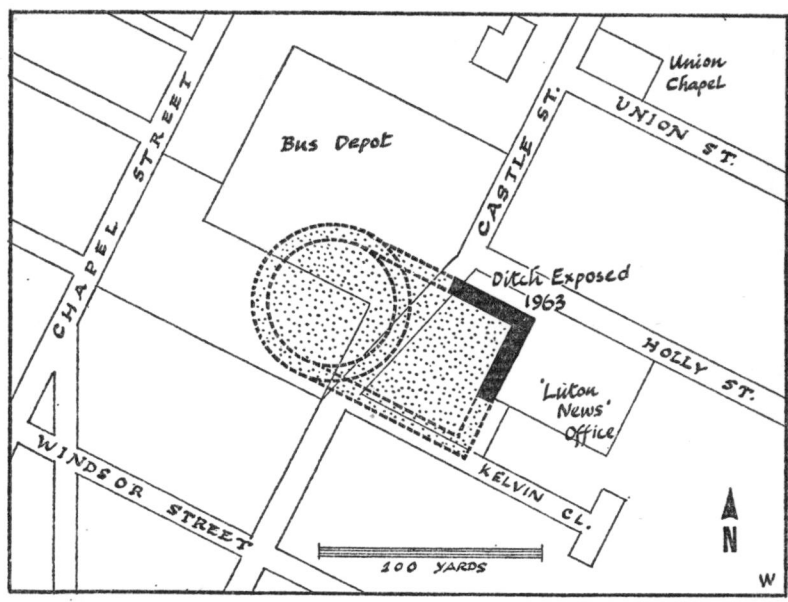

The approximate position of Robert de Waudari's Castle.

which had supported the posts showed quite clearly. The castle only stood for fifteen years before it was pulled down in 1154.

We know nothing of the organisation of the people of Luton at that time, but we can be sure that they looked on Waudari with the natural distrust of countrymen for a foreigner. Matthew Paris, a monk of St Albans Abbey who died in 1259 and wrote a history of the abbey and its surroundings, described Luton at this time as 'a place abounding with parishioners, and richly endowed'. From this we can assume that the town was already big and was probably already beginning to assume the crossroads plan which was a main feature of its layout in the eighteenth century.

THE SCHEMING ABBOT

Although Biscot belonged to St Albans Abbey the abbots were dissatisfied. They dearly wanted to add Luton Church with its rich endowments to their possessions. Matthew Paris tells us that about 1153 the eighteenth Abbot of St Albans, Robert de Gorham, worked out a plan for securing the church. The Abbot was related to Robert de Waudari, lord of the manor of Luton and was also very friendly with Gilbert Cymmay, the clergyman. Whilst Gilbert was dying the Abbot made frequent visits to him, and persuaded him to surrender the church in favour of the Abbot's nephew Geoffrey. The Abbot then turned his attention to getting Waudari's agreement. He had almost succeeded when fate temporarily intervened.

In 1153 Duke Henry of Normandy, the son of Empress Matilda and Count Geoffrey of Anjou, arrived in England. Although only 19 he was a great soldier, and as grandson of Henry I had a stronger claim to the throne than King Stephen. He had two choices before him; either to defeat Stephen in battle, or to force an agreement whereby he should be recognised as Stephen's heir. After Henry had 'captured a number of towns and very many castles . . . he arrived at the town of Bedford, where the king's supporters had taken refuge in a very strong castle, and after heavily plundering the town delivered it to the flames'. Moving southwards, Henry met Stephen at Wallingford in August 1153. A truce was agreed, and in Winchester three months later a charter was drawn up in which Stephen declared Henry to be his successor on the throne. Although it is not written in the Charter of

Winchester some sort of verbal agreement was made that all the mercenaries who were introduced into England by Stephen, should leave the country and their estates returned to the lawful owners who had held them during Henry I's reign. At the same time the castles of the foreigners should be destroyed.

In Luton Robert de Waudari had to leave the country and in the following year, 1154, his castle was pulled down. The Abbot of St Albans realised that no one would accept that the now dead Gilbert Cymmay and the banished Robert de Waudari had granted the church to him, and so he had to begin his plotting over again. Robert, Earl of Gloucester, had died, but his son William, Earl of Gloucester, had succeeded to the family title and the manor of Luton. The Abbot now began to press the Earl and at last persuaded him to transfer the church and all the land formerly held by William Chamberlain to the abbey. The Abbot had to pay 8 marks for the grant, and the Earl insisted that the widow of William the Chamberlain should be allowed to live on the land during the rest of her life. He also stipulated that the abbots of St Albans should pay half a knight's fee to the Earl of Gloucester each year. The Earl was not done with the Abbot yet, however, for he soon came back to petition for the lifting of the knight's fee. This was agreed to, but only after the Abbot had paid a further 20 marks.

To make quite sure that the Luton church belonged to the abbey, the Abbot next persuaded King Stephen to confirm the grant. The King did so on condition that certain of the profits of the church should be used for entertaining strangers visiting the abbey and St Alban's shrine. At about this time annual pilgrimages to the shrine were a binding obligation for the people of Luton. It was also decided that two priests should be chosen by the abbey to serve the church of Luton and that they should be paid out of the church's endowment.

The Abbot's Palace

The Abbot must have had a passion for Luton, for although he was a much travelled man and had visited the Pope in Rome and had been the foremost English abbot at the Council of Tours, he now found time to build a summer palace on St Anne's Hill, south-west of Rutland Crescent, overlooking the town. The palace, with its chapel dedicated to St Anne, was built of stone and was not demolished until 1689.

In 1155 King Stephen died and Henry II was proclaimed king in accordance with the Charter of Winchester. One of the first acts of his reign was to proclaim that all the land that had belonged to his predecessors should now be restored to him. So he became lord of the manor of Luton and held it throughout his reign. Earl William of Gloucester didn't seem to object to losing Luton, but the poor Abbot was distraught. For three years he followed the King about the countryside petitioning for the church of Luton to be restored to St Albans Abbey. At last, in 1158, the King gave way and issued a charter confirming that the churches of Luton and Houghton were once more the property of the abbey. For the next eight years, until his death in 1166, the Abbot was able to enjoy the profits of the church that he had worked so hard to acquire.

FARLEY HOSPITAL

King Henry II had spent much of his life in France and whenever he crossed to England he sailed from the French port of Wissant, between Calais and Boulogne. Nearby, probably at the tiny hamlet of St Inglevert, was the Hospital of the Trinity – a resting place for travellers – and it is likely that the King rested there many times before and after making the Channel crossing. Perhaps after some particularly rough crossing he felt particularly happy to be safe at the hospital, because in January 1156, he gave some of the manor of Luton to monks from Wissant so that they could build a hospital and chapel on Farley Hill. The building stood in Farley Farm Road and its lands covered the whole of the Farley Hill Estate and Stockwood Park (in those days known as Wyperley). The name Farley means a bracken or fern-covered clearing in the woodlands. The hamlet of St Inglevert is still remembered in the Santingfield street names. French monks probably came to Luton soon after 1156 to build and run their hospital, and by 1198 we hear that the master of the hospital was a Frenchman called Mauger.

Another hospital, this time for sick people, was called 'The House of God, of the Virgin Mary and St Mary Magdalene'. This hospital was founded by one of the most famous archbishops in

English history, Thomas Beckett. It lay on the hill between the Vauxhall factory and the airport, very close to the site of the former Spittlesea Isolation Hospital.

Fairs and Market

King Richard I sold the manor of Luton to one of his Crusaders, Earl Baldwin de Bethune, for £80. Almost as soon as Baldwin took over the manor he found the Abbot of St Albans, John de Cella, making claims on it. These included the right to hold an annual fair in Luton, stalls in the market, various pieces of land including Crawley and Cowridge, and fishing rights between the Abbot's Mill Pond and the North Bridge. Rather to the Abbot's surprise, Baldwin agreed to all the Abbot's claims. As far as we are concerned the most interesting thing about the whole affair was the Deed of Confirmation which Baldwin produced. Its wording gives us an insight into life in Luton at the time:

> 'The fair ought to be the Abbot's on whatsoever day the feast of the Assumption shall fall, except the sale of gold, and of horses, and of tanned hides, and of men who of old were sold, and that the Abbot shall have sufficient stalls and two chests and one shop in the market.'

The fair began on the eve of 15 August and lasted a week. For many centuries it was held in the churchyard, and in good years was used by the country folk as a means of celebrating the harvest. The lord of the manor reserved the right to sell horses and hides. It is interesting to notice that it was also forbidden to sell slaves; a custom that must have originated during Saxon times. The market had always been held on Sundays and seems to have begun by the people meeting on Sundays at church. Earl Baldwin considered that this was a violation of the Lord's day and had it changed to a Monday. Ever since, Monday has been Luton's official market day. The market stalls were the familiar trestle affairs that we still see in street markets today. The chests were large lock-up boxes in which traders kept their scales, weights and other equipment. As to the shop, its modern counterpart is the mobile snack-bar with a let-down counter front. These could be wheeled away when the fair was over. We learn at a later period that these shops were the cause of many complaints when they were left parked in the streets on Sundays.

By this time a number of tiny farming hamlets were appearing round Luton. Two of these, Crawley and Cowridge, were mentioned in the Abbot's claim. Crawley was a small hamlet round a green opposite St Anne's Church. The green has now been almost entirely built over, and only one cottage remained in 1963. Cowridge has now been absorbed into Round Green. It lay to the west of where Northview Road joins Stockingstone Road and stretched almost to Crawley. Stopsley, too, was by this time a fair sized hamlet. It was first referred to in 1199 as *Stoppelee*, and derives from land belonging to a person called Stopp. Its cottages clustered round the green and sheep drank at the village pond.

Ramridge came into being a few years later. Its name became associated with the low north-south ridge along which Ashcroft Road now runs. It is not certain whether it means the ram or raven ridge. Cowridge, on the other hand, which forms the next ridge to the west is clearly the ridge on which cows grazed, whilst Crawley means a crow-clearing in the woods.

The Abbot's fishing rights on the river Lea ran from Mill Street to the mill pond beside the Church Mill near the roundabout between St Mary's Road and Crawley Green Road. It is difficult to imagine monks fishing in green meadows where the Public Library and Arndale Centre now stand.

6   Falkes de Breauté and the Thirteenth Century

WHEN King John came to the throne in 1199, Earl Baldwin was still lord of the manor of Luton. The Earl's 4 years old daughter, Alice, was pledged to marry William, the 11 years old son of the Marshal of England. It was agreed that when the marriage took place, the manor of Luton would form part of Alice's dowry.

In 1214 Alice and William Marshall were married, but Alice died two years later at the age of only 19; her husband retained the manor of Luton for a few months, then later in 1216, perhaps under compulsion from King John, he handed it over to Falkes de Breauté, a Norman of illegitimate birth who was a great favourite and supporter of the King. There was certainly something distinctly strange about the transaction, since the two men were on opposing sides, Falkes supporting the King, and William his barons.

THE SEVEN YEARS' INTERDICT

King John had quarrelled with the Church over the appointment of the Archbishop of Canterbury – Stephen Langton. As a result the Pope had laid the kingdom under an interdict. This meant that for seven years all the churches were closed; their altars were stripped and their doors locked so that no services could be held and no masses sung. Marriages had to be conducted in the church porches and funerals took place silently in unconsecrated ground. Only baptism and confessions for the dying were allowed. At the same time, John had annoyed his barons by making them pay their rents and taxes with great regularity. In 1215 his enemies combined to make him seal the document of sixty-three clauses known as the Magna Carta – the Great Charter.

Once the document was sealed, King John raised an army of mercenaries (hired soldiers) and began to attack the castles of those barons who had made him grant the charter. One such unfortunate baron was William de Beauchamp, whose castle at Bedford was seized in the King's name, by Falkes de Breauté. In fear of the King's revenge, the barons invited the French king, Louis VIII, to take possession of England and depose King John. Louis was only too glad of a chance to invade England and sent over his army under his son, the Dauphin.

Meanwhile King John died and his 9 years old son was crowned King Henry III on 28 October 1216. In December of that year, the French army was at St Albans, where the Dauphin demanded homage from the Abbot. When this was refused, the French threatened to burn the abbey and the town, and only went away after the Abbot had paid them 80 marks. A month later, on 22 January 1217, Falkes de Breauté attacked St Albans and robbed the abbey of 100 pounds of silver and then followed the French to Lincoln where they were later beaten in a decisive battle and sent home.

The Most Hated Man in England

In a very short time Falkes de Breauté became one of the most hated men in England. He was described as impious, ignoble and base, a man with immense power, the keeper of numerous castles, the sheriff of seven counties, and the lord of vast estates. Typical of the stories told of him is one concerning the monks of Old Warden Abbey near Bedford. The monks claimed a certain wood which Falkes disputed, so he sent his soldiers to the abbey and attacked the monks. One of them died, others were wounded and thirty were dragged off to Bedford Castle.

Luton Castle

By 1221 Falkes had erected castles at Eaton Bray and Luton 'to the grave danger of Dunstable and the neighbourhood'. The Luton Castle stood on the southern side of the parish church. It covered most of the area from the church to Lea Road, with the river forming its boundary on the eastern side, and the College of Technology on the west. A substantial mound of earth still covered this area at the beginning of the present century, and

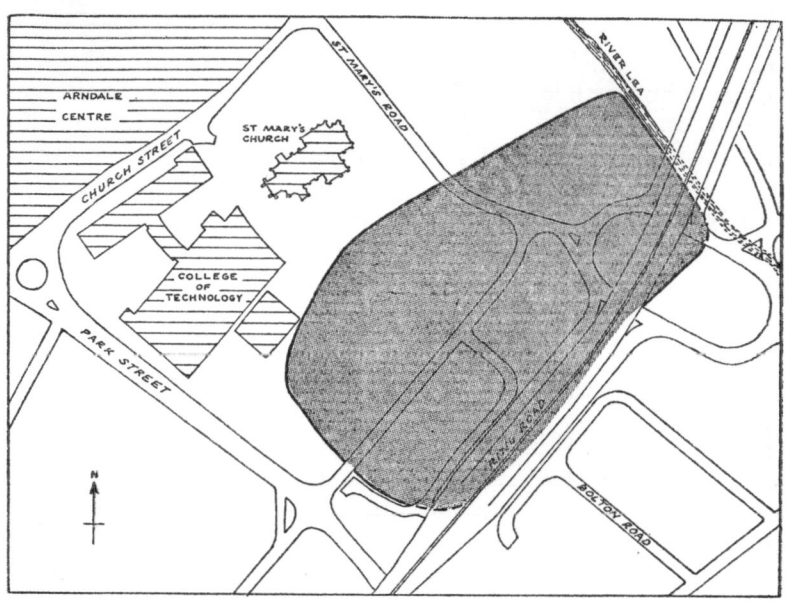

Falkes de Breauté's Castle lay within the shaded area.

records show that the castle moat bounded the southern side of the churchyard at the same time.

In 1221 Falkes dammed the river near his castle, causing the water to overflow onto the church lands, where it flooded houses and stopped the Abbot's mill from grinding corn, as well as blocking the King's highway. When the Abbot complained, Falkes replied, 'I am only sorry that I didn't wait until the corn had been housed, so that the water might have destroyed it completely.'

When King Henry became of age in the eyes of the Pope in 1223 he ordered the surrender of all royal castles. By April of the following year all the royal castles had been placed in the hands of the bishops, although Falkes managed to retain Bedford Castle and other castles in Wales.

A JUDGE IS KIDNAPPED

In the spring of 1224 Falkes was summoned to the shire court of Bedfordshire for disseisin at Luton – that is, without reason, seizing land belonging to other people and claiming it as his own. Falkes failed to appear at the court on a number of occasions and made himself liable to a sentence of outlawry. During Whit week (2–8 June) three justices, Martin Pateshull, Thomas de Multone and Henry de Braibroc gave judgment against Falkes in thirty-five cases of disseisin. On 17 June, when Falkes had his last chance to appear at the court or be outlawed, he sent his brother William Martel de Breauté whom he had left in charge of Bedford Castle, to kidnap the judges. William succeeded in capturing only Henry de Braibroc, the other judges escaping, and carried him off to Bedford.

De Braibroc's wife hurried to the King at Northampton. Falkes was solemnly outlawed, and Henry, now 17 years of age, gathered together a great army and made with all haste to Bedford. After a siege of eight weeks the castle fell, and William de Breauté, eleven knights and all his men at arms were hanged on an improvised gallows.

Falkes had not been at Bedford. The King's men found him near Chester where he yielded himself to the young King's mercy. Because of his past services to King John his life was spared, but he lost everything else, and two years later he died of poisoning at St Ciriac in southern France, where he had joined Simon the Crusader on his Albigensian Crusade.

All the accounts of Falkes's wickedness come from the monks and the clergy, so perhaps he wasn't quite as bad as they made him appear. Indeed some of the peasants who hated the clergy, might have thought of him as something of a hero.

It is interesting to note that Falkes held land in Surrey known as Falkes Hall. This name was transformed into Vauxhall in the sixteenth century, and has now reappeared in Luton in connection with the motor industry.

The Lady of the Manor

Falkes forfeited the manor of Luton, and after reverting to the King for about a year, it was restored to William Marshall, Earl of Pembroke, in 1225. The Earl saw to it that the manor paid £5 each year to the Dean and Chapter of St Paul's for prayers for the soul of his first wife, Alice. In the previous year William had married the King's sister, Countess Eleanor Plantagenet. In 1230 he was made captain-general of the King's forces in Brittany, and in 1231 he died at the early age of 41, leaving Countess Eleanor as the first 'Lady of the Manor'.

WILLIAM OF SOMERIES

In the same year the *Dunstable Chronicle* records the death of William of Someries. This is the earliest reference to the De Somery family whose name is perpetuated in the ruins of Lord Wenlock's fifteenth century gatehouse and chapel. In the field to the west of Lord Wenlock's building, erroneously known as Someries Castle, is a rectangular earthwork which represents the thirteenth century home of William de Someries, whilst extending over the field to the south of the earthwork, are the traces of an extensive village, perhaps deserted at a time of plague.

The rectangular earthwork consists of a mound of earth 33 m square, on which a house of some size must have stood. Behind it, on its western side was a small yard, whilst a larger yard lay in front of it, on the eastern side. The house and yards were surrounded by a rampart 94 m long and 65 m wide, which probably supported a wooden fence. It was protected on the outside by a ditch. The main gate was on the eastern side, where the earthwork is somewhat irregular; an old drawing shows a cottage on this spot in the eighteenth century. There is no evidence for a Norman castle having ever stood on the site; instead a fortified manor house seems to have existed there for four or five hundred years.

A similar earthwork existed at Limbury known as Gibbet Stretch Close. This may have been the site of the manor house of Biscot which was granted to Robert Fitzwalter by the Abbot of St Albans in 1211, and which passed to Walter Fitzwalter on his father's death in 1234. The Gibbet Stretch Close mound consisted of a mound of earth measuring 41 m by 23 m, with a higher mound in one corner, which according to tradition, later supported a gibbet or gallows. The manor house probably looked very similar to that of William de Someries, being constructed mainly of timber, wattle and daub. It was surrounded by a water-filled moat, which, together with a similar moated site in close proximity, both south of the river Lea, was destroyed without record in the construction of Runfold Avenue during the post-war years.

The Grey Friars

In 1224 the first party of barefooted Grey Friars landed in Britain. These men were followers of St Francis of Assisi, who believed that the only way for members of the church to help the poor, was by living like them and with them in squalor and misery in their villages and towns. The friars were very popular amongst the peasants, where their Bible teachings and their aid and comfort for the sick were greatly appreciated. Jealousy often arose between the local priest and the friars, and they frequently had to preach on village greens because they weren't allowed into the church. One such group of friars built themselves a monastery at Dunstable directly opposite the priory. The Prior would have liked to have kept them out of the town, but the friars were immensely popular and were backed by the royal family, so the Prior had to put up with them.

One of the Grey Friars was appointed master of Farley Hospital in 1228, and in 1247 the vicar of Luton, Adam de Biscot, resigned from the church in order to join the friars. We can imagine him giving up the comparative luxury of his vicarage, to go out with bare feet to preach the gospel and beg for his food from village to village.

The Pope's Ambassador

In 1244 Pope Innocent IV sent to England a new Papal Nuncio or ambassador called Master Martin. He was apparently an intolerable fellow who began to gather large sums of money from the people for the Pope's use. Many people objected and a great number of barons and knights assembled at Luton and Dunstable in June 1245, apparently for the purpose of holding a tournament, but really to plot against Master Martin. Tournaments usually led to trouble and King Henry forbade them to hold it, but the barons did not leave until they had chosen Fulk Fitz Warin to take a message of defiance to the Papal Nuncio in London. Matthew Paris tells us that Fitz Warin sought out Master Martin and ordered him to leave the country. 'By whose orders?' demanded Martin. 'By the orders of the whole body of armed men who have lately met at Luton and Dunstable. If you will take sound advice you won't wait here another two days, or you and your followers will be cut to bits!' Martin, terrified, rushed to King Henry for safe conduct to France. The King is said to have replied, 'The devil give you a safe conduct to hell!' However, the palace marshal led him safely to the coast, and he was not seen in England again.

SIMON DE MONTFORT

We have seen that when William Marshall, Earl of Pembroke, died in 1231, his widow the Countess Eleanor became the lady of the manor of Luton. On 6 January 1238 she was secretly married to Simon de Montfort, one of the most important men in thirteenth century England. The following year Simon became Earl of Leicester. Simon came from the south of France, and after his marriage to Eleanor was sent to Gascony in France to restore law and order there. This was a difficult job which took a long time and made a number of enemies for both Simon and King Henry. The King was not satisfied with the way that Simon had managed his affairs and in 1252 made him stand trial for five weeks at Westminster. In the end the King had to admit that all the evidence pointed in Simon's favour, but he refused to give Simon back his French job, nor could there be friendship between them again.

Henry III was an extravagant and devout king, but he mis-governed England in a muddled and confused fashion, which caused many of the nobility led by Simon de Montfort to attempt to curb his powers, and to set up a council of earls, barons and church leaders in his place. They particularly objected to the King bringing his friends from France and setting them up in good positions in England. In 1258 the King attended a council held at Oxford which put forward some important ideas for re-forming the government. The most important of these were that two knights should be chosen from each county to discover and report to parliament any wrongs committed by the royal officers; also that parliament should meet three times a year. At this time the word 'parliament' simply meant a 'parleying' – a conference between the king and his nobles. But even so, here in the middle of the thirteenth century was the beginning of the Parliament that we know today.

In 1261 King Henry refused to abide by the decisions reached at Oxford in 1258, and in the following year the Pope supported him. In 1264 civil war broke out between the King and the barons and on 14 May the King and his son Edward were taken prisoners at Lewes. For a year Simon de Montfort ruled England, but in May 1265 Prince Edward escaped to Wales where he mustered an army, and on 4 August Simon's army was trapped at Evesham in Worcestershire where it was quickly beaten. Simon was killed and the King was restored to power.

We don't know how often Simon visited the manor of Luton which had passed to him when he married Eleanor. Certainly he was there in November 1257 because he made a gift to the church. On 13 April 1275 Eleanor died in the convent of Montargis in France and the manor of Luton was returned once more to the heirs of William Marshall, Earl of Pembroke. The manor of Luton was valued at £85 8s $6\frac{1}{2}$d at Eleanor's death; $97\frac{1}{2}$ acres (39.5 hectares) of it were the property of Eleanor herself, whilst 39 acres (15.6 hectares) were leased to her tenants for a rent of £14 13s 7d a year. Another $5\frac{1}{2}$ acres (2.2 hectares) consisted of meadow with pasture and woodland. Meadow was the name given to grass set aside for haymaking, hence the concern in the nursery rhyme for 'The sheep in the meadow, the cows in the corn'.

When Countess Eleanor died the manor of Luton was given back to the heir of the Earl of Pembroke. This was Sybil de Ferrers, and the manor was divided equally between her six daughters.

CRIME IN THE THIRTEENTH CENTURY

In view of Simon's concern with affairs of national importance, it was impossible for him to manage his Luton manor himself, and so he appointed two stewards to run it for him. These were Henry Blundell and Thomas del Hoo. The stewards, or bailiffs as they were called at the time, had many jobs to do beside running the Earl's household. Not least amongst them was the apprehension of criminals.

In 1247 the bailiffs caught Ralph le Berker in the act of stealing five sheep. They put him into the Earl's prison, from which he escaped. After chasing him to Ely, they caught and hanged him. When the matter was later brought up at Bedford Assizes, the Earl was fined for not keeping a stricter guard on his prison.

Two other prisoners, Joan, the daughter of Emma, who had

stolen some cloth, and Gilbert the Fleming, both escaped from the same prison and fled to Luton Church where they claimed sanctuary. Here they could remain in safety for forty days, or carrying a cross in their hands, they could leave the country by the quickest available route. Once more the Earl was fined for allowing his prisoners to escape.

At Limbury Chapel, which stood close to where Leagrave Junior School now stands, 'William, son of Alice, drew his bow and shot an arrow at Roger le Ken', in 1247, 'so that he fell down dead.' William came from Houghton Regis and all the villagers were fined for Roger's murder. The people of Biscot, Bramingham and Limbury who were present at the time and didn't capture William were also fined for letting him escape.

FAMINE

In the last few years before his death in 1259, that inquisitive monk of St Albans Abbey, Matthew Paris, recorded in his *Chronicle* some interesting details of local affairs. In 1253 he tells us that there was a great shortage of corn and prices ranged from 5s a quarter at St Albans to 13s 4d at Dunstable. In the following year corn was abundant and cost only half-a-crown a quarter. From February to May 1256, storms, wind and rain reduced England to a muddy marsh and 'rendered the earth barren and fruitless so that many farmers sowed fresh seed in their land'. The wet spring was followed by an equally wet harvest. The corn was ruined and many people died of starvation. Two years later another disastrous harvest caused widespread famine and poverty. For the poor folk times were lean indeed:

' "I have no penny", quoth Piers, "Pullets for to buy
Nor neither geese nor piglets, but two green [new] cheeses,
A few curds and cream and an oaten cake
And two loaves of beans and bran to bake for my little ones.
I have parsley and leeks and many cabbages,
And by this livelihood we must live till Lammas time." '
[August].

FOOD IN PLENTY

We can contrast the frugal diet of the peasantry with the food required by Prince Edward, fourth son of Edward I, who stayed at King's Langley in Hertfordshire with his followers in 1294. The prince's servants took possession of all food, cheese and eggs brought to Luton market and then, when insufficient had been collected, they visited the private houses, helping themselves, and seldom paying or giving a receipt for what they had taken. Beer and bread were taken from the Luton bakers and brewers, and more was demanded, special bakings and brewings having to be arranged.

LIFE ON THE MANOR

For the common people of Luton life began as soon as it was light in the morning. After a brief meal of bread and ale the menfolk went out into their fields, to mow hay or cut corn. The great fields were divided into strips of land and each man cultivated some of them. Each year the men drew lots for their strips. Some of the strips were on the good land at the foot of the hills, others by the river where they were liable to become flooded, and others on stony ground which provided a poor crop. By drawing lots, each man felt sure of getting some of the good land. But land was short; as children grew up and demanded their share, so the strips became narrower, and often tenants tried to steal land from each other. Meanwhile the women milked the cow, fed the hens, made the beds and cleaned the mud floors of their chimneyless houses. The men had their mid-day meal in the fields, more bread and ale, with cheese and perhaps an apple. The afternoon passed by and the men returned home for an evening meal of soup made from beans and peas, bread and cheese. The meal over, the men would stroll outside to see that the cow or pigs were in good health. Perhaps they might pull a few weeds from their front gardens, planted with cabbage, onions and parsley, or attend to a loose shutter or broken latch on their tiny thatched cottages. Beyond the houses stood the church, with its stone tower and round-arched windows, where the townsfolk met for mass on Sundays. The church was surprisingly big and was used for other purposes besides mass. The Manor Court was probably held within its walls and even Miracle plays were performed from time to time. Weapons were kept there, and the fire-hook used for pulling thatch from burning houses. Nearby was the stone house where Hugh de Baneburgh, the vicar, lived.

The Manor House

The manor house stood some distance away, perhaps surrounded by a moat crossed by a drawbridge. Like the cottages, its walls were of wattle daubed with clay, but strengthened with great oak beams cut from the woods perhaps near Farley. It contained a great hall, with a kitchen and cellar, and a gallery at one end used for sleeping. Outside the main building were stables and outbuildings, with a yard for poultry and perhaps a dovecot for pigeons – a useful source of fresh meat during the winter. A royal manor like Luton probably had a bakery, brewery and laundry, as well as a private chapel close by.

The Peasants

A number of the folk in Luton were villeins or 'unfree tenants'. Although they were not slaves, they were not free to come and go as they pleased. They held 30 to 40 acres of land on condition that they worked so many days each week on the lord of the manor's land. The only way that a villein could leave his land was by payment of a fine to his lord, or by running away. If the villein who escaped could avoid being caught for one year, he was then a free man. His only difficulty was where to go; there was little point in moving on to another manor, unless it was to escape from a cruel master. Without their lord's consent villeins could not give their son or daughter in marriage, sell an ox or cow, or cut down an oak or ash. They must buy a licence for all these things. Similarly, permission was required to educate or apprentice a son, or to become a monk or priest. There were clearly many things that villeins could not do, but they had their rights too. There were rights of pasture on which cattle were allowed to graze; rights of pannage in which pigs were allowed to grub for acorns in the woods; rights of estover – the gathering of timber by hook or by crook, that is, as much timber as they could knock off, or pull down from standing trees, for implements and tools, from the wastelands of the manor; rights of public holidays and feasts at Easter, Whitsun, Michaelmas and Christmas.

Most of the Luton folk were cottars – owning a cottage and garden, and little else. Since they owned less than the villeins they owed fewer services to their lord and so they could find time to work for a living.

The Luton people were no better nor worse than their fellows in other villages and towns. They had their troubles and worries and many of these would come before the Manor Court for settlement. The court was presided over by the lord's steward who heard of the various misdemeanours that had taken place since the court last met – a man found poaching rabbits, men taking timber from the lord's wood, permission for a boy to be bound apprentice, and so on. Occasionally a crime was committed of such magnitude that it was sent to the Sheriff at the County Court in Bedford. For example:

'On the night of 24th April, 1275, felons and thieves came to the house of Thomas of Barton in Stopsley within the parish of Luton, tied Thomas up, gave him a wound in the head on the left side of the crown with a pick axe and left him for dead, so that he died soon after lunch the following day. The same night the said felons gave Thomas's daughter Joan, aged 12, a wound near the crown, so that she lay speechless, dying on 30th April; wounded his other daughters Cecily and Agnes, leaving them for dead, and then carried away all the goods of the house. At dawn the next day Agnes went to Richard de Sedefold's house and raised the hue, to which the neighbours came.'

In spite of Agnes raising a hue and cry the murderers seem to have escaped, and the coroner had to pass a verdict of murder by felons unknown.

In 1285 Nicholas le Hayward – (Haywards were appointed to take charge of the meadows, woods and ditches of the manor) – imprisoned the lepers of the Hospital of St John the Baptist at Luton and set fire to the house of Richard Attewynche. In Nicholas's absence the court outlawed him. It is interesting to notice that a hospital for lepers existed, probably out of town for fear of spreading disease, possibly in the region of Norton Road.

During the thirteenth century many large manors were unofficially divided up into smaller ones. This happened at Luton, where such new manors as Stopsley, Haverings, Woodcroft and Hoo came into being at about this time. We have also seen that the rest of the manor was divided up between the six daughters of Sybil de Ferrers; so that by the reign of Edward I there were a large number of small manors, from which the King was able to claim only a much reduced revenue.

In the records of taxes imposed by the King in 1297, we learn that Luton was producing $15\frac{1}{2}$ tons of grain each year. Luton now kept 1,473 sheep, 112 cows, 175 oxen and horses and only 115 swine. The corn was valued at about £12 a ton, swine 1s 6d each, sheep 1s, cows 5s, oxen 6s and horses 4s to 6s 8d. Luton's $15\frac{1}{2}$ tons of grain was about half of the total produced in four towns of the county – Leighton, Bedford, Dunstable and Luton.

7 The Fourteenth Century

ABOUT Eastertime in 1309 a tournament was held at Dunstable – probably the lists were set up on the flat land at the foot of the Downs close to the Luton boundary. Tournaments – mock fights – were favoured by the nobility as a sport and a war-practice for about 500 years, although the clergy never tired of pointing out that such sport damned the participants to hell. We know very little about the proceedings in 1309, except that Sir Giles Argentein, one of the most illustrious of jousters, participated, together with John de Somery and John de Aygnell, of Someries and East Hyde in Luton.

For the majority of Luton folk the fourteenth century was a period of great distress and misery. In 1314 and 1315 the country was swept by famine, the result of six successive years of bad harvest, which caused starvation and death to many Luton people. In 1317 the sheep and cattle of the town died in hundreds from some form of foot-and-mouth disease. A contemporary writer gives us this description:

> 'The beastes and cattel also by the corrupt grane whereof they fed, dyed, whereby it came to passe that the eating of flesh was suspected by all men, for flesh of beasts not corrupted was hard to finde. Horse flesh was counted great delicates, the poore stole fatte dogges to eat; some (as it was sayde) compelled through famine, in hidden places did eat the flesh of their owne children, and some stole others, which they devoured.'

THE GREAT FIRE

In 1336 a great fire swept through Luton. Most of the town was built of wood, and the houses were roofed with straw, reeds and the like. As soon as one house caught fire, sparks and flames spread to the next. Consequently the greater part of the town was destroyed and hundreds of families were made homeless. When the tax collectors came to Luton in July the townsfolk were excused their payments until Michaelmas Day (29 September). Four years later 200 houses were still ruined and uninhabited, and 720 acres of land uncultivated. It is clear that tools, seed, barns, animals, and inhabitants, besides the houses, must have perished in the fire.

TITHES

Throughout the Middle Ages one of the most crippling services that the peasants had to provide for the church was the payment of a tax known as a tithe. The church claimed a tenth of all a man's possessions and his labour. The demand was based on the story of Jacob's ladder in the book of *Genesis*, where Jacob vowed to God 'of all that thou shalt give me I will surely give the tenth unto Thee'. When corn was cut a tenth went to the church, when you pulled your onions a tenth were set aside, if you gathered wood every tenth stick must not be burnt. Since no man was expected to be completely honest about this, the church took the man's second best beast when he died, in order to make sure that they hadn't been too badly cheated. Since at the same time the lord of the manor took the best beast, little remained for the man's widow and children.

Some of the villeins managed to accumulate small sums of money with which they paid their lords instead of working for them. In the time which then became their own, they could devote themselves to raising sheep, a job which was becoming increasingly profitable. In 1343 wool from Bedfordshire was selling at between £7 7s and £9 7s per sack. English wool was exported and taxes paid on it helped to finance the English wars against France, which had begun in 1339.

In August 1346 the battle of Crecy took place and a number of Luton men fought on the side of the victorious Edward III, including David de Assheby, Roger de Loring, Henry de Bereford, Richard de Havering, Alexander de Stopsley, John Augnel, Thomas de Hoo and Edward de Kendale.

THE BLACK DEATH

In the autumn of 1347 the Black Death swept through Europe,

bringing about a long lull in the French war. To most people in England this plague in France was the reward of the Frenchmen for their sins, but when it appeared at Melcombe Regis in Dorset in the summer of 1348 the complacent English began to have second thoughts. The bubonic plague was carried by black rats, and quickly spread through England, killing large numbers of people all over the country. Men and women died within a few hours of contracting the disease. At first their throats became inflamed, then their chests burnt within; they would vomit and spit blood and their breath turned foul, carbuncles developing under their armpits. A Florentine doctor tells us that there was always a possibility of recovery as long as the blood spitting did not begin. There was no cure for the plague because no one knew what caused it. Men fell down in their homes, in the streets, at church or at work, and few people would nurse them or bury their bodies. The churchyards were filled and trenches were dug into which bodies were shovelled by the hundreds. A monk of St Albans wrote:

'Scarcely the half of mankind survived. And towns that were formerly very thickly populated were left destitute of inhabitants, the plague being so violent that the living were scarce able to bury the dead.'

Today children still play a game about the plague, although they have forgotten its meaning:

'Ring a ring a-roses,
A pocketful of posies,
Tishoo, tishoo, we all fall down.'

The 'ring a-roses' refers to a red rash which appeared on people's bodies as soon as they had caught the disease. The posies were sweet smelling flowers and herbs used to hide the stench of decaying corpses, whilst sneezing was a frequent symptom before the victims fell down dead.

We do not know how many people in Luton died of the plague, but a third of the population is likely to be a conservative estimate.

In January 1349 the Bishop of Bath and Wells wrote:

'The contagious nature of the present pestilence, which is spreading itself far and wide, has left many parish churches, and consequently the people of our diocese, destitute of curates and priests.'

Such was the case at Luton. The vicar, John de Luton, died of the plague at the beginning of 1349, and his successor Andrew Power died before the end of the year. Richard de Rochele next filled the vacancy, but fled after only a very short stay. In the following year (1350) William de Chaumbre, a clerk only in deacon's orders, was appointed vicar.

At St Albans Abbey the Abbot and forty-seven monks died – over three-quarters of the whole community. The new abbot was perhaps the greatest of all, Thomas de la Mare. He was one of King Edward III's Privy Councillors, and a great friend of the Black Prince.

DISLIKE OF THE MONKS

To the ordinary people the Abbot and his monks were their oppressors, and they often went out of their way to humiliate the clergy. Although many lords were allowing their villeins to buy their freedom, the monks, ever the most conservative of landlords, could have none of it. The Prior or Abbot was the servant of his church, and whether he wanted to or not, he was unable to give his men their freedom because they constituted church property and therefore something which he could not give away. Even so, the peasantry often had good cause to despise their extortionate landlords, for the monks sometimes lived lazy, drunken, lecherous lives, whilst the villeins had to work from dawn till dusk on the church lands for little reward.

THE ABBOT'S CELLARER

Abbot de la Mare sent his Cellarer into Bedfordshire to collect dues and rents. One Monday morning whilst he was on his way from Hexton back to St Albans, the Cellarer stopped at Luton market. Philip de Lymbury – a knight of the district – and some of his men were in the town. Philip, 'in hatred of the Abbot and in utter contempt of religion', seized the Cellarer and placed him in the pillory in the market place where he was ridiculed by all the townsfolk. The Abbot was furious and prosecuted the knight, but the Duke of Lancaster intervened in the dispute and a settlement was reached to the satisfaction of the church. Philip was ordered to make an offering on the altar, but whenever he approached it, blood gushed from his nose. The superstitious congregation considered that this was God's punishment for offending those whose job it was to serve him. Early accounts of the story do not tell us whether Philip tried to make his offering in Luton church or St Albans Abbey.

THE PEASANTS' GRIEVANCES

It must be remembered that the abbey owned quite a lot of land in Luton – the church and its mill nearby, the manor of Dallow, and land at Biscot, Crawley Green, Ramridge End and East Hyde. For a hundred years the tenants had been discontented with the demands made on them by the abbey. They particularly objected to a demand that all their corn should be ground at the Abbey Mill and many of them set up hand-mills of their own. On at least three occasions the Abbot's men seized the hand-mills and laid them down as a floor in the Abbot's parlour.

When the Black Death finally subsided the remaining peasants began to realise that they were important units in the social system. The harvest was rotting and there were not enough hands to gather it. Without the peasant's labour, not only he, but his betters also, must starve. He could ask for higher wages, and, if he didn't get them, flee to another town where men were so desperately needed that no questions were asked. Five men from Sharpenhoe fled to Luton in 1352 where they found work as carters, merchants and reapers. Unfortunately for them, their old master traced them, had them arrested and the court ordered them back to Sharpenhoe. A law had been passed in 1349 called the 'Statute of Labourers' which made this possible.

In many parts of the country men seized the strip fields of their dead neighbours until their lands grew big enough for them to employ labour and form a new class of society known as yeomen.

During the years which followed, discontent was spread further by the preaching of John Wycliffe and John Ball. Wycliffe pointed out that the common people gave a great deal to the church, but the church gave them little in return. The clergy had grown far away from the ideals of Christ, and Wycliffe's followers attempted to represent the apostles of Christ, walking like the Grey Friars before them, barefooted through the countryside, dressed in poor clothes, and begging for food. Wycliffe translated the Bible into English so that the ordinary folk could understand it. The priests were furious because up till then they had been able to interpret it as they pleased. Now anyone could read of the simple life Christ had led and compare it with the luxurious life of the church leaders, and then begin to ask awkward questions. The Abbot of St Albans had copies of Wycliffe's bible publicly burnt outside St Peter's Church in St Albans.

John Ball attacked the church and the state, and his sermons were based on the popular jingle:

'When Adam delved [*dug*] and Eve span [*spun*]
Who was then a gentleman?'

'Since everyone has descended from the same parents, Adam and Eve,' said Ball, 'how can some people claim to be better than others? Why should some men be lords, and others slaves?'

The Peasants' Revolt

In 1380 a poll tax of 1s a head for all persons over 15 except beggars, was levied to pay for the French wars. This proved to be the straw that broke the camel's back. A shilling was a very hard burden for the poor to pay. The common people could stand it no longer, and began to congregate together with revolt in their hearts. Some of the Luton men marched to St Albans, others to Dunstable, and there they 'joined up with other protesting folk like themselves'. The Peasants' Revolt had begun. The amazing thing is that similar risings broke out simultaneously in Essex, Kent, and Norfolk.

The St Albans party, led by William Grindcobbe, marched to London where they talked with Wat Tyler the leader of the revolt. He advised them to return to St Albans, which they did, smashing abbey property and burning the royal charters on which the Abbot's power rested, and which bound the villeins. Next day the Abbot's prison was broken open and the prisoners released. A charter was extracted from the Abbot giving the peasants the right of free pasturage on abbey waste-lands, permission to hunt and fish in woods and ponds, abolition of the milling monopoly and the right of the town of St Albans to free municipal government without hindrance from the abbey. The Abbot signed and sealed the charter which was witnessed on the Abbot's side by Sir William Hoo of Luton. 'The fools believed that all were now as noble as the family of the King himself, and that there were to be no more masters upon earth', wrote the abbey scribe. On 14 June Wat Tyler was murdered, and a few days later King Richard II – only 14 years of age – rode to St Albans with an armed force, and restored law and order. On 15 July William Grindcobbe and fifteen others were hanged and drawn, then they were left swinging on the gibbets for 'as long as they could last'. In another part of the town John Ball the preacher was also hanged, drawn and quartered. An Inquisition quashed the Abbot's charter and the rising seemed to have been in vain.

For many years to come the abbey and the common folk were at loggerheads – abbey property caught fire, its animals were stolen, and its goods were destroyed. Life would have been a lot easier for the peasants if the rebels had won, but a rising of such magnitude could not pass unnoticed and before the end of the next century the troubles of the peasants had disappeared and passed into the pages of history.

THE 'MOAT HOUSE' AT LIMBURY

Sometime between 1370 and 1400 the 'Moat House' at Limbury was built. Originally this was a residential hall consisting of a large hall proper, separated from a bower by a cross passage. The walls were constructed of timber and wattle with a facing of brick and Totternhoe stone. The roof timbers of the hall are still preserved and consist of decorated arch-braced collar beams. The original covering was thatched. Behind the existing house stood a courtyard with kitchens and stables ranged round it. The whole building was surrounded by a moat with rounded corners and may have been crossed by a drawbridge on the north side. The fourteenth century hall was divided up into smaller rooms and floors somewhere about the beginning of the seventeenth century. On the wall of the cellar an inscription had been scratched recording that on 23 July 1666, hailstones as big as golf balls fell around the house. A modern copy of this can be seen in the bar of the present restaurant. The original house was probably built by the 'de Bereford' family, though the Ackworths lived there from about 1400 to 1548. John Ackworth was one of the founders of the Guild of the Holy Trinity in 1474, and a brass on the wall of the north transept of Luton church shows him with his two wives.

Below his effigy are seventeen small figures who may represent eight brothers and nine sisters of the Guild of the Holy Trinity.

Luton Parish Church

It will be appropriate to complete our survey of the fourteenth century by looking at the greatest surviving monument of the period that our town can provide – the parish church. It was during the fourteenth century that the works of the earlier churchbuilders in Luton were pulled down and an almost entirely new building erected in their place.

The church is dedicated to St Mary and is cruciform in plan. Its total length, including the tower, is 55.48 m and its width in the transepts is 30.78 m. The nave is 12.2 m high, whilst the tower is approximately 30 m high. These dimensions make St Mary's the largest church in the county and one of the biggest parish churches in England.

The most prominent feature of the outside of the church is the tower, decorated in a chequer-board pattern of knapped flint and soft Totternhoe stone. The flint was used with the stone in order to retard the weathering process. The chequering also appears on the walls of the aisles, transepts, vestry and porches, but most of this is modern facing work. Almost all the buttresses of the church have been restored, but the pair at the south-west angle of the south aisle and the north-western buttress of the north transept seem to be original fourteenth-century work. The transept buttress still shows signs of mediaeval tooling.

The best way to describe the interior of the church is to imagine that we are walking round the building. As we make our journey we will look at the more important features of all periods.

The Nave

We enter the church through the fourteenth-century north porch, and walk to the centre of the nave. If we turn and face the chancel and the altar, we notice on our right the Late Decorated arches of about 1360; on our left, separating the nave from the north aisle are three arches whose pillars have been carved without capital or abacus but whose arch moulding is carried down without interruption to the plinth. This achieves a sense of great height. The clerestory windows high above the nave are of the Perpendicular style. If we walk towards the chancel, we can see above the transept arches some amusing corbel heads traditionally claimed to represent Henry VIII and Anne Boleyn.

On entering the chancel our attention is naturally drawn to the altar with its mosaic reredos, based on Leonardo da Vinci's painting of *The Last Supper*. It was made in Venice and set up in 1883, and though it is a fine example of mosaic work, it tends to be somewhat garish by modern standards. The east window, rebuilt in 1866 by G. E. Street to replace a delightful round-headed window of the early eighteenth century, purports to be a reconstruction of the original thirteenth-century triple-lancets, whose sills were found in the wall when the earlier window was taken down.

A blind Perpendicular window in the north wall of the chancel also contains mosaic work. It is probable that it was blocked up in 1461 when work on the Wenlock chapel was commenced, and the vestry that it supplanted was moved further east to its present position. Near the filled-in window is a Late Decorated Easter Sepulchre – an arched opening in the wall in which models representing the Crucifixion were once displayed at Eastertime.

In the south wall of the chancel are four beautiful stone sedilia – seats for the clergy during high mass. Normally not more than three sedilia are found in churches, and it is likely that one of them

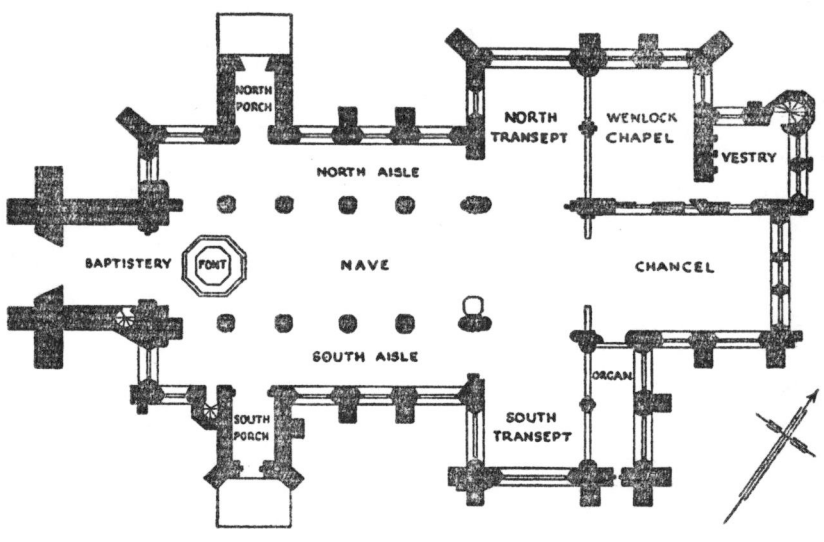

once contained a piscina – a stone basin in which the priest could rinse the vessels of the sacraments. Over the sedilia are carved eight coats of arms, together with the motto of John Wheathampstead, Abbot of St Albans from 1420–40 and again from 1452–61. The motto is proof enough of the Abbot's connection with the work; it reads 'Val-les-La-bun-da-bunt-val-les' (*valles abundabunt frumento*) and alludes to Psalm 65 v 14, 'The valleys shall stand so thick with corn'. There is some doubt as to the owners of the other coats of arms depicted, though the first and eighth are those of Abbot Wheathampstead himself. They are described heraldically as 'gules a chevron or, between nine ears of wheat tied in three parcels, or'. These arms were adopted by the former Luton High and Grammar Schools.

West of the sedilia is a beautiful arched recess known as the Barnard Chantry. It was erected by Richard Barnard, vicar of Luton, between 1477 and 1492. The vicar's name is carved in the form of a rebus (picture writing) over the arches, a muzzled bear is repeated three times standing for the syllable *Bar* and a hand is shown holding a box of spike-*nard*, a sweet smelling, but costly ancient ointment.

Before we leave the chancel it is worthwhile looking at the choir stalls which are nearly 600 years old. One still bears a link to which a Bible was once chained. The armrests are finely carved with animals and birds, and are in surprisingly good condition.

The Wenlock Chapel
The chancel is separated from the Wenlock Chapel by 'a wide and lofty arch, divided into two by a slight pier'. This is the celebrated and very delicate Wenlock screen. The whole chapel was built for Sir John Wenlock in 1461. Above the screen is carved a great shield encircled by the Garter bearing the Wenlock arms.

Under the screen are two tombs. One belongs to Lady Alice Rotherham, the mother of Thomas Rotherham who became Archbishop of York in 1480. The other commemorates William Wenlock, Master of Farley Hospital from 1377 to 1391, who is seen dressed in a priest's cassock and mantle, and is holding two strips bearing prayers in his hands. It is unlikely that either tomb was ever intended to stand under the screen, the spaces having probably been intended for Sir John Wenlock and his first wife Elizabeth.

Under the windows in the north wall of the Wenlock Chapel are two canopied altar tombs. One is almost certainly that of Sir John Rotherham (brother of the Archbishop) who died in 1492 or 3. Henry Cobbe suggested that the other might have belonged to George Rotherham who died in 1579 – but the architecture of the tomb suggests that it is earlier than that date. On the wall above these tombs is a funeral helmet attributed to Sir John Wenlock who died at the battle of Tewkesbury in 1471. It appears, however, to be a sixteenth-century great helm adapted and remodelled with spike for crest and mantle, as a funeral helmet which may have been carried as late as the seventeenth century. The vizor is missing, but the 'buff' or chin guard is of a fifteenth century pattern, and thus may possibly be the only piece which could be part of the Wenlock armour. Another helmet on the west wall of the chapel is a 'close helmet' of the sixteenth century.

The Wenlock Chapel is separated from the north transept by two Decorated arches and a fine, carved oak screen. The lower part of the screen is carved in linen-fold style of the late fifteenth century and was probably moved into its present position from some other part of the church. The frieze above it is poorly mitred at the mullions and may well represent domestic carving of the late sixteenth century, perhaps brought from Luton Hoo. There is a tradition that the screen was the gift of the Marquess of Bute but this cannot be substantiated.

Between the wooden screen and the Wenlock screen is a well-worn staircase which once led to the rood screen loft above the chancel which was removed at the Reformation.

THE NORTH TRANSEPT
The north transept contains a late fifteenth-century Perpendicular window. Its glass commemorates James O'Neill, vicar from 1862–96, who was largely responsible for the church's restoration. In the north transept is the brass of John Ackworth, already described (page 83); and another bearing the legend:

'Here lyeth the body of Daniel Knight,
Who all my lifetime lived in spite.

Base flatterers sought me to undoe
And made me sign what was not true.
Reader take care whene'er you venture
To trust a canting false dissenter.
Who died June 11th, in the 61st
Year of his age, 1756.'

During his lifetime Daniel Knight had been forced to make a public apology to Samuel Marsom, a Luton Baptist, but in his epitaph he retracts and gets his own back!

THE SOUTH TRANSEPT
Let us now cross the nave into the south transept. The west wall and most of the south aisle are probably of Norman transitional work and were erected before the end of Henry II's reign. The arch and its piers leading into the south aisle from the transept are undoubtedly of transitional work (1130–50) and are the oldest existing feature in the church. The south pier of the arch has a Norman, cushion-shaped capital. It has been suggested that this is one of the original Norman piers which supported the chancel arch of Earl Robert's church completed in 1137. Close to the arch is a piscina of about 1330 with ball-flower decoration down its sides.

On the eastern side of the south transept was the Hoo chapel. It is now occupied by the organ, but was probably the chapel of the Guild of the Holy Trinity established in 1474. The panelling which separates the Hoo Chapel from the south transept is supposed to be the original rood screen of the church, but it has been so heavily restored and repainted that it is difficult to see any trace of the original work.

There are two recesses in the wall of the south aisle. One contains a thirteenth-century coffin lid found in the churchyard. The other, under the westernmost Decorated window, contains an effigy of a priest wearing a chasuble, alb, stole and maniple. There is good reason to believe that the figure represents Richard Barnard who founded the chantry in the chancel.

THE BAPTISTRY
The great arch separating the nave from the tower is 9 m high and

was built about 1300. Immediately east of the tower stands the fourteenth-century Baptistry, which was probably built about 1320. It is octagonal in shape, 6 m high and 3 m wide, and is constructed of Totternhoe stone. It has been described as one of the most beautiful Baptistries in England, although close inspection shows that it was not very well made. This may be partly due to the removal of paint and gilt from the stonework, since it was covered with these from time to time, and led one writer to believe that it was made of wood. The Baptistry was moved to the south transept in 1823 to make way for a wooden gallery which extended from the tower to the middle pier of the nave, and was entered from doors above the north and south porches. In 1866 it was returned to its present position when the gallery was removed. The font, which dates from about 1250, is of Early English style, and is made of Purbeck marble. The eight small columns supporting it are modern. There is *no* foundation for the legend that the Baptistry was given to the church by Queen Philippa, wife of Edward III.

Finally, we should remember that in the Middle Ages, the church walls would have been covered with paintings, giving a remarkable impression of colour to the whole building. These paintings were often an integral part of the architecture of the building. Not only did the pictures illustrate scenes from the Bible, but the lives of the saints were also depicted. At Luton the life of St Mary must have been dealt with in great detail. Unfortunately there are none of these paintings to be seen today, although St Albans Abbey and Chalgrave church (near Toddington) are still richly decorated.

8 *The Fifteenth Century — Some Great Men*

LUTON'S claim to fame in the fifteenth century lies in its connections with three men who played leading roles in the national life of the time – Sir Thomas Hoo, Sir John Wenlock, and Thomas Rotherham, Archbishop of York.

Before we look at the great men, let us consider the ordinary folk of the town once more. The fifteenth century was a period of war: first the Hundred Years' War with France, and then the Wars of the Roses – a period of civil war. A first impression would suggest that it was almost impossible to live a normal life during such disturbing times, but such an impression would be wrong. The fighting wasn't continuous and the common folk had little to do with it. Fighting had become a job for professional soldiers, and many nobles who had been to France had built up private armies which did the fighting for them. The people of Luton could continue to cultivate the land and breed sheep – their loyalties going to the lord of the manor and those in power whom he supported.

The end of the fourteenth century had seen the building of the parish church, whilst the beginning of the fifteenth century saw gifts pouring into it. In 1412 the will of a chaplain called John Spitele bequeathed six handwritten service books, a gilt chalice, a Communion cloth and silk vestments. John was buried in the churchyard close to the north door, and a brass commemorating him is one of the oldest in the church. In 1430 we hear that the church had a peal of five bells, and in the will of Rev John Penthelyn who died in 1444, we read that he left money for the chimes of the church clock. In the same will the rectory at Luton is described as having four rooms – a hall, pantry, kitchen and sleeping chamber. John Hay of Stopsley, who died in 1455, paid for the restoration of the north aisle and was buried there, but his tomb was destroyed by later restorers.

Although the townsfolk were not much troubled by the wars, they did have trouble from robbers, particularly when travelling along the roads in wooded country. In 1431 the chapel of Farley Hospital was broken into by three men who stole some relics of St Luke the Evangelist. The men had already committed a similar crime at Dunstable, and were chased as far as Barnet, where one was killed with an arrow, the second wounded, and the third escaped, but was caught in London with the relics in his possession.

THE COURT LEET

Crimes of this sort, and the much milder, everyday troubles of the town, were settled at the Court Leet. The frequency with which these courts met varied from manor to manor – on some it was once or twice a year, on others every three or four weeks. In Luton once or twice a year seems to have been the rule. Everyone in the manor over the age of 12 had to attend, unless he had permission to be absent or had sent sufficient excuse. Defaulters were fined. It was agreed by law that the court had to be held on the manor itself, and in a fixed place. At St Albans the Abbot held his court 'under an ash tree in the middle court of the Abbey'. Since the Luton court was also presided over by the Abbot he may have preferred to hold that court in the open air also – perhaps in the churchyard, with the church handy, should it choose to rain.

We can imagine quite a stir in the town whenever the Court Leet was called. If it was a fine day we can be sure the menfolk swore about the waste of a good working day, whilst the women would be all agog for any new scandal that the court might disclose. As the Abbot took his place at the head of the proceedings, his usher would call for silence by repeating the word 'Oyez!' three times. Then the jurymen would be sworn in, and the court proceedings would begin. The names of all the manor tenants were called out and fines imposed on the absentees. Next the court proceeded to fine offenders. William Grenefeld and John Wells, both brewers, were each fined 4d for selling ale above the agreed price. Thomas Fuller, Richard Godfrey and Robert Potter were fined 2d each for reselling beer at a profit. Two poachers, Richard Long and Henry Sternell, were each fined 20d for fishing in the Abbot's mill pond. As each case was called and dealt with it was taken down by the Clerk of the Court. A few of these court records, or Court Rolls as they are called, have survived. The examples just quoted occur in the Luton Court Rolls for 1455.

SIR THOMAS HOO

Let us now consider the careers of the famous men who were connected with Luton. Sir Thomas Hoo led an important, if not very exciting life. He was still a boy when he inherited the Luton Hoo estate in 1410. (The Hoo seems to have been established as a separate Luton manor late in the twelfth century.) When Thomas came of age in 1415 he was serving as a pageboy to Thomas Beaufort, the Duke of Exeter. He fought under the Duke at the Battle of Agincourt in 1415 and was with him at the Siege of Paris in 1421. He was well known at the court of Henry V and his Queen in Paris, and was still in attendance on the Duke when King Henry died at Vincennes in 1422. Four years later Thomas Beaufort died, and in his will, he left his favourite war-horse 'Dunne' to Sir Thomas.

In 1429, at the same time that Joan of Arc was crowning Charles VII King of France in Rheims Cathedral, Sir Thomas was made High Sheriff of Bedfordshire and Buckinghamshire. Six years later he was back in France suppressing a rebellion at Craux. The King honoured his work there by appointing him Chancellor of France. After preliminary negotiations by John Wenlock, Sir Thomas arranged for the marriage of King Henry VI to Margaret of Anjou on 24 May 1443. He was rewarded for these services by being made a Knight of the Garter, and was given large estates in Sussex. Soon afterwards he was created Baron Hoo and Hastings and during the next six years he took a prominent place in Parliament. He died on 13 February 1455, at Hastings Castle, and was buried in Battle Abbey.

SIR JOHN WENLOCK

When Sir Hugh Mortimer died in 1403 the manor of Luton passed to John de Cressy in whose hands it remained for 64 years until 1467 when it was sold to Sir John Wenlock. Sir John had already inherited half the manor in 1433.

Sir John Wenlock was a great soldier. In order to understand his story we must first look at national events in England. In the

1450s the English people were very discontented. The lower classes were heavily overtaxed to pay for the disastrous French wars; whilst the nobles were furious at the mis-government by which they had lost France – in 1431 the English had burnt Joan of Arc; many soldiers considered that Joan was a saint and that by putting her to death they were courting disaster. Within twenty years the whole of France, except Calais, had been lost. In 1445 King Henry VI had married Queen Margaret. Unfortunately he suffered from fits of insanity, and in 1454, during such an attack, the Duke of York was made Protector. When the King had recovered the Duke was dismissed, but York, rather than lose his new found power, decided to take arms against the King. The struggle for control which followed was called the Wars of the Roses.

The Wenlock family came from Much Wenlock in Shropshire. At the time of Henry V's death in 1422 John Wenlock was Constable of Vernon-sur-Seine, midway between Rouen and Paris. After a disputed election in 1433 he became Member of Parliament for Bedfordshire. In 1440 he was with Lord Fanhope in Brittany where he was accepted as a member of the royal household, and during the following years he carried out numerous diplomatic assignments in France. He was made Constable of Bamborough Castle, and Chamberlain to the Queen. By 1449 he had made enough money to be able to lend the King £1,033 6s 8d, in those days a tremendous sum. The Duke of York, after his dismissal in December 1454, began to amass an army which marched on London in May 1455. The King's supporters, including John Wenlock, were called Lancastrians. They marched out of London and met the Yorkist army at St Albans. The Lancastrians were beaten, and Sir John Wenlock was so badly wounded that he was carried off in a cart 'sore hurt'. He seems soon to have recovered, because later that year he changed over to the Yorkist side and was made Speaker in Parliament. The Lancastrians held their own parliament at Coventry in 1459 and Sir John together with the Duke of York and others was attainted – that means, they were sentenced to death or outlawry, for not supporting the King. The Duke of York escaped to Ireland and Sir John to France. In June 1460 the Yorkists invaded England, landing at Sandwich. At the end of the year the Duke was slain, and his son Edward, Earl of March, continued the struggle. In the following spring Edward was acknowledged as King Edward IV, although King Henry VI was still alive. Sir John Wenlock was made a Knight of the Garter and created Baron Wenlock. Other honours poured upon him – Chief Butler of England, Treasurer of Ireland, Chamberlain of the Duchy of Lancaster, Steward of Berkhamsted Castle and Lieutenant of Calais.

By 1470 Sir John had returned to the Lancastrian cause and had joined the Earl of Warwick in France. In April 1471, in company with King Henry's Queen Margaret and her son Prince Edward, Warwick and Wenlock landed with an army at Weymouth. Troops from the west country rushed to join them. On 3 May they arrived at Tewkesbury. Next day King Edward and his army arrived and a great battle followed. Wenlock was in charge of the centre of the battle, together with Prince Edward and Sir John Langstrother. The Lancastrians were defeated and Sir John Wenlock was killed and buried in Tewkesbury Abbey.

The Tudor historian, Holinshed, reported that Wenlock had been killed by the Earl of Somerset, because he failed to give him all the support he needed, but there seems to be no truth in this legend.

John Wenlock had been married twice. His first wife, Elizabeth, died about 1461 and it is said that he built the Wenlock Chapel in the parish church to her memory, though it is not known whether she was buried there. A verse originally inscribed on one of the chapel windows, suggests that Sir John intended to be buried there himself with Elizabeth. It read:

'Jesu Christ most of myght,
Have mercy on John Le Wenlock Knight,
And on his wife Elizabeth,
Who out of this world is past by death,
Which founded this chapel here,
Help *them* with your hearty prayer,
That they may come to that place,
Where ever is joy and solace.'

The Wenlock Chapel had originally been the Someries Chapel, and in order to rebuild it we are told that Sir John had first to buy the manor of Someries. We do not know when this transaction took place, but as early as 1438 Sir John was described as 'of Someries'.

SOMERIES MANOR HOUSE

The fortified manor house of Someries, sometimes erroneously referred to as a castle, lies two miles south-east of the Town Hall, on the Luton Hoo estate. Someries is quite an early example of a brick building in England, and today consists of a very ruined gatehouse and chapel. John Leland, writing in 1552, tells us that this house was begun but never finished, and it is unlikely that there was ever much more than the building that we can see today.

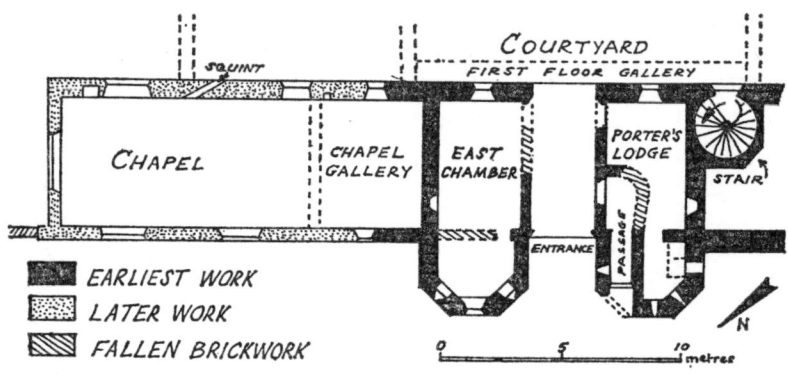

It is likely that the old half-timbered manor house of William of Someries which adjoined the brick building was occupied from the thirteenth century until it was pulled down by Sir John Napier in 1742. This helps to explain why the chapel and gatehouse are not mentioned in an inventory of 1606 which lists the rooms of the house as a 'dairy, poultry house, farm house, Queen's chamber, inner chamber, Le Grayes chamber, chamber at the gallery end, gallery end next the great chamber, great chamber, clock chamber, children's chambers, maids' chamber, inner chamber next the maids' chamber, Miss Elizabeth her chamber, Mr Cheyney his chamber, chamber next, the Cheyney's, great parlour, little parlour, hall, smiths' chamber, wells' chamber, cook boys' chamber, kitchen and hall'.

The existing buildings are constructed of the so-called 'Flemish' or 'Statute' bricks which measure about 23×10×5 cm. True Flemish bricks had been imported into London and East Anglia from the middle of the thirteenth century, but these were extremely expensive inland and it is probable that the Someries bricks were made locally, perhaps by Flemish immigrants. Small quarry pits in the vicinity may well be the original clay pits from which the bricks were made, and it might be possible to see here the origins of the local brickmaking industry which was particularly thriving at the beginning of the nineteenth century. A distinct change in the baking of the bricks used to construct the chapel can be seen on its outside, about 2 m from the ground. Such a feature suggests the work of brickmakers unfamiliar with local clay.

The gatehouse originally consisted of a central passage with a vaulted brick roof. Opening on either side of it were two large rooms. The eastern room was at one time divided into two. The part at the rear of the gateway containing a fireplace and large window. The smaller front section looked onto the gate-approach.

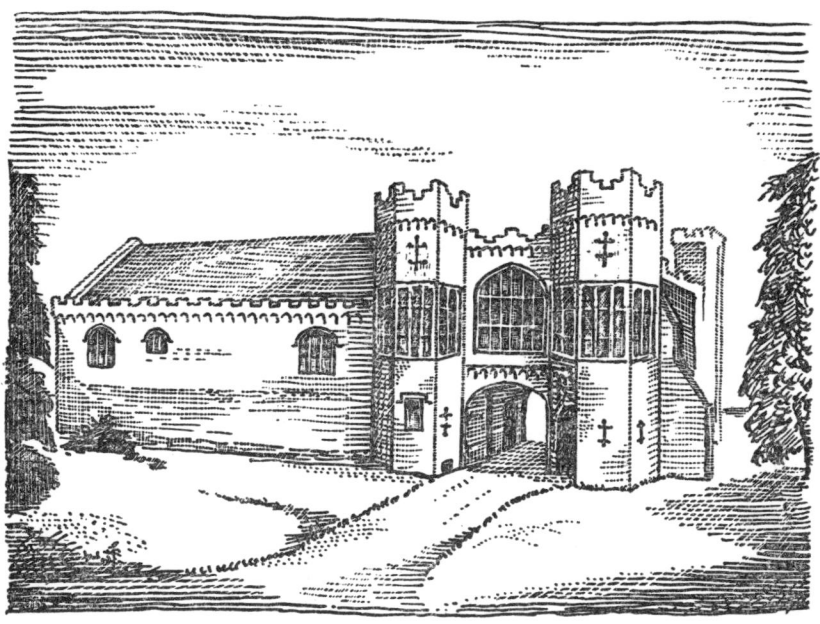

Gun-ports overlooked the road outside. The room on the west of the central passage was similarly divided into two, and was reduced in size further by a small passage which entered the building to the right of the main gate. There was no original access to the chapel from the ground floor of the gatehouse. To the west of these rooms was a tower containing a circular staircase which led up to at least two floors and also led down into the cellar, the entrance of which has now been filled in. A large room existed on the first floor of the gatehouse and two doors led out of it, one into the chapel gallery, and the other on to a covered way, now destroyed, which ran along the southern side of the building. It is probable that a rectangular plan had originally been envisaged for the manor, constructed around a courtyard.

The chapel was 15 m long and 5.5 m wide. There is good reason to suspect that its western end was taken down and remodelled at a later date. The east wall of the chapel contained a window of four lights, with niches for statues on either side of it. In the north wall were two windows, one larger than the other, which were later bricked up; perhaps at a time when the chapel was being used for some secular purpose. Close to the east window, but in the south wall, is a piscina with a stone drain. Next to it is a window of three lights, and adjoining it a squint set at an angle, so that the ladies in the adjoining room could observe the service without entering the chapel. When the chapel was remodelled a partition was built across the western end cutting off some 4.5 m. Above it, a gallery was erected; the holes cut to hold the timber floor joists still being clearly visible. The original chapel door would have led into the area that had been partitioned off, so a new door was constructed some feet to the east. It now seems likely that the gatehouse was the earliest structure but it is difficult to be certain without excavation.

Who Built Someries?

We must now consider who began to build the brick manor house at Someries. John Leland, who died in 1552, antiquary to King Henry VIII, wrote of the building:

> 'A fair place within the Parish of Luton called Somerys, the which house was sumptuously begun by the Lord Wenlock

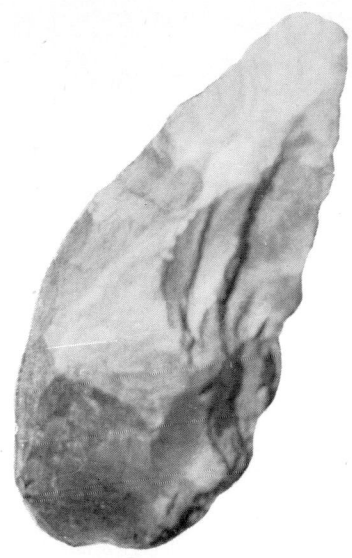

▲ *Flint hand-axes from Luton made by Acheulean man about 250,000 years ago. Half-size*

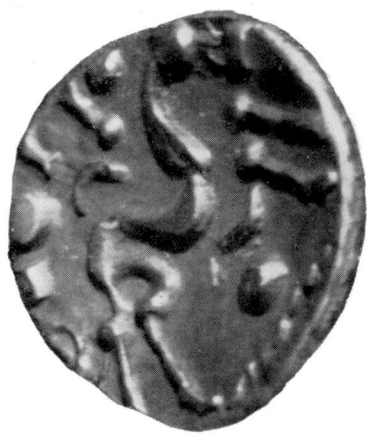

▲ *Coins minted for the Iron Age Chieftain Conubelinus (A.D. 15–40) found at Leagrave in 1960. The name of the chieftain CVN, can clearly be seen on the left-hand coin. The stylised horse was probably a tribal symbol. Enlarged four times*

A

Excavation of the Neolithic earthwork called Waulud's Bank at Leagrave in 1954. The trench has been cut across the henge ditch. The dark line across the far end of the trench marks the position of the palisade. In the foreground is the edge of a hut

B

▲ *Roman triple vases from Leagrave, probably used in connection with the worship of household gods. About 4 inches wide*

▼ *Two of the burials from the slaughter cemetery on Galley Hill, excavated in 1961*

C

A 'Buckelurne' (9 inches high), and square-headed brooch (about 7 inches across), from the Saxon cemetery found under Argyll Avenue in 1925

D

▲ *The section of the Anglo-Saxon Chronicle recording the Battle of Bedcanford. The translation reads: 'Year 571. In this year Cuthwulf fought against the Britons at Bedcanford and captured four villages, Limbury, Aylesbury, Benson and Eynsham; and in the same year he passed away.' The manuscript is preserved in Corpus Christi College, Cambridge*

▼ *Two pages from the Register of the Guild of the Holy Trinity. On the left hand page can be seen the Arms of Archbishop Rotherham, together with pictures of a Lute and Ton Barrel; a rebus, or play on the name of Luton. 1474*

E

▲ *The organ and gallery in the west end of the church c. 1860*

▲ *Early eighteenth century window in the chancel c. 1860*

LUTON PARISH CHURCH

▼ *The Wenlock Screen*

▼ *Fifteenth century wooden screen*

F

The Moat House before restoration, at Limbury (built 1370–1400), showing the carved rafters with the earlier thatch, and inscription originally in the cellar

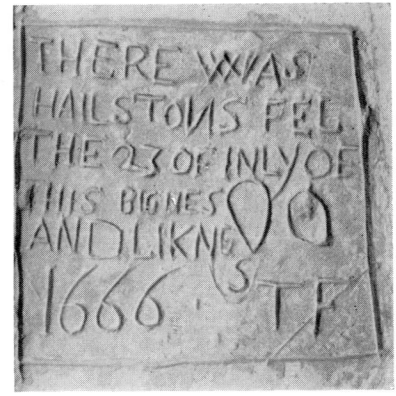

THERE WAS
HAILSTONS FEL
THE 23 OF INLY OE
THIS BIGNES
AND LIKNES
1666 · S TF

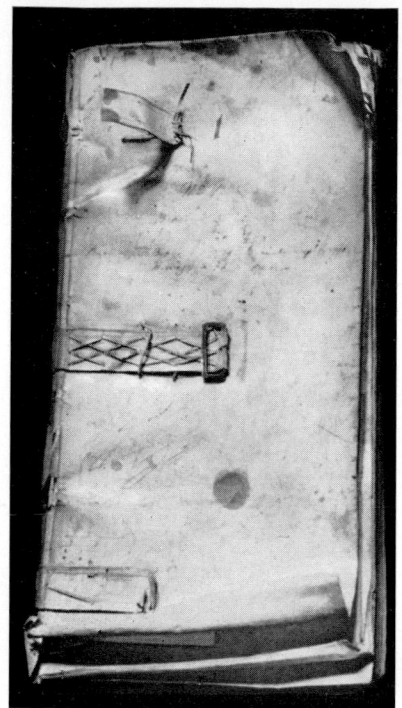

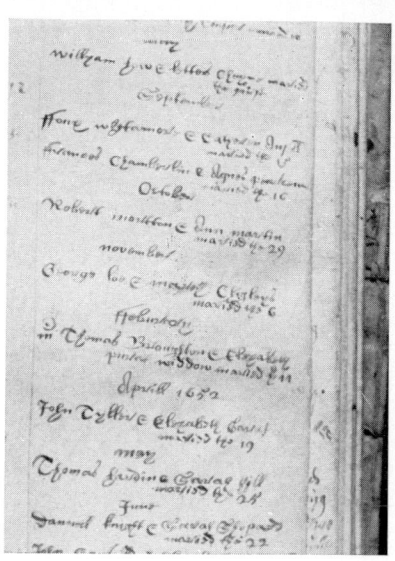

An early register from the Parish Church

▼ *A Court Leet – tenants paying their rents in 1903*

▲ *Someries Gatehouse from a watercolour by Paul Sandby (1725–1809). The farmhouse on the left was the home of Joseph Conrad, the novelist, for a short time*

▼ *Luton Parish Church from the south-east about 1827*

Farley Farm, in the early nineteenth century, probably on the site of the old Farley Hospital

Stockwood House, built by John Crawley in 1740, and demolished in 1964

J

▲ *George Street looking towards Market Hill about 1820, from a drawing by Thomas Fisher*

▼ *George Street in 1855, looking towards the old Town Hall*

K

▲ *George Street, late nineteenth century, filled with wooden hat-crates*

▼ *Luton's first Town Hall, opened in 1847 and gutted by fire in 1919*

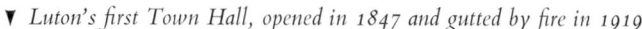

L

By-Election 1911, declaration of the poll. The victorious candidate was Mr Cecil Harmsworth, a Liberal. Most men were wearing straw boaters. The clock had been installed in 1856, to commemorate the ending of the Crimean war.

M

▲ *A plait dealer about 1900*

▼ *Wooden hat-crates outside the old Great Northern Station, Bute Street, about 1910*

N

▲ *The original Vauxhall factory in Kimpton Road, 1910*

▼ *The original Skefko factory in Leagrave Road, 1911. In the background is Maiden Hall farm with Blow's Downs in the distance*

O

▲ *1905. The first Vauxhall made in Luton. Three cylinders and chain-driven*

▼ *Luton policemen, in straw helmets, with the successful election candidate, Cecil Harmsworth, in 1911*

P

but not finished. The Gate House of Brick is very large and fair. Part of the residue of the new Foundations be yet seen, and part of the Old Place standeth yet. It is on a hill not far from St. Anne's Hill.'

This is hardly the detailed description expected of a man who had seen the buildings. It is more likely to be based on hearsay. But since it was written within two generations of Lord Wenlock's death, it is likely to contain some truth in its statement that it was begun by Lord Wenlock, who failed to complete it. A detailed study of the building by Terence P. Smith suggests that Wenlock began to build the gatehouse in the ten years after 1448, but that he was unable to complete it due to his attainder. However, with his return to favour in the years after the Yorkist success at Northampton in 1460, he resumed work on the chapel, employing different builders, but died in 1471 before he had carried the work much further. The ruined walls on the western side of the gatehouse never extended further west than they do today. Their foundations end quite clearly at this point, and the wall at the northern angle has been constructed as a buttress to hold the gatehouse in position.

Terence Smith has also suggested that the workmen responsible for constructing the brick manor house belonged to a group of craftsmen living in eastern Hertfordshire or western Essex, who were also responsible for building Rye House (Hoddesdon, Herts) and Faulkborne Hall and Nether Hall (both in Essex). The quality of all their work was very fine and shows considerable western-European influence. Perhaps there were foreign craftsmen amongst those responsible for the construction of Someries. However, when building activity came to a sudden end in 1459 and the workmen were set-off, they seem to have decided to have no further dealings with the turncoat Wenlock. He had to look elsewhere for the men to build his chapel, and the change in style and bricks can be clearly seen.

In 1605 King James I stayed at the mansion as the guest of Sir John Rotherham. The Crawley family bought Someries in 1629 and it remained in their possession for about 100 years. Soon after 1740 much of the building was pulled down and its bricks went to build Someries Farm and the adjoining buildings and cottages. Engravings made in 1787 show it looking much as it does today. At the beginning of the present century Joseph Conrad, the novelist, lived for a short time at Someries Farm.

As John Wenlock had died fighting against King Edward IV, his lands were forfeited and granted to Thomas Rotherham. Born in 1423, Rotherham rose to become Archbishop of York in 1480 and a cardinal. Writers in the past have suggested that all or part of Someries was built by Rotherham, but this no longer seems likely, and there is no documentary evidence to support it. He would certainly have had little time to live at the manor, and consequently gave it to his brother Sir John Rotherham and his nephew Thomas, who probably came to live at Someries about 1472.

THE GUILD OF THE HOLY TRINITY

On 12 May 1474 Bishop Rotherham obtained a licence from King Edward to found a religious guild in connection with Luton church known as the Guild of the Holy Trinity. His brother, John Rotherham, John Ackworth of Biscot, John Lammer (Vicar of Luton), Richard Stopisley, Alice Rotherham (mother of the Bishop) and seven others are all addressed in the original licence and must have been founder members. Guilds played an important part in the Christian life of medieval towns. Their members paid an annual fee or subscription which was used to help members who fell sick or were too old to work. The guilds built chapels, supported schools, organised religious processions, burnt candles at certain altars and generally helped one another in an effort to live a Christian way of life.

The Guild of the Holy Trinity founded a chantry in the church, with two chaplains to sing masses for the souls of the founder and members at an altar of the Holy Trinity in the southern part of the church – perhaps in the south transept or behind the organ in the Hoo chapel. A register of the guild with a beautifully illuminated frontispiece is now in the possession of the Marquess of Bute. It covers the years 1475 to 1546, and it shows us that the guild was one of the richest in England, with kings, queens, bishops and abbots amongst its members. All the members of the guild were known collectively as 'The Brothersed', and 'Brothersed House', the great hall in which the guild held its social activities stood at the corner of Castle Street and George Street where the *Red Lion* stands today.

The closing years of the fifteenth century were comparatively uneventful in Luton. In 1483 William Catesby was appointed steward of the St Albans Abbey manors and a judge in the Abbot's courts, which included Luton. Catesby's family owned manors at Hayes and Northwood in Luton. William Catesby was an adviser of Richard III and figures in Shakespeare's play of that name. In 1492 Thomas Ramridge of Luton was made Abbot of St Albans, and was buried in the abbey on his death in 1519. Unfortunately nothing is known about his life.

Many Manor Houses are Built

We have looked at the brick built mansion of Someries. By the end of the fifteenth century many lesser manor houses existed within the Borough. In his *History of Luton* William Austin lists 'a large manor-house at Leagrave, three at Limbury, two at Biscot, six or more at Stopsley, two at Cowridge, one at Lammers [between the junction of Lynwood Avenue with Hitchin Road, and Stopsley Junior School], one at Ramridge [Rickyard Close], one at Nether Crawley [south of Turner's Knoll], one at Crawley Green, one at Haverings [now under the airport runway], one at Eaton Green, one at Luton Hoo, one at Whipperley [Stockwood], one at Farley and three at Hyde'. Almost a dozen large houses stood within the town of Luton, too, besides the hundreds of cottages belonging to the ordinary folk of Luton. Around the town were the large open fields where every cottager held a little land and the right to pasture his sheep and cattle. By 1474 the town probably held as many as sixty malt-kilns, some on farms and some in taverns, where ale was brewed with water from the river Lea. We must remember that before the introduction of tea, ale was the main drink for young and old, though at that time it was made without the hops which strengthened it, and gave us the 'bitter' brewed in the town today.

9 The Sixteenth Century

EARLY in the sixteenth century we frequently find mention of the names of Thomas Crawley and John Sibley. Both families were great landowners in the town for the next 400 years. The will of John Sylam of Bramingham Manor contains rich gifts to the church and a legacy of 750 sheep, besides those animals remaining in his personal effects. From this we can assume that sheep farming was becoming very popular on the hills around Luton.

In 1502 Edward Sheffield, a relative of the Speaker of the House of Commons, was installed as Vicar of Luton. Later he was made Canon of Lichfield, Rector of Camborne in Cornwall and Rector of Yatt in Gloucestershire. Since he lived and died in Luton he could have seen little of his other parishioners and was clearly one of the absentee clergymen, so common in the sixteenth and seventeenth centuries.

Little of note seems to have happened during the early years of the century. In 1529 George Ackworth of Biscot Manor represented Bedfordshire in Parliament. For twenty-one years from 1537 a Welshman called John Gwynneth was Vicar of Luton. Gwynneth was a doctor of music and wrote a number of religious songs and tracts, all of which have now been forgotten although copies exist in the British Museum.

BRICKMAKING AT LUTON

The earliest reference to brickmaking in the Luton area occurs in 1541. At that time Barnard Spayne was manufacturing bricks and tiles. We don't know where his land was, but it may have been in the area of the Mixes Hill pits at Round Green. As lord of the manor, Sir Thomas Rotherham claimed that clay was a mineral, and that only he had the right to extract it. He sent his men to break up the freshly made tiles and to remove 200 loads of newly dug clay. Spayne tried to bring an action against

Rotherham's men, but since Sir Thomas presided over the Court Leet, the men were protected and the case was dismissed.

Soon after 1535 a copy of the Bible, printed in English, was set up in the parish church in accordance with the order of Thomas Cromwell, Vicar-General to Henry VIII. The Bible was chained to a desk in the chancel of the church. (A copy of one of these chained Bibles is still to be seen in the church archives.) The cost of providing the Bible was paid for, half by the vicar and half by his parishioners. Thomas Cromwell was also responsible in 1538 for making it necessary by law to register all births, deaths and marriages. It was the parson's job to enter, every Sunday in the presence of the churchwardens, the details of baptisms, marriages and funerals that had taken place in the parish during the past week. He also had to see that the registers were kept securely in a chest sealed with two locks. The earliest surviving Parish Registers in Luton date from 1603, though we can be fairly sure that some were kept long before that date.

In 1694 a charge of 3d was made for every christening, which the poor found hard to pay. Another charge was made for every funeral, and a graduated scale was worked out ranging from £50 for a duke to 4s for the ordinary folk. The vicar had to charge 2s to record a birth and 2s 6d for marriages. These too were on a similar graduated scale. All the money collected went to pay for wars against France. In order to make sure that the vicar didn't cheat, the tax collectors had free access to the register and were authorised to fine him £100 for failing to register any event.

In 1539 the abbey of St Albans was surrendered to Henry VIII and from that time onwards Luton church and the abbey lands at Luton passed to the Crown. The change-over seems to have had little or no effect on events at Luton at all, and the Rev John Gwynneth continued as vicar for the following nineteen years.

THE DISSOLUTION OF THE GUILD OF THE HOLY TRINITY

In 1547 all chantries, hospitals and guilds became the property of King Edward VI. Under this grant the Guild of the Holy Trinity at Luton and certain minor chantries were seized for the King. The commissioners found the guild in a very poor way. Its two priests were so 'meanly learned' that they were deprived of their livings, and pensioned off at £5 a year each. Luton was described as a market town of 1,200 communicants, so we may assume a population of about 2,000 people at that time. In the same year Parliament directed that all images were to be removed from churches. This must have happened at Luton though no record of the event survives.

Luton probably suffered from an absentee clergyman in 1558 when George Mason became vicar. Mason was a favourite of Queen Elizabeth I and held three livings in the London area. At the same time he was a prebend of St Paul's and a canon of Windsor. He was succeeded in 1563 by Thomas Rose, the first married priest to hold the living of Luton.

When William Camden visited Luton about 1586 the choir of the parish church was roofless and overgrown with weeds. Since the dissolution of St Albans Abbey no one was sure whose job it was to make repairs. The chancel remained in this state until 1603, when, as a result of a complaint in the Exchequer Court, it was decided that Robert Kettle, President of Trinity College, Cambridge, and George Wingate of Biscot, who jointly held the rectorial tithes, were bound to make the repairs.

Throughout its existence the Holy Trinity guild had kept detailed records of its accounts. These give some interesting details about the price of food in the earlier part of the sixteenth century. Mutton could be bought for $\frac{1}{4}$d a pound and beef 2d a pound. A lamb could be bought whole for 1s 4d, a goose for 3d, a chicken $1\frac{1}{4}$d and a rabbit $1\frac{1}{2}$d. At the same time milk was 1d a gallon and beer 1s 10d a barrel.

The court records are equally informative and we learn that adults who spun tops in the street in 1528 were liable to spend a day and night in the stocks. Most of the tradesfolk seemed to have come before the court at some time or other for attempting to sell flour, bread, meat or beer at an excessive price. We hear of a butcher in 1528 being fined 10s for cheating his customers by swelling up veal and mutton, and twenty-one women beer sellers (tiptatores) who were fined for making excessive profit on beer. Four butchers and a fisherman were also in trouble for selling goods above the official market price. Those townsfolk who held land on either side of the Lea were compelled to keep the river clear of weeds and choking mud. Failure to comply could bring a fine of 3s 4d or as much as 40s for a persistent offender.

By the end of the sixteenth century the main occupations of the townsfolk were malting and farming, particularly sheep farming for wool rather than meat. As we shall see malting provided the raw material for a vast number of inns which came into being during the following centuries.

LUTON HOO PARK

The Reformation had affected Luton little as it had no monastic house to be dissolved and life continued to go on comparatively undisturbed in the now considerable market town. In his *History of Luton Church* Cobbe shows that the vicar, John Gwynneth, although he remained sympathetic to the Roman Catholic faith which he was able to practise openly again in the reign of Mary Tudor, had during the earlier reigns of Henry VIII and Edward VI observed the Protestant changes which had been made. It is not known whether he died, retired or was forced to resign when Elizabeth ascended to the throne in 1558.

After the death of Elizabeth the new king, James I, seems to have shown a special interest in Luton and in 1605 visited Sir John Rotherham who was still at Someries. James was anxious to obtain money by any means he could and had a note made on his return that a Mr Robert Sandig who had a house and land at Luton would be a suitable person from whom to get a loan. Robert Sandy or Sandby to whom James obviously referred had recently bought the Hoo estates and changed his name to Napier. In 1611 James came to Luton again but this time to visit Robert Napier to whom he gave a baronetcy and also gave to Robert's son, another Robert, a knighthood. A few years later, in 1623, Sir Robert was given permission to fence off 300 acres of land at the Hoo to make a park. At the same time Sir Robert also became lord of the manor and acquired the gift of the living of the church which, since the dissolution of St Alban's Abbey had passed to the Crown. These privileges and honours must have cost a great deal of money but once established at the Hoo the Napiers became one of the largest and most influential land-owners in the district.

The elder Sir Robert Napier died in 1637 leaving four cottages on Tower Hill for the poor people of Luton. Thirty-five years earlier Edward Vaughan had left three cottages, also on Tower

Hill, for the same purpose. Tower Hill stood on rising ground at present occupied by the Town Hall above what is now Manchester Street. Until well into the nineteenth century it was, like its namesake in London, to be a popular venue for open-air meetings.

It was about this time that the Crawley family began to play an important part in the town's affairs. This, without any doubt the oldest Luton family, had its origins in Nether Crawley which was close to where the *Somerset Tavern* now stands in what is still appropriately named Crawley Green Road. As early as 1332 there is reference to Thomas de Crawley in a document and from 1445 the descent of the family can be traced continuously. They had added considerably to their holding of land around the town, no doubt as a result of profitable sheep farming. The latter played an important part in the rural economy of this neighbourhood in the sixteenth century. In 1611 Thomas Crawley purchased from Sir John Rotherham the land adjoining the church from Park Square to Lea Road and built a large house there. The Rotherhams were at this time becoming impoverished having already sold the Hoo to Sir Robert Napier. In the meantime Francis, son of Thomas Crawley and the most famous of all the family had, in 1608, married Elizabeth, daughter of Sir John Rotherham.

Thomas Crawley died in 1629 and Francis bought Someries from Sir John, his wife thus returning to be lady of the house in which she had spent her childhood. Sir John then moved to Essex although some members of the Rotherham family continued to live at Farley which they were to hold for many more years to come.

10 Luton at the time of the Civil War

SIR FRANCIS CRAWLEY AND SHIP MONEY

LUTON was to play a part in the events that led to the Civil War. The town was situated on the border of the Eastern Association, an area which, with London and the other big towns in the country, was the most favourable to the Parliamentary cause. This cause in the impending struggle was no doubt supported by the local traders and independent farmers but the members of more important landowning families would be Royalist. Among these was Francis Crawley who was a lawyer of some note and had in 1632 been made a judge. It was at this time, some eight years before the actual beginning of the war, that Charles I, like his father James, was striving hard to raise money without calling a Parliament together. In 1635 he appointed twelve judges to advise him on the legality of imposing Ship Money in time of peace. This was an old tax that could be put on coastal counties in times of danger, such as war. Sir Francis Crawley, who had been knighted in the meantime, was among the judges who advised the King that he alone could decide whether the tax was necessary and could impose it upon the whole country if he thought fit. Charles did so and this led to the famous trial of John Hampden for refusing to pay the Ship Money and Sir Francis was again one of the judges who passed sentence on Hampden.

When Charles called the Long Parliament in 1640 it proceeded to impeach Sir Francis and five other judges, but this was not carried far as the situation had become one of war. In 1645 when the Parliamentary forces had the upper hand a resolution was made in Parliament that the five surviving judges, including Sir Francis, should 'cease from being Judges, as though they were dead'.

When the war began in 1642 Sir Francis Crawley and Sir Robert Napier hastened to join the King at Oxford leaving it a simple matter for Parliamentary troops to occupy for a time both Someries and the Hoo. There were no major military engagements in the neighbourhood but from time to time movements of troops. These led to small skirmishes one of which took place in 1645 in the streets of the town. A party of Cavaliers came in demanding that £250 be raised before they left. The news spread quickly to a small Roundhead garrison at Markyate which sent troops to the rescue. There was a brief encounter in which four of the Cavaliers were killed and twenty-two captured with their horses which would have been more welcome to the opposing side than the prisoners as at this stage in the war they needed horses badly. We are told that as the Royalists fled hastily from the town the womenfolk, glad to see them go, ran after them throwing money at them.

With the main engagements of the war finished Sir Francis Crawley had his estate returned to him in 1646 and was allowed to live at Someries once more by paying a fine of £958, a large sum of money in those days. All the fighting was, however, not over for in 1648, with the King in the hands of the victorious New Model Army, a second civil war commenced with the Scots coming to the aid of the Royalists. In July of that year there passed through the town northwards a considerable Royalist force some of which were delayed at an inn known as the *Prince's Head*, later the *Duke's Head*, which stood at the corner of Manchester Street and Bridge Street. They were surprised at the arrival of troops of the New Model Army after which there was a sharp battle in which six Royalists were killed and nine wounded. Those who were lucky enough to escape hurried on to join the main force.

The second civil war was soon over to be followed by the execution of the King in 1649 and the establishment of the Commonwealth. Sir Francis Crawley died fourteen days after the death of the King he had so faithfully served.

An Unwelcome Minister at the Church

The later years of the war and the period of the Commonwealth brought many changes in matters of religion. The Book of Common Prayer could no longer be used in churches, bishops were abolished and clergymen allowed to be each in charge of only one church. These changes pleased many including some of the clergy but most of these just accepted the change being prepared to wait until such time as the Prayer Book could, as they hoped, be used again. Others disliked the changes very much indeed and some clergy gave up, or were deprived of, their livings.

In the early years of the war the vicar of Luton was John Birde, who also held Cheddington which he chose to keep rather than to be the incumbent at Luton. One wonders why? He was followed at Luton by Samuel Austin who soon left as he found so much division in his congregation. Then for a period of about eighteen months came Thomas Attwood Rotherham, a cousin of Lady Crawley, but following his stay there is some doubt for about three years as to who was in charge of the church. With no bishops to ordain new clergy and with so many clergy deprived of their livings a time came when ministers, who were wholeheartedly in favour of the new form of worship but had not been ordained, were put in charge of churches. They were usually even less acceptable to those who clung to the old ways than were the clergy who had more or less willingly adopted the changes. One such minister who had not been ordained, John Jessop, was appointed to Luton church in 1650.

Jessop had many difficulties including the holding by some people of private services in their own homes using the Prayer Book. This was apparently permissive for the family alone but the inviting of neighbours to join in these services diminished the congregation which Jessop himself managed to attract to the church. Matters came to a head in 1658 with the death of Lady Crawley, the widow of Sir Francis. Her son John, who had fought in the civil war in the Royalist cause, insisted that due to the family's ownership of Someries they had a right to have her buried in the church. To this Jessop agreed provided that the burial service in the Prayer Book was not used. Having given no previous notice of their intentions John Crawley and his friends forced open the church door and carried out the burial service in the form they wished it to be. John Jessop had no alternative but to report the incident to Oliver Cromwell drawing attention at the same time to other ways in which his authority in church matters in the town was being flouted. The Protector ordered that John Crawley should be brought to London in custody to appear before him and that Jessop should also attend bringing with him witnesses. Fortunately for Crawley the Protector died before he could appear and with Cromwell's death the Commonwealth began to disintegrate.

It is interesting to note that after the Restoration in 1660, when both the bishops and the Prayer Book returned, John Crawley was ordained (it is possible that he was so already) and until his death was rector of Barton-in-the-Clay. Needless to say John Jessop was removed as minister at the church as Sir Robert Napier lost no time in using his privilege of the gift of the living, now restored to him, to present it to Thomas Pomfret. John, a son of Thomas Pomfret and a poet of some note in his own time, was born in Luton during the time that his father was vicar.

During the period of the Commonwealth Sir Robert Napier had erected his own private chapel at the Hoo and it was no doubt to this that Jessop referred in his report to Cromwell. In 1674, fourteen years after the Restoration, the chapel was consecrated.

John Crook, the Quaker

The period of the Commonwealth brought many changes in thoughts about religion. Most people were prepared to express these new ideas within the church but others, including John Crook, sought more extreme means. Crook was a captain in the Parliamentary army whose regiment, after the execution of Charles I, bought Beckerings Park, near to Ridgmont, where he lived in a large house. He was appointed one of the civil magistrates who did most of the work previously done by the justices of the peace. In 1654 he joined the Society of Friends, soon to be called Quakers, being from his important position a very valuable early convert. He was soon to be visited by and become a close associate of George Fox, the founder of Quakerism. The Quakers had what appeared to be strange views as they did not want a church at all as such, refused to take oaths and to do military service. They suffered persecution even during the Commonwealth with the result that Crook was in gaol no fewer than eight times, the first in 1655. In 1657 there was a three-day meeting of Quakers from a wide area at Beckerings Park and yet another the following year, thus beginning the yearly meetings which have been a feature of the Society of Friends ever since. Crook wrote about thirty books some of which had a wide circulation.

At some time after 1661, being deprived of Beckerings Park, John Crook came to live in a large house on Park Square in Luton where he was again visited by George Fox. At this time the Quakers had a Meeting House at Sewell which Crook attended. He died in 1699 while on a visit to his daughter at Hertford and was buried at Sewell.

John Crook's life was in some respects similar to that of the more famous John Bunyan but the two men had very little sympathy with each other's views. Bunyan was an Independent, as Oliver Cromwell had been, and thought that each individual church was a separate entity which should work out its own government to suit its own needs. John Jessop could well have been, and probably was, an Independent. It was at Samshill, near Harlington, that John Bunyan was arrested in 1660 for preaching, the result being that he spent a long continuous period in gaol. Here he wrote *The Pilgrim's Progress* which is considered by some to be related to places in the Bedfordshire he knew so well. There is, however, no definite evidence that Bunyan visited Luton although it is almost certain that he must have done so.

THE FIRST BAPTIST COMMUNITY IN LUTON

Thanks to the influence of Bunyan the Independents, or as they were to be known later the Congregationalists, grew in strength in Bedford and the north of the county while the Quakers, partly due to the early enthusiasm of Crook and his contemporaries, were comparatively strong in the middle of the county until about half way through the eighteenth century. The Baptists had a church at Kensworth. Except for their belief in adult baptism there was little to distinguish the Baptists from the Independents as their systems of church government were almost identical. So much, however, did they both differ in their outlook from the Church of England, from which they held that they had been ejected by the Act of Uniformity of 1662, that they, in common with the Quakers, usually called the places in which they worshipped Meetings, or Meeting Houses, rather than churches. Together they were known as Dissenters or Nonconformists, the latter in time becoming the more usual apellation.

The church at Kensworth, which had members from a wide area including Luton, Dunstable and St Albans, split from time to time, as did all healthy Nonconformist churches, to form new churches. This could be due to growth but it was more often the result of a division within the church on a minor matter of doctrine or a seemingly small question of church government. One such schism came in the Kensworth church in 1690 on the choice of a new minister and Thomas Marsom led a number of members, living over almost the whole area served by the church, away to form a new church in Luton.

Thomas Marsom then purchased land off Park Street where a church was built, although it is safe to assume that Baptists were meeting somewhere in Luton before the church was ready to be used and most probably before the split in the Kensworth church. There is a long tradition with Luton Baptists that they met at Dallow Farm, which may well be true, but not that these gatherings were in secret for, although things were being made very difficult for the Dissenters, there was no need for that. The Marsoms, who were originally ironmongers with premises on Market Hill, were a family of some standing in the town. The Thomas Marsom who founded the Luton church was not a full-time minister and it was indeed to be some time before one was chosen. When he died in 1726 the Baptist minister from Hitchin, in a funeral service which was afterwards printed, referred to him as 'your aged pastor . . . a minister for over fifty years' but made no reference to him ever having been imprisoned. This leaves much doubt as to whether he was in prison with John Bunyan which it has sometimes been claimed that he was.

There was a similar breakaway of Baptists at Dunstable from the Kensworth church in 1708 probably on a matter of doctrine but in the meantime the church at Luton was growing in numbers and was enlarged. As members came from a wide area new or branch churches were formed, as at Chalton in 1732 and at Thorn in 1742, this latter to become fully independent in 1751 as the Chalton church had been from its beginning.

The local Baptists were mainly traders and independent farmers. Samuel, the third son of Thomas Marsom, was described as 'a gentleman of great substance in the world being a linen draper, a solicitor-in-law and likewise an eminent minister of the gospel'.

When he died the minister of the church at Chalton was unable to hear the sermon preached with the 'audience so great and I so little'. How much the early Baptists were concerned with worldly affairs may be seen in the minute book of the Luton church which in addition to expulsions and suspensions for normal human failings included others such as 'lack of financial integrity in business'. Not only those concerned in business affairs must have been pleased when in 1678 the town got its first regular postal service with three deliveries each week to and from London.

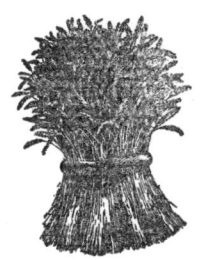

11 The Eighteenth Century — New influences affect Luton

The Affairs of Some Families, Old and New

IN 1712 the Crawleys ceased to live at Someries. Richard Crawley held an important position as Registrar of the Admiralty so to be nearer to London they lived at Northaw, near to Barnet. The Someries estate was sold to Sir John Napier in 1724 after which time the house fell into a state of decay. Shortly afterwards John Crawley, the then head of the family, decided to return to Luton and proceeded to have a new house built at Stockwood in the neighbourhood of which the family had acquired more land. Pending the building of Stockwood he lived for a time at Rothamsted in nearby Harpenden. The new house was completed in 1740 and was to become the home of the Crawley family until the present century. About forty years after it was built the house was given a facing of Coade stone and red tile which gave it an attractive colourful appearance.

In 1742 Sir John Napier, the last baronet of the family, died and as he was childless the estate then passed to his aunt who lived only another ten years. She left it to Francis Herne, who soon decided to sell the now large estate with all that went with it. It was purchased in 1762 by John Crichton Stuart, third Earl of Bute, who was one of the most remarkable men to be associated with the town.

The Third Earl of Bute and Extension of Hoo Park

Bute was born in 1713 in Scotland and came to London as a comparatively impoverished young man. He fell in love with and married Mary Wortley Montagu, a rich heiress. The Butes returned to Rothesay Castle to live for a period on limited means, but later returned to London and formed a close friendship with

Frederick, Prince of Wales, who died in 1751. Bute continued to be on friendly terms with the Princess of Wales, who sought his advice on the training of her young son, the future George III. George became King in 1760 and soon proceeded to appoint Bute to the Government with the hope that he would end the Seven Years War. In 1762 Bute became Prime Minister and in the following year gained great popularity in securing peace.

In the meantime (1761) Lady Bute's father died and she inherited £1½ million. The Butes thus became one of the wealthiest families in England. It was with this wealth that the Hoo was bought and a similar estate at Highcliffe in Hampshire. Thanks to John Wilkes, and the disappointment of the City of London with its terms, the peace treaty for which Bute had striven was loudly criticised. Protected by a gang of prize fighters he soon became the most unpopular Prime Minister the country has ever had and he was hounded out of office in 1765.

Bute set to work to improve the Hoo which he had rebuilt by Robert Adam, one of the greatest architects of the period. He increased the park from 300 to 1,500 acres which has had the effect of sterilising the growth of the town southwards and forced it in later years to extend in every other direction. The park was laid out by 'Capability' Brown, probably the greatest of all landscape gardeners. Brown had the stream widened to make two lakes and had clumps of trees planted that gave a vista with the impression that the whole of the surrounding countryside was part of the park. The laying out of the park must have involved an immense purchase and exchange of land. It is considered, almost with certainty, that this hastened the enclosure of much that remained. If this were so the tenants were saved the great expense of an Act of Parliament which was the alternative means of securing the enclosure of the open fields. It is in any case useful to note that at this period of enclosures there was no general enclosure award for Luton and that in the following century there was still a considerable amount of common pasture and waste left in the manor.

It is as a scientist that Bute has the greatest claim to fame. Linnaeus, the Swede, had just produced a classification of members of the natural world which Bute countered with a rival and ingenious scheme of his own. This he propounded in a most expensive book, *Botanical Tables*, of which only twelve copies were printed. His gardens at the Hoo and Highcliffe were used to demonstrate his ideas and it was the need he felt for more botanical gardens that prompted him to persuade his old friend, the Dowager Princess of Wales, to convert the gardens of her palace at Kew into the present Royal Botanic Gardens. It was appropriately Bute who suggested the first director.

When the gift of the living became vacant in 1779 it was presented by Bute to his youngest son William, who lived in a mansion at Copt Hall, near to Someries, and needless to say a curate did most of his work. The curate at this time was Coriolanus Copplestone who died in 1800 at the age of 84. He lived in Hog Lane (now Chapel Street) where he augmented his stipend by keeping a private school. Notwithstanding any possible neglect of his pastoral duties Lord William Stuart met with the approval of some people with whom his father was still unpopular. One of these was Samuel Johnson for whom it did not help matters that Bute was a Scot. While staying at Southill in 1781 he was overcome with a curiosity to see the Hoo. Having found that Bute was away he came to observe 'this is one of the places I do not regret having come to see. It is a very stately place indeed; in the house magnificence is not sacrificed to convenience, nor convenience to magnificence. The library is very splendid, the dignity of the rooms is very great and the quality of the pictures is beyond expectation, beyond hope'. He refused to walk through the shrubbery as it was 'a very foolish use of the ground' and with regard to the famous botanical garden he remarked 'is not *every* garden a botanical garden'. Before he returned to Southill he dined well at an inn in Luton drinking the King's health – it was 4 June, George III's birthday! Lord William Stuart later became Bishop of St David's in 1795 and in 1800 the Archbishop of Armagh.

The Hoo on which Bute had bestowed so much care was damaged by fire in 1771 and towards the end of his life he spent much of his time in retirement at Highcliffe. It was there that he fell down a cliff while studying plants and never fully recovered from his injuries. He died in London in 1792 and was buried at Rothesay. The new earl was his son, another John, who by marriage had already acquired Cardiff Castle with estates in the vicinity of Cardiff which with subsequent development brought more wealth. He was created Marquess of Bute in 1796.

About 1700, Daniel Brown, a Quaker, came from the north Bedfordshire village of Podington to settle in Luton. He set up in business as a maltster and bought a house in Park Street. During the next 200 years the Brown family were to be prominent as farmers, millers, corn merchants, timber merchants and even engineers and greatly affected the fortunes of the town. The Luton Quakers were still attending the Meeting House at Sewell but later, about 1712, a new Meeting was started at Dunstable. It was not until 1741 that they began to meet regularly in Luton but the first Meeting House in the town was not built until 1748. In 1799 this had become too small for their needs and a larger one was built close by and this, which is supposed to have been the first slated building in Luton, served the Friends here until 1963 when a new Meeting House was opened in Crawley Green Road.

Methodism comes to Luton

At this time the Dissenters and the Quakers were making little attempt to 'spread the gospel', the urge to do so coming mainly from within the Church itself. One of the prime movers was John Wesley who had a friend and firm supporter in William Cole, who in 1752 bought a mansion at Sundon which had previously been owned by Lord Sundon. Wesley visited Cole here having lost his way completely on the hills which he had to cross as the roads were so bad. Cole was High Sheriff and appointed Wesley to be his chaplain. William Cole later came to live at the fine vicarage in Luton which was then vacant as Dr Prior, the vicar previously to Lord William Stuart, was also headmaster of Repton School and Lord William himself lived at Copt Hall. Needless to say Wesley came to visit his friend in Luton to find Coriolanus Copplestone, the curate, sympathetic but not the Parish Clerk. He refused to have the bells rung when Wesley preached in the church in 1772. With such growing hostility here and elsewhere some of Wesley's followers were leaving churches to worship alone. To assist those in Luton William Cole built a chapel for them opposite the church in Church Street where the Masonic Hall now stands. Wesley himself preached here four times in a building which was to serve the needs of Methodists in the town for nearly forty years.

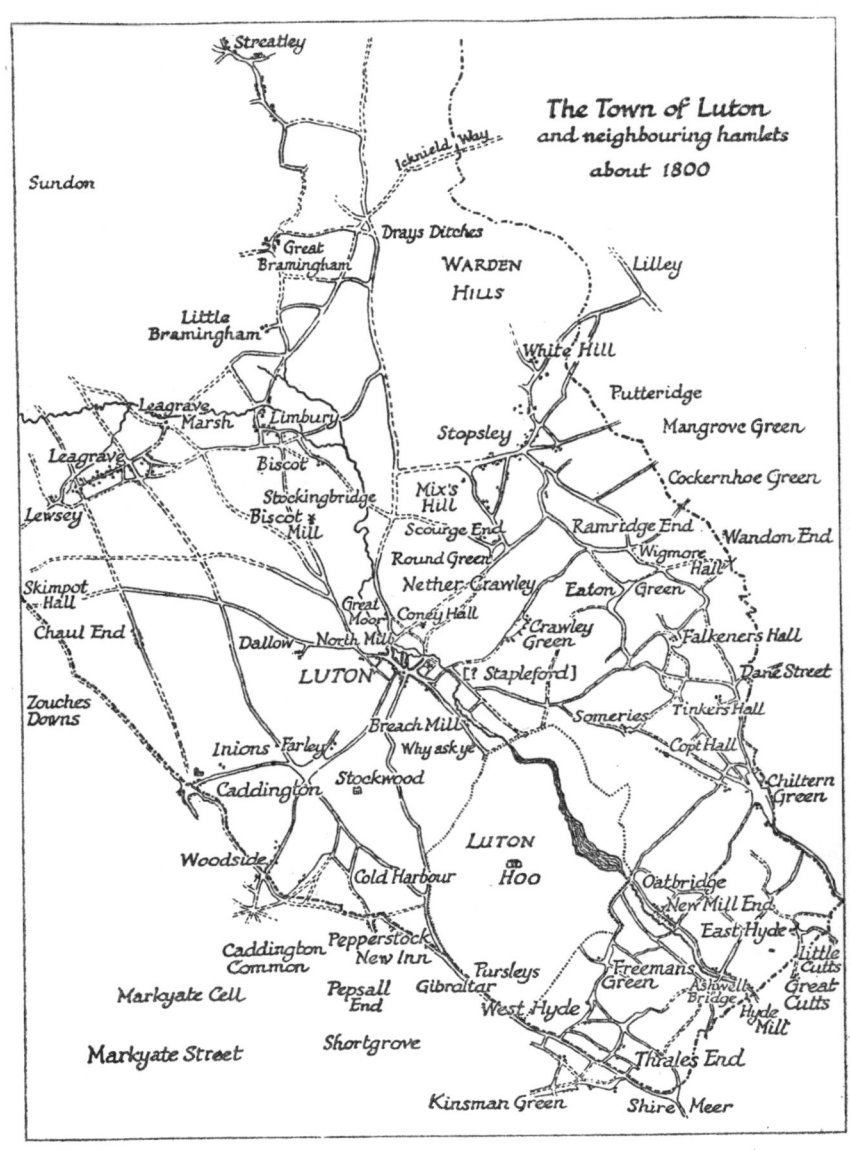

The Town of Luton
and neighbouring hamlets
about 1800

LUTON IN 1801

The township of Luton in 1801 was exceedingly small and extended from the present Lea Road to Bridge Street with a few side streets built up for a short distance on each side. The names of many of the streets changed later so it may be useful to give those by which they were then known.

George Street – High Street or North Street.

Upper George Street – Dunstable Lane.

Manchester Street – Tower Hill, although this was applied also to the site of the present Town Hall and the area above it, now Gordon Street.

Market Hill – Chipping Hill.

Chapel Street – Hog or Hogg Lane. It was also at one time Beggars Lane.

Park Street – from Market Hill to Park Square was Common Street and beyond Park Square it was South Street or Sheep Street.

Lea Road – Blackwater Lane.

A feature of the town was a number of narrow lanes, most of which have now disappeared with the re-development of the town centre.

Barber's Lane ran from opposite the Market House to High Town, crossing the river by a footbridge.

Smith's Lane ran from the top of the Market Hill down to the river. Few lanes can have had more names – Pepper Lane, Rosemary Lane, Park Lane, Pork Pie Alley, Baths Alley being among the more respectable applied to it.

Love Lane ran from the Bedford Road to Hitchin Lane and disappeared when the railway came. A small part still remains in Coupees Path.

St Anne's Lane, known also as Sonning Lane and School Lane, ran from Park Street to the church and is still there at the side of the College of Technology.

There were also a number of cul-de-sacs known as yards with cottages in which many people lived.

Luton was still a small town. The population of the whole parish, which included all the surrounding hamlets as well as the town, was 3,095 and that of the town itself was only about 2,000. Park Square – it had no name then – was in some senses Luton itself with the North Mill and the *Fox* its northern extremities. Guildford Street and all the intervening streets now demolished – Williamson Street, Bute Street, Cheapside, Waller Street, John

Street – had not yet been laid out. Likewise there was not yet King Street, George Street West, Wellington Street and Park Street West. Castle Street was there, it seems to have had no other name, with Pikes Close its only connecting link with Hog Lane. There were a few cottages in High Town, soon to be known as Donkey Hall, and at Coney Hall (hence 'The Rabbit') a short distance along the road to Bedford.

To the north of the town and extending from the new road to Dunstable to the old road to Bedford was the Great Moor. This was the pride of the town but it restricted any immediate development in this direction. On the town side of the North Mill was the Little Moor, stretching on either side of the river down to the footbridge in Barber's Lane. This was enclosed in 1808 allowing an important development of this area.

There was a pond in the middle of Park Square called the Cross Pond, and the Long Pond, lined with a row of trees, occupied the lower part of Park Street as far as the Pound, which was then at the corner of Lea Road. Houses lined both sides of Church Street for much of its length and there were trees on the east side of George Street. A row of buildings (Middle Row) stretched from the Market House on Market Hill to the bottom of Chapel Street. On each side of George Street there were comparatively large houses and a farmhouse stood near the bottom of Wellington Street.

Three water mills were still working on the sites of the Domesday Mills. The North Mill, later to give Mill Street its name, stood between the Great and Little Moors but it was more often known as Freeman's Mill only because the owner was named Freeman. The Brache Mill, owned by the Quaker Browns, was off the present Osborne Road and the Hyde Mill was of course separated from the town by the Hoo Park. There were at least five windmills. Rye Mill stood at the top of Cromwell Hill on the Old Bedford Road and another closer to the town near Villa Road. In High Town there was a windmill near Welbeck Road (called until recently Windmill Street) and yet another stood in Windmill Road. Biscot Mill remained until the present century. The windmills were vulnerable to fire and gales – all of ours were at some time either burned or blown down.

The traders of this period include grocers and drapers but no butchers. There were a watchmaker, sackmaker, basketmaker, glazier and cooper, meeting the obvious needs of a small market town. In addition to hat manufacturers there were a fellmonger, dealing in animals' skins and hides, and a wool dealer. This latter owned, apart from the millers and corn dealers, probably the biggest business in the town. His big warehouse stood in Barber's Lane and contemporary accounts speak of the house adjoining as 'John Hay's mansion'. This was the area of the property later owned by John Waller and it is probable that John Hay's house was afterwards his.

The Origins of the Luton Hat Industry

In 1689 the inhabitants of Luton, Dunstable, Studham, Whipsnade, Caddington, Eaton Bray, Sundon, Wingfield, Totternhoe, Kensworth, Great Gaddesden, Redbourn, Flamstead and Edlesborough petitioned Parliament to reject a Bill which would force people to wear felt hats at certain times of the year. They claimed that they represented over 1,000 families, on which were dependent 14,000 persons, engaged in the making of straw hats. Thirty years later a similar petition from an even larger area asked for import duties to be put on chip (wood shaving) plait from Holland and plait and hats from Leghorn, pleading that the continued importation would ruin poor people employed here in a similar manufacture for 'time out of mind'.

There is evidence here that the hat industry in Luton and the neighbourhood around it is a very old one and it is also clear that this was closely connected with another craft, namely the making of straw plait.

There is a tradition that straw plaiting was first introduced into Scotland by plaiters from Lorraine by Mary, Queen of Scots. They are said to have found the Scottish straw unsuitable and in consequence travelled south to Luton where Sir Robert Napier allowed them to settle. There is unfortunately no reliable evidence to support this theory.

The Hat Industry during the Period of French Wars

When the long war with France began in 1793 the supplies of hats from Leghorn were cut off as Italy soon fell into the hands of the French. A prohibitive tariff was imposed on both plait and hats so there arose an incentive to home producers to make a hat that was comparable with the finest Leghorn. It was first of all necessary to improve the fineness of the plait and a small tool known as a straw splitter was invented. This was used to split the whole straw into a number of smaller straws of uniform width and these were then plaited to make a plait as narrow as $\frac{1}{4}$ in from which could then be made a better quality hat. Thomas Waller, a Luton plait dealer, showed the greatest initiative in securing an improved plait and while the war was still in progress he visited twice a week a large camp for prisoners of war at Yaxley, near Peterborough, and employed the prisoners in making a good quality plait. When the war had finished he made two visits to Tuscany to study the manufacture of the Leghorn plait.

One obvious result of the growth of the straw hat industry was a rapidly increasing demand for plait. Thus more and more plaiters were required. Most of them learnt their craft at the plaiting schools, the first of which were established about the year 1800. Soon almost every south Midland town and village had its plaiting schools. It is reckoned that a total of at least 10,000 boys and girls were in attendance at any time during the first half of the nineteenth century, and, when trade was booming, 13,000.

The children were supposed to learn reading, writing and arithmetic as well as plaiting. In the best plaiting schools they actually did so. But no one insisted that the men and women who ran the schools should be qualified. When factory inspectors subsequently visited the schools they found many masters and mistresses in charge of them who could not only neither read nor write but could not plait. The parents paid 2d a week for their children's education, provided the straw and later sold their children's plait.

The children were set to complete a certain length of plait daily. They attended school – all too often a terribly overcrowded cottage room – from nine o'clock until twelve and from two o'clock until five. Sometimes they worked an extra three hours in the evening, though the evening session was in some schools for evening pupils only.

The plait markets became a picturesque feature of the nineteenth century town life in the south Midlands. Let us imagine the scene on market-day, Monday in Luton. George Street's narrowness

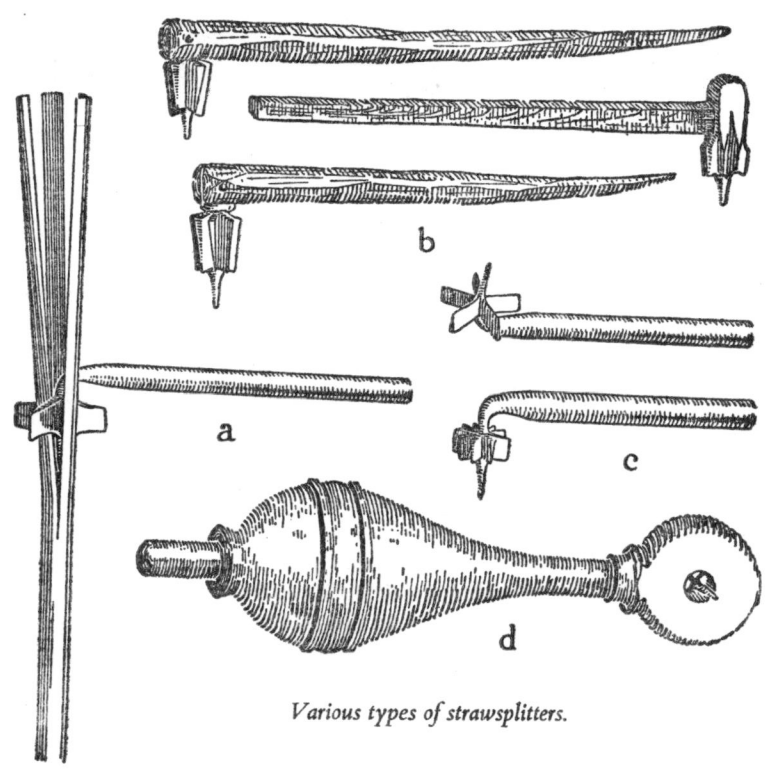

Various types of strawsplitters.

is emphasised by the large number of stalls which crowd it: the stalls of straw dealers and plait dealers. The plaiters are comparing prices in order to buy their straw at the lowest price and sell their plait at the highest. The bonnet-sewers and hat manufacturers are also comparing prices; they want the cheapest plait consistent with quality. And the plait dealers are taking care not to be cheated into paying for greater lengths than they actually receive. They have been swindled too many times already.

LUTON LEADS THE ENGLISH STRAW HAT INDUSTRY

The increased production of plait was made possible only because of the greater demand for hats. Before the war these had been made mainly in the homes of those engaged in the industry and they had to find a market as best they could. There were a few makers with bigger establishments in Luton and more in Dunstable which already had a reputation for a better quality commodity; this probably more because of its position on the main road, the hats being sold in the yards of the coaching inns. In Luton Edmund Waller, a brother of Thomas, opened a warehouse for the purchase of hats from the domestic workshops and was soon to be followed in this line of business by the family of Coupees and others. This method of business was unique to Luton. In Dunstable it was the factories alone which were to develop. It was also to be the first big turning point in the modern development of Luton, for in the eighteenth century it was a typical market town serving the needs of an essentially rural community and neighbourhood and specialising in corn; but by the time the peace came it was already a thriving industrial centre. In 1793 hats had played a small part in its livelihood and after 1815 corn was still to play an important part for some years, but a significant change had come.

THE RETURN TO PEACE

When the war ceased the hat industry was still protected by a considerable tariff and this, with the improved techniques introduced during the war, enabled it now to withstand the foreign competition. Hats had been made for many years in London where the manufacturers had also supplemented their production with purchases from Tuscany and the south Midlands. After the war a number of these firms saw the need to get nearer to their supply and opened branches in both Dunstable and Luton. Among these were Munt and Brown, Welch, Willis, and Elliott, but the firm of Vyse, which came to Luton in 1826, was the largest and had the greatest influence. The Vyse family was to play an important part in the life of the town, with which the firm only recently severed its connection.

The larger firms such as Vyse and the merchant-manufacturers such as the Wallers were soon joined by smaller units, which in some cases grew rapidly, and when the tariffs were finally removed in 1842 the industry had become so firmly entrenched in Luton and Dunstable and to a lesser extent in St Albans and other towns in the neighbourhood that, whilst it suffered temporarily, it was soon able to re-establish itself.

12 The Nineteenth Century — Luton before the railway

IMPROVED COMMUNICATIONS

THE growing town with its expanding hat industry needed better communications with the outside world. Its most important road passed through from St Albans to Bedford and at one time this must have followed the river and approached the town by Park Street, but had been diverted probably when Napier laid out the Hoo Park. It left by the route of the present Old Bedford Road and by so doing crossed the river only once by a ford on the far side of the Little Moor. A bridge was built here (i.e., in Bridge Street) in 1797 and this became the first bridge in Luton. As people had been drowned at the ford in times of flood this was a great improvement. This road was put under a Turnpike Trust in 1727 which was set up to improve the road in the whole of its length through the county. In 1774 the trust was amended and a new one formed for the road from St Albans to Clophill only. Local men of some substance were appointed to the trust and they were concerned only with providing a better road and not with making a profit from the tolls. Our toll gates were at Gibraltar Farm, in London Road, and at some place north of the town in the vicinity of Bridge Street.

In 1832 the New Bedford Road was opened. The old road had been quite unsatisfactory – a lane winding over the Barton Hills. The new road took three years to construct, the most difficult and costly stretch being the Barton Cutting, which replaced the steep hill on the old road.

Dunstable had previously been reached either by travelling along Dallow Road and then taking a track through Skimpot or alternatively through Leagrave and by part of the old Icknield Way. The present road to Dunstable was made in 1784.

The road to Hitchin was always as it is now, the continuation of Church Street by Hitchin Lane (now Hitchin Road). In the eighteenth century there were two streams at the end of Church Street one of which had been the mill stream of the old Church Mill. The river had to be diverted to make one channel only and a further bridge was built over this in 1799. The only other road out of the town of any consequence was a continuation of Hog Lane (Chapel Street) to Caddington and Markyate.

The improved roads made possible a better coach service and in 1794 the Ampthill Flyer was starting from Ampthill in the mid-afternoon and reaching Luton in the evening. Here the passengers from Ampthill to London had to stay the night at the *Old Bell*, which was situated at the corner of Hog Lane and George Street and was the town's oldest coaching inn. In the morning it began a twelve-hour journey to London and by this means was able to make the return run from London to Ampthill twice a week. The single fare from Luton to London was 12s if one faced all weathers and travelled on the outside of the coach and 21s if the passenger had the luxury of an inside seat. In those days an agricultural worker earned only about 8s a week so it is not surprising that ordinary people travelled little. It was not until 1810 that Luton got its first direct coach service to London and the journey time was then reduced to nine hours. This was, until the railway came near to the town, the quickest connection we had with the rest of the country.

It is astonishing that with these inadequate communications the hat industry flourished, a gas works was opened and even an engineering works was promoted in Luton in the early years of the nineteenth century.

Some other improvements in transport had been made in the eighteenth century with the construction of the Grand Junction Canal through Watford, Hemel Hempstead, Tring and Leighton Buzzard in 1793, and the making of the rivers Ivel and Flitt navigable as far as Biggleswade and Shefford by 1760.

Hat workers in Luton used to make the journey once a week by horse and cart or with a hand cart to the canal at Leighton Buzzard to collect coal. This was the most convenient collecting place as there were steep hills on the roads to all the other towns on the canal system.

In the nineteenth century came the railway, but not to Luton, for the compilers of the 1851 Census Return observed that it was the largest town in the country without either the railway or some means of navigable water transport. The dates at which the town's smaller neighbours obtained the railway (with their populations in 1851) may be of interest: Hemel Hempstead (7,073) 1837, Berkhamsted (3,395) 1838, Leighton Buzzard (4,465) 1838, Bedford (11,693) 1846, Dunstable (3,589) 1848, Hitchin (7,077) 1850. Luton's population in 1851 was 10,648 and she was not to get the railway until 1858. The reasons why it was so long in coming and the differences it made when it came will be dealt with in a later chapter.

LOCAL GOVERNMENT AND A NEW SYSTEM OF POOR LAW

Since the Elizabethan period the local government of villages and of towns which were not boroughs had been in the hands of the Vestry but by the nineteenth century any direct connection with the church itself was very slender. The churchwardens had to call Vestry Meetings which were attended by the chief ratepayers whether they were churchgoers or not. The Vestry Meeting then appointed constables who, since they were generally part-time, were usually ineffective in keeping law and order, and overseers. These latter were very important as one of their main functions was seeing that the aged, infirm, orphans and those without work were provided for. There was a workhouse, sometimes more than one, in each parish where those unable to fend for themselves, or with no one to care for them, were housed and usually given some work to do. The Luton Workhouse was off Park Square in the neighbourhood of the present Park Street West. It was also the duty of the overseers to see that roads were maintained and that any matters of sewage and refuse disposal were dealt with. Work of this kind was often given to men out of work in return for payments to keep them from starving. The Vestry could also supervise a school and do various other things if allowed to do so. This latter was important as the Justices of the Peace sitting in Quarter Sessions had to sanction any rate raised by the Vestry but on the other hand if the Vestry was not doing what the justices thought necessary they themselves could order it to be done and fix the necessary rate.

The Poor Law as it had been controlled by the overseers was felt to be too costly and inefficient and in 1834 parishes were forced to combine to make Poor Law Unions for the joint control of their poor relief. The new system was more efficient but dreaded by the poorer people, who feared going into the new and bigger workhouse. The Luton Poor Law Union included the parishes of Barton, Caddington, Dunstable, Eaton Bray, Houghton Regis, Humbershoe, Kensworth, Luton, Streatley, Studham, Sundon, Totternhoe and Whipsnade. Humbershoe (pronounced Humbers-hoe) was that part of Markyate on the west side of the Watling Street and at that time in Bedfordshire. The new work-house was built in Dunstable Road near to the corner of Dallow Road and was opened in 1836. Luton people soon observed that thirteen steps led to its front door! It is now part of St Mary's Hospital.

The new Poor Law had one advantage over the old as the new Board of Guardians was in part elected by the ratepayers and in this respect it was a beginning of democratic local government.

Luton gets a Board of Health

A second change arose out of a national concern regarding the unnecessary loss of life in the growing industrial towns due to epidemics of cholera, typhoid and smallpox. It was obvious that these were caused by the bad housing conditions of the poor and by inadequate water supplies combined with ineffective sewage disposal. An Act of Parliament of 1848 had made it compulsory for many towns with a high death rate to have a local Board of Health or allowed one to be set up if 10 per cent of the inhabi-tants of any town petitioned for it. The Vestry was strongly opposed to Luton having such a board but someone had organised a petition. As there was no local newspaper at this time the full story of the crisis is not known and it is to be hoped that somebody will be able one day to present a full account of it. Notwithstand-ing the good work done by the Vestry it was for the ultimate good of the town that it now had a more representative body to control its affairs.

The Board of Health, like the Guardians, was partly elected and had nearly all the powers that a Town Council then had. The town's sewage disposal was a major problem. At one time a great deal of this had found its way into the Long Pond in Park Street where it had to wait for a heavy fall of rain to wash it down Blackwater Lane (Lea Road) into the river. In the place of this crude system dumb wells were now attached to the houses, but these were all too often very close to the freshwater wells. It was not until 1870 that Luton had a piped water supply. One of the first tasks of the Board of Health was to provide a sewage works off Windmill Road, close to Osborne Road, with a refuse disposal yard near by. The sewage works were to remain there until 1886 when the river board demanded their removal to a new site now covered by the present Vauxhall works.

In 1866 the lord of the manor leased the market tolls to the Board of Health which at once proceeded to get the greater part of the market off the streets. This was done on condition that the town erected a Corn Exchange on the site of the market hall, the new building to revert to the lord of the manor after seventy-five years. Middle Row, the block of houses in the central part of what is now Market Hill, was pulled down and the Corn Exchange, only the base of which now remains, was erected in 1869. In front of the Corn Exchange the town placed a water fountain in memory of Lionel Ames, a very popular neighbour, who lived at The Hyde. The Ames family resided there for many years and seems to be remembered mainly for the great height of its members. The Ames Memorial, always known as the 'Pepper Box', was a feature of the main street.

The pulling down of the market hall coincided with developments elsewhere in the town. In addition to the almshouses on Tower Hill which had already been described as bad property there were cottages belonging to the parish on Market Hill which must have been in an equally poor condition. These were temporarily exchanged for some cottages in Lea Road and a common trust formed about 1869 to provide better almshouses in Chobham Street for six married couples and six single persons. The Tower Hill almshouses were then destroyed. The trustees appointed to manage the new trust included the churchwardens and overseers as it was still nominally in the control of the Vestry.

In the meantime Robert Hibbert, who lived at The Hyde for about twenty years, in 1819 gave a row of cottages in Castle Street, almost opposite the *Red Lion Hotel*, to provide for twenty-four poor widows. This charity, unlike the previous ones, was not in the control of the church. In 1885 there was an exchange of land and new almshouses were provided in what is now appropriately known as Hibbert Street. These, which have separate flats for twelve women, have since been modernised and in addition to having bathrooms have a central flat for a warden. This was by no means the end of Hibbert's philanthropy but the limit of that which directly affected Luton. Much of his income came from a sugar plantation in Jamaica in the days before slaves were emancipated. His concern for the welfare of his own slaves is said to have made him unpopular with other slave owners as it made slaves generally discontented.

It was also in 1869 that the Board of Health decided to build the Plait Halls in Cheapside and Waller Street to take the large plait market away from the main street. These two streets had only recently been laid out in the area which had been John Waller's house and garden. Shops had become more numerous thus making the shambles which had previously been at the side of the old market hall no longer necessary. Livestock continued to be sold on market days on the verges of Park Street until 1882 when a cattle market was opened off Castle Street.

Another example of the initiative of the Board of Health is shown in the forming of a Fire Brigade. There had previously been a purely voluntary fire fighting service and William Austin records that at one time the fire engine had been kept under the gallery in the church. In 1864 the Board made the maintenance of the service its own responsibility.

One of the last achievements of the Board of Health was the provision of public baths in Waller Street in 1872. The washing baths were indeed very much needed for at this time very few houses had bathrooms. It was in keeping with the morals of the Victorian age that there were two swimming baths, one for men which was small enough and the other for women which was ridiculously restricted. The baths, almost as soon as they were built, proved inadequate for a town which had no other facilities for swimming.

PUBLIC UTILITIES

The powers of the Board of Health were limited and many

services had to be provided by public utility companies. This involved the provision of the capital by public-spirited persons who would be content with a fixed and moderate return so that any additional profits could be ploughed back into an improved service.

The first such local public utility came before the days of the Board of Health in the Luton Gas and Coke Company. Gas began to replace lighting by oil or candle in Luton in 1834, when the gas company was founded. The gas works in Dunstable Road, so long familiar to Lutonians but now gone, bore the proud motto 'Ex Fumo Dare Lucem' (out of smoke came light). The introduction of coal-gas to the town might be said to be the first of many innovations which were to improve greatly the standard of comfort of ordinary Luton people.

Reference has already been made to the need for a piped water supply and this was met in the same way by the forming of the Luton Water Company in 1865. By 1870 the company had bored deep wells to reach a pure water supply and had laid a system of water mains throughout the town.

A more unusual kind of public utility was to be seen in the forming of cemetery companies. During the first half of the century the churchyard was still used for burials and there were burial grounds adjoining the Baptist Meeting House in Park Street, the Friends Meeting House, the Union Church, the Wesleyan Church in Chapel Street and the Ebenezer Particular Baptist Church. These were often near to dwelling houses and could contaminate freshwater wells. Pressure was exerted by the Board of Health and in 1854 two cemetery companies were formed, one to lay out a cemetery in Crawley Green Road for the use of the Church of England and the other, to provide a cemetery, with no respect for sects, or better still regard for all, at the top of Rothesay Road. Needless to say these were to be known as the church and chapel cemeteries respectively. In 1864 the Quakers started a burial ground of their own, also in Crawley Green Road.

Luton had its Town Hall which, in keeping with so much else in those days, was the property of a private concern, the Town Hall Company. It was a pleasing building in Georgian style built in 1847 on the same site as the present Town Hall. At the end of the Crimean War in 1856 a public subscription was raised to put a clock on the front of the building to celebrate the return to peace. One of the rooms on the ground floor was rented by the Luton Literary Institution whose main function was to provide a library for its members. Most of the rest of the ground floor was used by the Court of Petty Sessions which had previously been held at the *George Hotel*. This court, which had been in being since 1830 to serve an area wider than the town itself, superseded the very old Court of the Hundred of Flitt which incidentally had also met in Luton. The change thus made was virtually the end of the hundred system which had existed since Saxon times. In 1839 Luton had its full-time police who were part of the newly-formed county force. They were so effective in dealing with crime that the Court of Petty Sessions in Luton, as elsewhere, soon became known as the Police Court. On the first floor of the Town Hall, approached by a wide staircase, was the hall itself, a large room which was used for meetings of all kinds. There were shops and offices in adjoining buildings of the same style as the Town Hall itself.

EDUCATIONAL DEVELOPMENTS

There were a number of private schools in the town and neighbouring villages similar to that of Coriolanus Copplestone. Some better off Luton people were already sending their sons away to school, but for their daughters it was still another matter. There was a school for boys with working-class parents but when it began is not known. In 1673 Cornelius Bigland, a Luton barber-surgeon, left '£6 a year . . . in trust for clothing, maintaining, schooling and educating six poor children of the town for ever'. Twelve years later a similar bequest was made by Roger Gillingham. John Richards, a Luton tin-plate worker, was more specific in leaving, in 1731, property in trust for educating five poor boys at the Church school in Luton. It is on record that Joseph Freeman, master of the school, died in 1794 having had thirty-three children of his own. It has been thought that the school was at one time held in the vestry in the church but on the other hand St Anne's Lane, leading off Park Street to the church, was once known as School Lane.

An interest in educating poorer children developed during the period of the long war with France when it was realised that this could be done at low cost by using slates or sand trays instead of pens and paper and by training older children, called monitors, to teach the younger ones. In this way one master or mistress could teach as many as 200 children. The parents would only need to pay about 2d a week for their children to go to school which would about meet the salary of the master or mistress. All that would be needed was a building with some assistance in providing the limited equipment. The only trouble with this excellent plan was that the different kinds of churches and to some extent the political parties became involved.

The Nonconformists, supported largely by the Whigs, were the first to take action, wanting schools to be independent of church control. They were followed quickly by some of the Church of England who with much Tory support wanted education to remain under the control of the church. The former worked through the British and Foreign Schools Society and the latter through a rival National Society for Promoting the Education of the Poor in the Principles of the Established Church. Hence there were British (unsectarian) and National (Church) schools.

Bedfordshire was a Whig county with Samuel Whitbread, an MP for Bedford and a great advocate for education, one of the leading Whigs. He was responsible for the opening of a British School at Shefford which was followed quickly by another one at Woburn which had the assistance of the Duke of Bedford, another Whig. In 1809 the Marquess of Bute, then a Whig, provided land on Park Square for a British school to be built in Luton. The National Society had not yet been formed and if it had the Marquess might have acted differently. The new school bore the inscription 'Train up a child in the way he should go, and when he is old he will not depart from it'. About 125 boys attended the school in the daytime and a similar number of girls in the evening. There was a Sunday School at which the same subjects were taught as at the day school but this was less well attended. The master was paid £52 10s per annum for the first 60 boys and 10s for each additional boy and his wife £31 10s for supervising the evening school for the girls. These were high salaries for those days. Although it had started as a British school the school soon came under the control of the church.

A report in 1818 mentions six other 'pay' schools in the town, three for boys and three for girls, attended by 255 children, and a number of plaiting schools. The 'pay' schools were probably private ones attended by better-off children.

A turning point in education in Luton came in 1833 with a Treasury grant of £20,000 per annum to the two societies to meet not more than half the cost of building new schools. The managers of the Luton school immediately severed all connection with the British Society and joined the National Society to which it applied at once for consideration for a Treasury grant. One was given, leaving the rest necessary for a larger school to be met by subscription to which the Marquess of Bute again gave generous support. A National School for boys and girls was opened in June 1835 in Church Street to the great dismay of the supporters of the British school system who would have no hope of obtaining a similar grant. They raised funds to build a British School in Langley Street in 1836, Daniel Brown, a Quaker, providing an adjoining school for infants.

The Methodists were equally interested in education. The Wesleyans, who like the Anglicans favoured a church control, set up a committee which in 1854 opened a school in a room of their new church in Chapel Street. The Primitive Methodists on the other hand were as one with the Baptists and Quakers in matters of education and let their old church in High Town Road as a British school when they built a new one adjoining it in 1852. With four schools now in the town most children were having some education for which their parents still paid but the length of time they stayed at school was all too brief for much to be learned. The growth in the number of schools was also not so much due to a desire for more education as it was to a rapid increase in the population of the town.

The National School was soon overcrowded and those in control of it were concerned because twice as many children were now attending schools other than their own. They applied for another grant and once more faced the task of raising funds to build a bigger school. This was done in 1857 when Queen Square School was completed. They then sold the old school in Church Street to the Quakers to pay off part of the debt they had incurred. The Quakers turned it into an Adult School.

In 1814 the Park Street Baptists rebuilt their church and the new building is of some interest as it was octagonal in shape and was consequently known as the 'Round Meeting'. There were soon divisions in the Park Street community and a new church was formed called the Union Church as it brought together two kinds of Baptists who could for the time being agree to differ. Their church, built in Castle Street in 1836, is a pleasing building and is a good example of architectural design of its period. In 1846 there was yet another schism at Park Street and a number left to form the Ceylon Baptist Church in Wellington Street. The differences at the Union Church were now to become widened to the extent that one group within the church could no longer be considered to be Baptists. They broke away in 1865 to become Congregationalists and in building King Street Church were to give the town one of its landmarks. These were breaks of live rather than decadent communities and each new church when formed seemed to vie with the rest in forming branch churches in the villages and building mission halls in the town. In 1866 the Round Meeting was blown down in a severe gale and the present church was built on the same site four years later.

The doctrines of the Baptist church at Dunstable, which had broken away from the church at Kensworth shortly after Thomas Marsom had led his followers away, caused them to become Particular or Strict Baptists. Those of the Dunstable church who lived in Luton began a new church in Rosemary Lane in 1803. They also grew in numbers opening another church in Ebenezer Street in 1833 which was to serve them until their present church was built in Hastings Street in 1853.

The Methodists also grew in strength. The original church built in Church Street for John Wesley soon proved to be too small so a larger one was built in 1814 in Hog Lane – it was not long before this was re-named Chapel Street as the Methodists at this stage preferred to call their places of worship chapels. Another section of Methodists then appeared in the town. These, the Primitive Methodists, were more free in their form of service than the Wesleyan Methodists and they usually appealed much more to the working class. Their first church was built in 1838 in High Town Road, then a growing part of the town known as

Donkey Hall. It is supposed to have received this name at the time the Round Meeting was built when an enterprising person carried bricks from the previous building on a donkey along Barber's Lane to build a house in High Town. In 1852 a new church was built in High Town Road adjoining the previous one and in the same year the Wesleyan church in Chapel Street was rebuilt. The new church here was a fine building which was able to seat a congregation of 1,800 making it one of the largest Methodist churches in the country. A second Wesleyan church was built in 1863 in Waller Street, again near the town centre, but the Primitive Methodists built their second church in 1864 in Brown Brick (later to be known as Park Town) which was another growing part of the town. The Methodists had even more zeal than the Baptists in forming branch churches on the outskirts of the town, in its hamlets and in the neighbouring villages. Lay, or as they were more usually known, local preachers, had a full programme or 'plan' of services to attend. This growing activity of the other sects must have been of great concern to those connected with the Church of England.

Until the middle of the century the parish church was expected to serve the whole of the needs of Luton, which included not only the township itself but the growing hamlets of Leagrave, Limbury, Stopsley, Chiltern Green and East Hyde. So long as the Butes held this lucrative living they presented it to their relatives or absentee vicars few of whom showed much interest in the church. A change came after the Butes left the Hoo and sold the living to various patrons who appointed a succession of vicars most of whom had a greater awareness of their pastoral duties. Among these was Thomas Peile who was vicar from 1857 to 1861. Dr Peile, no doubt under a certain amount of pressure, surrendered a great deal of his income to enable new churches to be built at East Hyde in 1859, Stopsley in 1860 and a new one in the town itself, Christ Church, also in 1860. The East Hyde church had in fact been built in 1841 as a chapel-of-ease attached to Luton church much of its cost being met by the Marquess of Bute and the Ames family. In 1859 it became a separate parish as Christ Church and Stopsley were from the time their churches were first built.

In 1862 the living was purchased by James O'Neill for himself and he was to hold it for thirty-five years. During this period still more new churches were built and new parishes formed, Biscot in 1866, St Matthew's in 1875 and St Paul's in 1892. Out of the new parish of Christ Church, yet another was formed in St Saviour's in 1893.

O'Neill, who found the church in a dilapidated condition, effected a considerable restoration which we have already described. He was a striking character who brought new life to the church in Luton. Since his death he has become a legendary figure and will later receive more of our attention.

The Effect of the Churches on the Life of the Town

The churches had a great influence on the social life of Luton and did much to build up its schools; but their effect upon its economic development was greater still. The Quakers were the merchants of the town and the Brown family throughout the century were the biggest corn millers. Another member of the same family started the large firm of timber merchants in 1817, and yet another joined forces with a fellow Quaker in 1840 to form Brown and Green, an engineering firm which specialised in making bicycles and later almost anything in iron from baths to lamp-posts. It was a son of the Green of the firm, J. W. Green, who in 1869 took to brewing and began the merger of local breweries which was to culminate into our present extensive brewery. Until about this time Quakers had looked upon brewing as a respectable form of business, but they were now searching their consciences. The other nonconforming sects, except the Particular Baptists, were beginning to launch the campaign for total abstinence, so J. W. Green decided to join the Church of England, of which he became one of the most distinguished adherents in the town.

The early hat manufacturers, including the Wallers and the Coupees, were mainly Baptists as were many of the shopkeepers and craftsmen. Richard Vyse is said to have gone to the parish church on Sunday mornings and to Park Street Baptist Church in the evening and if this were so it speaks much for the respect that the members of the various churches had for the beliefs of others.

In the first half of the century the Methodists entered little into the life of the town and appear to have been building up through their class meetings a basis of living by Christian experience. Later they were to be the biggest force in the town, rivalled perhaps only by the newly-arrived Congregationalists.

The Church of England had a weakening hold in the town in the early years of the century and what strength it had came from the land-owning community. As Luton grew and the professional classes became more represented these tended to be Anglican. This added support, with the help of the more vigorous incumbency of James O'Neill, assisted the church to regain much lost ground.

The various professions had long been represented in the town but it was not unusual for a man to carry on a trade side by side with a profession. There was also a difficulty in describing a profession. Samuel Chase in the late eighteenth century is described as a surgeon and man-midwife. The Chases were originally Baptists but later members of the family who stayed in the town and became solicitors joined the Church of England. By the middle of the nineteenth century the various professions were obtaining legal recognition in return for restrictions on their part of those qualified to practice in them. Some families tended to stay in the professions as others did in trade. It is perhaps not surprising that Luton sent few of its sons to have distinguished careers in the armed forces.

THE DEVELOPMENT OF BANKING IN LUTON

Banking apparently began in Luton with Leonard Hampson who was originally in partnership as a lawyer with John Griffiths. The firm was already engaged in banking in a minor way when Charles Addington Austin, a nephew of Griffiths, came from Hertford to be articled to it. When Griffiths died Hampson took another partner, Edward Williamson, into the legal side while Austin and he carried on the banking. The new arrangement led to Hampson and Austin's, or the Luton Bank. We lack information on the date when it was formed but Luton Museum has fortunately two notes issued by the Bank dated 1821 and 1822. It was, however, short lived and when Leonard Hampson died in 1824 leaving no heirs, Austin lacked sufficient capital to carry it on and the bank failed. C. A. Austin and Edward Williamson then formed a partnership and became the town's leading solicitors.

In the meantime five Quakers had in 1812 formed the so-called Bedfordshire Leighton Buzzard Bank and following the failure of the Luton Bank they opened an agency in a room at the *George Hotel* where they conducted business one day a week. In 1827 two of the partners, Joseph Sharples and William Exton, took over part of the business, including the Luton agency, to form the Hertfordshire Hitchin Bank. A full branch was opened in Luton in 1839 with Robert Marsh as the manager. More Quakers were then brought into the firm which eventually became Sharples, Tuke, Lucas and Seebohm. About 1866 Benjamin Seebohm became manager of the Luton branch and was finally succeeded by the Latchmores towards the end of the century.

In 1859 they bought John Waller's very fine house on the Market Hill and built what was to be known in Luton as 'The Bank'. It was also about this time that the gardens of Waller's house were taken over and developed into Cheapside, Waller Street and John Street. The bank was ultimately to become the Corporation's bank and provided, through its customers, the capital for the public utilities that were playing an increasing part in the town's activities. Our Luton Quaker banking families – the Marshs, Lucas's, Seebohms and Latchmores – were an influence in the business and philanthropic life of the community especially in educational work. They were all very much intermarried and as William Exton's daughter had married a Barclay it was not surprising that the firm became part of Barclays Bank in 1896.

The bank did have one rival, for in 1839 the London and County Bank (later to be incorporated into the Westminster Bank) opened a Luton branch. It did not move to its present position until 1896 at which time Chapel Street was widened. The next bank was to come in 1898 with the Capital and Counties Bank (to be later incorporated into Lloyds Bank).

C. A. Austin, the partner in the Luton Bank, was a member of a well-known family of Luton solicitors. He himself was from 1862 until his death in 1872 clerk to the justices and steward of the manor, succeeding his partner Edward Williamson in both of these offices. He was related to Thomas Erskine Austin, who was clerk to the Board of Guardians for many years and as a young man had been very active in the movement to get the railway to Luton. William Austin, the Luton historian, was T. E. Austin's son. An example of T. E. Austin's enthusiasm for railways is shown well in the journey he made as a young man in 1838 by horseback to Leighton Buzzard from whence he travelled by train to London to see Queen Victoria's coronation. He returned to Luton on the same day and this could well be the first time a Luton person visited London and returned in one day.

In the middle years of the century a number of important traders began to appear in the town and their ascendancy to some extent reflects a decline in the importance of the market. One of the oldest shops in Luton is Blundells which was begun by members of a family with long connections with the neighbourhood. They were mainly Nonconformists, prominent in the civic life of the town, and had farming connections. The drapery business was started in 1852 and when Cheapside was developed they occupied the corner site.

Gibbs and Dandy's claim an even longer history as they arose out of the ironmongery side of Brown and Green's business which we have seen was formed in 1840. There is no doubt a hidden history behind many other local trading firms whose names are now familiar.

13 The Nineteenth Century — Luton after the railway

THE RAILWAY AT LAST

BY the middle of the century the people of Luton had become desperate to have the railway. Between 1838 and 1858 many plans had been proposed but none of them had come to fruition. The most promising one came in 1844 when George Stephenson contemplated a line which would come from Leighton Buzzard and pass through Luton on a loop to give another route to London. He saw representatives of the town at the *George Hotel* on 11 May 1844, and outlined his plan. He met a barrage of objections mainly concerned with the Great Moor which he said would have to be intersected by the line. The townspeople had already let the Little Moor go and had allowed the new roads to Bedford and Dunstable to cross the edge of the Great Moor but were unwilling to allow a further breaking up of the open space of which they were justifiably proud. Stephenson is supposed to have left the meeting in a very bad mood, vowing that Luton would not have the railway as long as he lived. The line he proposed was ultimately opened in 1848 but terminated at Dunstable. This brought the railway much nearer to Luton but with little benefit to those who wished to travel to London. A coach continued to take passengers to Watford to catch trains there, it being quicker than the alternative route.

Hopes were raised again in 1855 when a company was floated to construct a line from Dunstable to pass through Luton to Welwyn where it would join the Great Northern line and give a connection to King's Cross. There was a great surge of local interest and businessmen soon raised £20,000 of the necessary capital and James Waller and Henry Tomson were appointed directors of the company. Tomson was a member of a prominent local farming family and had recently started a corn mill in Luton. The town was soon divided as to the best site for the station which both Waller and Tomson wanted to be between Dunstable Road and New Bedford Road. Others favoured a site at the top of Bute Street, even if this meant pulling down some cottages. This plan won the day and both Waller and Tomson resigned from the board of directors, to be replaced by Thomas Sworder and John Everitt, a hat manufacturer.

Needless to say there was great excitement when work on the railway began and there was a procession with a brass band, the Friendly Society men in all their regalia and the navvies with their pick-axes. This made its way to Bute Street where Colonel Gilpin, one of the members of parliament for the county, cut the first sod. The town went mad with joy when the first section was opened and the maiden journey was made to Dunstable on 3 May 1858. Once again there was a brass band and the train with twenty-two carriages was quickly crowded with passengers, many of whom had not bought tickets. Sitting on top and hanging on to the sides of the coaches they left on the very first railway train ever to leave Luton. Not for the last time the system broke down and most of the passengers had to walk home, but it must have been a memorable day. The return fare to Dunstable was, by the way, sixpence.

There was some delay with the remainder of the line to Welwyn but it was opened to traffic in 1860. The Luton, Dunstable and Welwyn Railway which was later taken over by the Great Northern Company was claimed to be the cheapest per mile of any constructed in the country.

From 1860 there were, every day, several through-trains from Luton (via Hatfield) to King's Cross; in other words, it was now possible to travel by rail to London without changing.

In 1857 the Midland Railway had extended its line from Leicester through Bedford and Shefford to Hitchin, reaching London by the Great Northern Railway, but by 1862 congestion on the latter forced the Midland to promote its own line to London from Bedford through Luton. The route involved cutting across the Great Moor and the then extensive Leagrave Common, but the town had learnt a lesson and objections were few; the prospect of a direct link with London, and with the Midlands and

North, outweighed other considerations. Construction was rapid: goods trains began to run through Luton on 9 September 1867, and local passenger trains on 13 July following. Long-distance trains were transferred to the new line on 1 October 1868, and the Bedford and Hitchin section at once assumed the role of an unimportant branch line.

The southern part of the Moor now cut off by the railway was taken by John Sambrook Crawley with the money which the company gave in compensation for the part of the Moor needed for the railway itself. In exchange he gave the town the huge open spaces between Old Bedford Road and High Town we now know as Pope's Meadow, People's Park and Bell's Close. The portions Crawley had taken were developed for the building of Crawley Road, Moor Street and Francis Street. The opening of the new line brought the long railway footbridge, one of the minor features of the town.

The Midland line specialised in passenger traffic and the carriage of coal leaving the Great Northern to concentrate on general goods traffic which it did with much success in meeting the increasing needs of the hat industry.

The coming of the railway was the second stage in the development of Luton.

The Hat Industry in the Railway Age

The hat industry expanded steadily in the early years of the century and it continued to do so even after the tariffs on imported hats and plait had been removed. In the early days the hat makers had attempted to undertake all the processes of manufacture, often using crude methods. As techniques improved specialisation followed and this was to be seen first in blocking. Slicken stones gave way to the box iron and by 1860 blocking machines had been introduced. Men now did blocking leaving the women workers to concentrate on sewing. It was also about 1860 that the first blockmakers appear. Bigger firms could employ their own blockmakers but with so many small manufacturers there would be a demand for blocks that could be met by independent makers. It was indeed a skilled craft and when once established it did much to assist the introduction of new shapes.

Dyeing and bleaching were also attempted by the makers

themselves with the result that the only colours were black, brown and blue produced by wood and vegetable dyes which were not, in any case, very effective with plait. The first independent dyers appeared in the middle of the century but a turning point came when Thomas Lye set up in business in Luton in 1857. His father had built up a plaiting business at Kirkby Malzeard near Ripon and he had already made visits to Luton to sell plait and buy hats to take back to Yorkshire. When he settled in Luton, aniline dyes, which were to be much more effective with plait, had been recently introduced and by developing them he was able to build up the business which still remains. It was to be followed by other firms and dyeing became an important complementary industry.

In its early days the hat industry had been able to exist on 'three shapes, three colours and three sizes' but by the time the railway came it had departed from this and a large measure of specialisation had appeared.

FURTHER DEVELOPMENTS IN THE HAT INDUSTRY

A big expansion of the hat industry followed the coming of the railway but more adequate transport was not in itself so much its cause as were some changes within the industry itself. Most of the trade at this time was in bonnets and these were sewn by hand, it taking some years to train a girl to be a good bonnet-sewer. The sewing machine had been invented in the 1860s and was soon adapted to meet the needs of various trades and it could be only a matter of time before straw hats would be sewn by machine. There were many technical difficulties, but finally in 1874 Mrs Stratford, wife of the Willcox and Gibbs' agent in Luton, accepted the challenge of the Singer Sewing Machine Company's agent and sewed a hat on a Willcox and Gibbs' machine in the conventional manner of beginning at the centre and finishing at the edge. One drawback with the machine was that the stitch was visible whereas a good hand sewer could conceal the stitch. French engineers had mastered this difficulty but their machine was a prohibitive price and it was left to Edmund Wiseman to invent a concealed-stitch machine in 1878 at a more reasonable cost. He later invented an improved machine, on the same principle, known as the box machine.

The first visible stitch machines were known as the 10 Guinea machines as they originally no doubt cost this amount, but they were soon reduced in price to about £4 retaining, however, their name. These were soon replaced by an improved model known as the 17 Guinea machine so called, not from its price, but to distinguish it from the earlier one. It took about four years to train a girl to become a good machinist and competent to work with all types but most were content to be able to manage one and were known as 17 Guinea machinists or box machinists, terms which puzzled many not used to the trade who imagined that the machinists were earning 17 guineas a week. Once a girl could master the machine she could sew six hats in the time that the hand sewer was sewing one.

The industrial revolution, which had come late to the hat trade compared with such industries as textiles and engineering, had some interesting consequences. The sewing machines were exceedingly cheap and the agents were prepared to let the hat makers buy them on easy terms or even hire them at very low charges. It was possible to drive them by steam power; indeed Vyse's had done this as early as 1877, but this did not of necessity increase their output and only made the operatives less tired. Machinery, which in so many industries had forced the small manufacturers out of business and concentrated production into a few larger firms, had no such effect on the Luton hat industry, which was still to remain domestic in its character. Homeworkers, known in the industry as outdoor hands, could use the machines as efficiently as the factory workers, and housewives throughout the town, even the wives of the professional class, would machine in the few weeks that the trade was busy.

Everyday Life in the Hat Industry

The industry had always been seasonal as so many women bought a new hat to wear at Easter and the hat makers were very busy from February until May, after which came the long 'dull season' when there was little work to do. In the busy season thousands of girls came into Luton from the villages to work for the week and return home at the weekend, but more came to stay for the whole of the season. A result of this was that the houses became very overcrowded and it was difficult to move for piles of hats and plait. Until about 1870 it was customary for the women and girls in the smaller factories to work until about ten o'clock at night and all night on Friday. The only redeeming feature of these long hours of work was that it lasted for only a few weeks of the year. It was not until 1866 that the Factory Acts applied to the industry but it became very difficult to enforce them as there were so many factories and workshops to inspect and the workers were as keen as their employers to evade the law. They wished to earn as much money as they could while there was work to be done.

The large number of small units in the industry had an interesting effect on the plan of the houses in the town. From the middle years of the century these were built with two very large rooms at the rear. One on the ground floor was used for the heavier operations of blocking and stiffening now usually done by men and the equally big room above this was used as a sewing room for the women workers. Some houses were built on this principle even in the earlier years of the twentieth century.

The industry employed many more women than men and much of the female labour came into the town for the periods when the trade was busy, but what employment was there for the men of Luton? The hat industry itself employed a number as blockers and stiffeners and there was always a lot of fetching and carrying to be done between the small workshops and the warehouses of the merchant manufacturers and this was done usually by the men, as was the packing of the hats in the warehouses. Blockmaking was also a male occupation and only men were employed in the bleaching and dyeing industry. Apart from employment in the hat industry itself some men in the hamlets and outlying parts worked on the land or at brickmaking, which still continued at Stopsley, or at the small lime works near the town. In the town itself there was work at the brewery, the few engineering works and in the maintenance of social services such as the railway, roads, the gas works, refuse collecting and, of course, building. Luton, however, continued to impress visitors with its large surplus of women and to have the reputation of being a place where the men were kept by the women.

A FRESH SOURCE OF SUPPLY OF PLAIT IS FOUND
Given the great expansion of the industry after the opening of the

railway and the adaptations of the sewing machine the reader may have wondered from whence was coming the increased supplies of plait. In its hey-day the plaiting country had covered a radius of twenty miles from Luton with a smaller area on the border of Essex and Suffolk and this could scarcely be extended. New sources of supply were being sought and about 1870 plait began to come from China. At first its only virtue was that it was cheap, for its quality was much inferior to best English and Italian plait. It soon improved in quality and thanks to the persistence of plait importers such as Charles Mees there was soon no inferiority in the Chinese supplies and all the standard English plaits were being successfully imitated. In 1891 supplies began to come also from Japan and the quality was, if anything, even better. This killed what hopes there had been of some miracle saving the English plaiting industry. In Italy there was a worse state of affairs, and the government had to face some serious riots in Tuscany.

The causes of the ruin of the English and Italian plaiting industries will better be understood when it is realised than an English plait-maker by plaiting $7\frac{1}{2}$ score (a score was 20 yards) of plait in a week could earn 6s 3d when the price of plait was 10d a score. This was a useful supplementation of an agricultural labourer's wage of 14s a week. The plait from the Far East was coming in at 3d a score and to compete at this price would have reduced the plait makers' earnings to 1s $10\frac{1}{2}$d a week.

The ruin of the plaiting industry meant prosperity for the hat industry for the cheaper plait combined with reduced costs of production effected by the sewing machine lowered considerably the prices of the hats and increased their production when new markets were found.

New markets were found in the development of an export trade and in this the railway was to be of great assistance. Some of the export markets were less sensitive to fashion than the home market and the latter was less so in those days than it is now. Hats could be made for foreign trade in what had previously been the long dull season.

FELT HAT MAKING BEGINS IN LUTON

Another dull season production was also being found by a few enterprising manufacturers in the finishing of felt hats. Felt hats, for both men and women, had long been made in London and on the borders of Lancashire and Cheshire, principally in Stockport and Denton. There were also a few firms in some Midland towns, chiefly Nuneaton and Atherstone. The firms in the felt-hat industry normally made the hats in all the stages of production from rabbits' fur or sheep's wool to the finished hat, e.g., the bowler. There was a halfway stage in the production when some of the more difficult processes had been completed and the semi-manufactured hat at this point was called a 'hood'.

The felt-hat manufacturers usually made a surplus of hoods, and some made hoods only. They were quite willing to sell them to Luton hat manufacturers. In this way some local firms carried out the finishing stages and produced ladies' felt hats. In 1877 three brothers named Carruthers came from Scotland and set up a factory to make felt hats, but for hoods they were able to meet but a fraction of the town's demands.

The effect of these changes was that while the busy season continued the dull period was broken by a short season in September and October for the finishing of felt hats and the export trade. It must, however, be stressed that straw hats accounted for most of the trade until 1914 and that the industry was still concentrated mainly in small firms and few of these were concerned in either the export trade or the finishing of felt hats.

Some New Industries Follow the Railway

With the railway came other changes. In 1871 Hayward Tyler's opened their factory on the site of an old cricket field. It was an old established firm having been originally formed in 1815 but in the middle of the century it had passed into the hands of the Howard family who made it into a limited partnership, a rare form of business undertaking. The firm, which had a siding on the Great Northern Railway, specialised in the making of soda-water machinery, to which it later added various forms of hydraulic engines including pumps. It is claimed that they made the first motor car in Luton but this was at a time when experiments were being made with steam-driven cars and the internal combustion engine was still in its early days. By standards of those times it was a large concern as it employed over 600 men, most of them new to the town. It was often known as the 'brass foundry' to distinguish it from Brown and Green's, now to be known as the 'iron foundry'. This was perhaps unfair, as the firm of Hayward Tyler had also an iron foundry as well as blacksmith's and whitesmith's shops. About ten years later came a smaller firm, Balmforths, which made boilers, and it too had a siding on the railway.

Self-help

Hayward Tyler's was a non-union firm, and trade union organisation was non-existent in the hat industry, so it is not surprising that there was little working-class activity as such in the town. The first did in fact arise out of Hayward Tyler's and the occasion was the work's annual 'beano' in 1882. They had been by horse-drawn brakes to Bedford and were making the last major halt at Silsoe on the return journey. This had the two-fold purpose of resting the horses and refreshing the passengers, but a more sober group of young men decided that all they could do usefully was to see the sights of Silsoe. To their surprise and interest they found a co-operative stores in a side street and this shamed them when they realised that the large town of Luton had not yet managed to achieve what had been done by a small village. On their return they secured the willing assistance of their employers and called a meeting in the work's chapel and it was there resolved to form the Luton Industrial Co-operative Society.

The chapel was an unusual institution of Hayward Tyler's and it is often said that all the men had to go there for morning prayers. The owners were, it is true, very religious men, Anglicans and Quakers, but the chapel was by no means compulsory and the short services held there each morning were conducted on alternate days by Church of England and Nonconformist ministers. They were discontinued in 1919.

To return to the co-operative society we must realise that it had little capital, which was in fact the total shareholdings of the few original members. They rented a shop in Chapel Street in which they took turns to serve until they had built up enough trade to employ a manager. The first shop having proved to be too big they soon moved to No 28 Dumfries Street where they stayed until 1888 when a shop in Hastings Street was opened. In the meantime they had been ruined by a dishonest manager and they had then to begin again, but their faith that they would ultimately succeed was more than justified when one realises the size and success of their society now.

Self-help was to be seen in other ventures too. As the town grew its social services increased and the professions began to grow in importance. Doctors and lawyers now had statutory recognition, but their fees were usually beyond the purses of the working class who would still go to the druggists or chemists in preference to the qualified doctor and some of these had a reputation higher than that of the medical men. Every family had its own cures for most of the ailments that beset mankind and some of these remedies were already known to be useless. This was a bad state of affairs but worse still was the constant fear of a prolonged illness with its subsequent poverty that might lead to the Poor Law Union. It was to meet these fears that Friendly Societies had been formed and membership of the Oddfellows or the Foresters would, in return for a weekly contribution, entitle the member to a sickness benefit and payment of his doctor's bill. The Friendly Societies were in evidence at the founding of the railway in 1858 but they were later to grow to sufficient strength to open a Medical Institute in Waller Street in 1893. Here they had a dispensary and employed two doctors to attend to the friendly society members. They also threw open the Institute to family membership and the medical benefits in this way would come to all the household. Samuel Pride, the secretary of the Institute, and G. Wistow Walker, a Luton schoolmaster and later mayor, deserve to be remembered for a lifetime of service to this worthy cause. In the meantime a local doctor would give medical attention to a whole family in return for a small weekly subscription, whether they were ill or not, and the threepenny doctor, as he was known, was the salvation of many.

The Temperance Movement

The Co-operative Society and the Friendly Societies were for the more provident but there were many who could not or would not provide for themselves the relative security offered. Poverty was still a serious problem, especially among the hat workers whose wages were irregular. A major cause was unfortunately but too obviously, drink. The nonconforming sects, having taken up the cause of total abstinence, launched a campaign to combat the drink evil and the Temperance Federation was the result. At the juvenile level there were Bands of Hope with light entertainment and recitations, with competitions very often not at all connected with alcohol, but at frequent intervals the message was driven home. The adults presented a more serious problem and for them there were attractive concerts and lantern lectures, anything in fact that would keep people out of public houses. The Quakers in their Adult School premises provided better facilities for games than any public house or club. The most active worker in the cause was T. G. Hobbs, who was otherwise an enterprising hat materials merchant and the publisher of the local time-table. Hobbs was a great traveller and a fellow of the Royal Geographical Society; he was also an excellent photographer and could consequently be relied upon to give one of a number of excellent lantern lectures. His most popular lecture was one called 'Sewing and Sowing' which was illustrated entirely by local scenes. The slides, and the script to be read with them, which could more appropriately have been called 'The Drunkard's Progress', are now fortunately preserved at Luton Museum. The most ingenious counter-attraction to drink devised by the movement was the 'Temperance Excursions' and for these they booked whole trains which started from Luton at about 6 am and took the passengers at the off-peak periods to Great Yarmouth, Brighton or Scarborough, at extremely low fares of about 4s. Once there, one could stay for a day, three days, a week or ten days and return to Luton at about 2 am in the morning. Thanks to T. G. Hobbs and his co-workers thousands of Lutonians saw the sea for the first time and enjoyed a well-earned holiday – it was also after all the most effective of all ways to hit the drink trade.

The Attack on the Public Houses

So effective was the temperance movement that it was able to influence the Licensing Bench to take a firm hold on the granting of licences to public houses. William Austin records that in 1871 there were 269 licensed houses in the town, one for every seventy-seven inhabitants or one for every forty-eight persons over the age of 13. Some of the public houses had a very bad record with regard to their direct connection with various forms of crime. The

Bench refused the renewal of the licences of thirty-eight of these, after which there was a marked decrease of crime in the town and the 'Luton System', as it was called, was quoted nationally and many temperance reformers came to visit us. This successful policy was pursued further and no new licences at all were granted with the result that as the town expanded all the public houses were concentrated in a small area. South of a line drawn from the *Sportsman* in Stopsley to the *Rabbit* in Old Bedford Road and from there to the *Fox* in Dunstable Road and the *Salisbury Arms* in Wellington Street (a casualty of enemy action by air raid in 1940), there was a public house on almost every street corner but north of that line none at all except in Leagrave and Limbury, and there were to be none until long after the Second World War. The drink question became a political one, for while both parties agreed that it should be controlled, the question of compensating publicans whose licences were refused became a burning one. The Conservatives, supported now by the brewers who had at one time been Liberal, wanted compensation from the national exchequer, but the Liberals wanted it from a tax on the public houses which remained. The bars of the licensed houses became rallying points for Conservative support, an unfortunate connection which Luton shared with most other places in the country.

THE CHURCHES IN THE RAILWAY AGE

In the second half of the nineteenth century all the then existing churches strove in their own way to meet the needs of a growing population and it would be tedious to enumerate all the new churches and mission halls that were built. The most striking figure in the religious, and to some extent the secular, life of the town was James O'Neill, the vicar of the parish church, to whom reference has already been made. That he loved the church, which was so very much his during his long incumbency, there can be no doubting. He restored it by removing a gallery, by doing away with the private pews and by reinforcing the already crumbling masonry. He gave greater character to the services by introducing more music and having spectacular processions within the church. The church, however, remained Low, as it always had been, with no change in ritual. Towards the end of O'Neill's long period at the church a young organist and choirmaster,

Frederick Gostelow, was appointed and soon made the church well known for the quality of its music.

James O'Neill was, however, a born fighter and uncompromising in any views that he held. He strove to draw attention to himself whether it be in driving around the town furiously in his Irish gig or in wheeling the crippled Miss Vyse around in her invalid chair. Almost immediately he came he plunged into a storm of controversy regarding a Rev C. B. Harris who had a very popular 'Wooden Church' in Albert Road within his own parish. He went to extreme measures to force Harris out of his church for which many people could see no just cause. Having succeeded the truth at last came out – Harris had married his deceased wife's sister, which may have been within the law of another country which would allow such an incestuous union but was contrary to a higher law, that laid down in the Prayer Book. He railed against the Salvation Army and almost incited violence against it but his greatest fight of all was his attempt to retain church control of education. Almost everyone admired the spirited manner in which he took up causes and to those who supported these causes he was their hero – but to those who did not agree with him it was a different matter.

The churches at this time were venturing into new forms of evangelism and in the Anglican community there was the CEMS (Church of England Men's Society) which was never very effective in Luton where the most successful venture was the PSA (Pleasant Sunday Afternoon) which filled the King Street Congregational Church. This gathering, which was presided over by H. C. Middle, a local schoolmaster, heard talks on subjects of social, political and scientific interest three Sundays out of four, to sugar the pill of a religious topic on the remaining Sunday. But its biggest attraction was the orchestra, which was without doubt the best in the town. Other Nonconformist churches usually had their men's classes held by progressive members of the church. In this way they came to grips with new disruptive forces such as Darwinism, theosophy, spiritualism and socialism. The Methodists went a stage further and at the Central Mission above the station all the services were cheerful and enthusiastic. The Quakers, however, being less set on conversion, were content with the Adult School with its small classes and some intent to educate.

The Sunday Schools had undergone a great change as with almost all children being educated elsewhere there was no longer a need to teach them to read and write. The schools now became channels whereby the children might learn to be regular church attenders. Good attendances would qualify one for a prize and many gained prizes in this way, which were often the only books ever to come into a home. The greatest attraction of all was the Sunday School treat and if the Sunday School was small it was by horse and brake to some place like Totternhoe Knolls or Bricket Wood, but if it were larger a whole train would be needed to go to Hatfield Park; Ampthill; or again, Totternhoe Knolls. So many children were affected that it was necessary to close the day schools in the catchment area of the Sunday School. The best attended Sunday schools were often those which provided the best treats and as this depended on the collections at the Sunday School Anniversary there was an incentive to make a good show of this.

The peace of the Victorian Sabbath was broken in Luton in 1882 by the appearance of the Salvation Army. Its methods seemed strange even compared with the new evangelism of the established sects and in the early days of the Army they were indeed extreme. The captain of the local corps at one period led his troops forth, he himself riding on a white horse. On the whole the churches, even if they disliked the tactics of the Army, counselled patience and tolerance, but on many occasions the mob in Luton broke up the Army meetings and rough-handled the Salvationists.

Of much greater consequence, although at the time it seemed of little importance, was the opening in 1884 of the first Roman Catholic church in Luton since the Reformation. The small corrugated iron building in Castle Street seemed trivial compared with older churches in the town, or even the new Temple of the Salvation Army, but a page in history had been turned.

THE FIGHT FOR THE CONTROL OF THE SCHOOL BOARD
The churches had played a large part in building up an educational system in the town but here, as in the country as a whole, the situation was far from satisfactory. The monitors had long since given way to pupil teachers who were scholars who had stayed at school to learn to teach. Teachers were paid according

to how well they taught, which meant how many of the children satisfied the school inspectors. Too few children went to school and many of those who did stayed too short a time. A system of compulsory education was badly needed but there were insufficient schools for that to be achieved. The Forster Education Act (1870) allowed two years in which bodies like the British and Foreign Schools Society and the National Society, and indeed any similar organisations which might be interested, could apply for grants to pay for the cost of new schools. If this failed in any area then School Boards would have to be formed to build sufficient new schools out of a rate raised for that purpose.

Those in charge of the British schools in Luton, mainly Baptists and Quakers, were willing to hand over their schools to the School Board if one was set up in Luton. They had support from Congregationalists and Primitive Methodists. The vicar, James O'Neill, with the vicar of Christ Church, thought that new schools could be built which would make a School Board unnecessary. Grants were applied for and funds hastily raised to build Christ Church School in Buxton Road and St Matthew's School in Havelock Road. O'Neill, largely out of his own pocket, built another school in New Town Street. The Wesleyans, with a school of their own, sat on the fence but Henry Blundell, the most prominent Wesleyan in the town, supported the principle of a School Board as did also an odd man out, the vicar of Biscot. With such divided opinion a poll was demanded in 1871. Only 493 wanted a School Board and 1,196, many worried about having to pay another rate, did not.

The Education Department was not satisfied that sufficient school places were provided and on 27 January 1874 an order was signed for a School Board to be set up to serve Luton and its hamlets. The first election for this – it was one of the very first by secret ballot – took place on 17 February 1874 and must rank as the strangest election in the town's history. There were nine seats on the board, the main contestants for which were a 'Prayer Book Five' led by James O'Neill and a 'Bible Five' one of whom was the vicar of Biscot. Each hoped to get its five elected and by so doing control the board. The Bible Five prepared well but the vicar wasted a lot of time protesting and trying in vain to get the election cancelled. When the election came O'Neill was easily top of the poll but all the Bible Five were elected! He then argued that the election was undemocratic as his five polled more votes than the other five. For some months the Prayer Book members of the board stayed away from its meetings in protest. The subsequent elections for the board were fought on the same basis with the church party at times gaining control. In time the heat in the contests died down as both parties settled down to build an education system in which each could have pride.

The board, a large one so far as these boards went, elected as its first chairman William Bigg, a Quaker and retired bank manager. One of the first things it did was to make education compulsory in its area for children up to the age of 13. This was six years before it became compulsory throughout the country. Parents still had to pay 2d a week for their children to be at school – education was not free until 1890. By making it compulsory the board put an end to child labour in the town. This had been an unfortunate feature of the hat industry, the many small units of which it was impossible for the factory inspectors to supervise effectively. It proved to be simpler to prosecute a parent for not sending a child to school than an employer for employing the child. At the same time the boards generally had great difficulty in getting unwilling children to school and appointed a new class of minor officials as School Attendance Officers. The one chosen in Luton bore an appropriate name, Mr Fetch. When fines failed bad offenders were sent to an Industrial School at Walthamstow and the very worst sent to face the stern discipline of a training ship, HMS *Formidable*.

In its early days the board used temporary premises but in time built a number of new schools: Biscot, to pacify the vicar of Biscot (1876), Leagrave (1876), Waller Street, its first major achievement (1877), Chapel Street (1880), Old Bedford Road (1883), Hitchin Road (1883), Surrey Street (1891) and its last, Dunstable Road (1898). By that time another change in the educational system was imminent. In the meantime the Wesleyans had closed their school but the church built one more, St Mary's Hall (1885) to replace a previously unsatisfactory building.

In 1890 the board made Waller Street School a Higher Grade School for boys in its other schools who had reached a required standard. This was very successful and was the beginning of secondary, or more advanced, education in Luton. Its success led the board to attempt to make the old British School in Langley Street a Higher Grade School for girls. This more or less failed because too few girls reached the standard necessary for them to attend.

The School Board came to an end in 1903 following the Balfour Education Act (1902) which put the control of education in the hands of the newly-formed county councils. The larger boroughs, which included Luton, were allowed to control the education of children up to the age of 14. This was now the responsibility of the Town Council which appointed an Education Committee for this purpose. Outwardly the change meant little as the officers and clerks of the School Board now became employed by the Town Council. It affected the town only as the education service in the hamlets – Leagrave, Limbury, Biscot, Stopsley and Hyde – became the full responsibility of the County Council as did the education of children over the age of 14 in the town itself. The change also meant that the Church schools which had previously only had Treasury grants could also be supported out of the rates. This annoyed some Nonconformists called Passive Resisters who showed their indignation by not paying the whole of their rates. This meant an appearance in court with an order of restraint. Something to the value of the rate not paid, usually a clock, was taken from the person's house to be sold by auction. The Passive Resister then paid a friendly policeman to buy it back. He had made his protest, the last of so many similar protests in the matter of religion which had been a feature of life in the town since the Reformation.

The Beginnings of our Hospitals
Notwithstanding their sharp differences of opinion Luton people could work together if the cause was worthy enough, and the need for a hospital was realised by all. Hospitals are a comparatively recent institution and in earlier days had been thought of mainly as places to which people could be sent if they were suffering from an infectious disease. In the eighteenth century there was one such, a pest house, on the middle of the Moor. It is, however, interesting to note that the former Spittlesea Isolation Hospital opened in 1892 was built almost on the site of one used for a similar purpose

in the Middle Ages. Spittlesea Hospital was, of course, controlled by the Corporation.

There was also the infirmary at the workhouse under the control of the Board of Guardians and intended primarily for bed-ridden paupers and girls in trouble. One knew it was there and sometimes thought of it, but did not speak about it as there was a stigma attached to it.

Until late in the nineteenth century operations were rare and the doctors qualified to perform them few, so Luton folk needing nursing attention either had it at home or went into a London hospital. The increase in the number of trained doctors in the town combined with the growth of the population led the Medical Officer of the Board of Health, Edward Woakes, in 1872, to move to get two houses in High Town Road converted into a Cottage Hospital. This so much fulfilled a need that in 1882 the trustees of the Marquess of Bute presented a site in Dunstable Road and subscriptions were raised for the building of the Bute Hospital.

Like the Cottage Hospital, this was a purely voluntary effort and received no grants from public funds. It was supported generously by subscriptions, and fêtes, garden parties, concerts and processions were organised for money to assist the hospital. Patients, who were attended by their own doctors, were asked to pay what they could afford and there was always a number of free beds. In the meantime a Children's Hospital had been opened in London Road in 1894.

LUTON BECOMES A MUNICIPAL BOROUGH

The local government of Luton in common with that of other English towns had been subjected to many changes. The Board of Guardians had been made responsible for the relief of poverty in 1834, the Board of Health for matters of sanitation in 1850 and the School Board for education in 1874. These had proved to be very effective bodies and provided between them most of the reasonable needs of a growing community. They did not, however, give the town the dignity that many Lutonians felt that it deserved. This could only come by securing Borough status, and Dunstable, with a population of a mere 4,470 compared with Luton's 17,821, had gained this distinction in 1864. True there had been something very strange in Dunstable's achievement, which had been gained on the strength of an old charter which it was claimed made her appear to be a Borough in the Middle Ages when she was not. Luton needed to make no such claim of this kind as her population was enough to merit the change of status.

It was the decision of the Town Hall Company to sell the building that brought the question to a head. The Board of Health was slow to buy, and but for the public spirit of George Lockhart and John Higgins, who had secured a provisional contract, it would have passed to another private company which might well have converted it to some other use than that for which it had from the first been intended. In short it might have ceased to be a Town Hall. In 1875 the Board of Health, under pressure, did in fact buy the Town Hall. However, the whole affair was the last straw which broke the camel's back. For some years the leading citizens of Luton had been wondering whether the board was adequate to cope with the town's growing-pains. They were now determined to press for a more efficient, dignified, and democratic form of local government. Luton was for the purposes of local government still a parish and only the church-wardens and overseers, long since shorn of any other effective power, could act. In response to a request that they should do so they called a public meeting in one of the Plait Halls in December 1874, to consider 'the desirability of applying for a Charter of Incorporation'.

There were objections to the proposal. It was argued that it would add to the rates and that Lutonians were not responsible enough to have self-government, but it was resolved by a large majority to apply for a Charter. A little over a year later, on 26 February 1876, the Charter was granted.

The first elections were held in May 1876 and there were three wards, North, East and West, each of which was represented by six Councillors. With six Aldermen the Council comprised twenty-four members.

The new Borough Council took over the whole of the work of the old Board of Health, but it was a completely responsible body having no over-riding jurisdiction by the magistrates. There were, it is true, elective auditors whose function it was to see that the accounts were in order, and they had to satisfy themselves that the rates were being spent on the purposes for which they had been raised.

The various officers of the Board of Health now became officials of the municipal borough. George Bailey, the Clerk of the Board of Health, became the first Town Clerk.

The Mayor, who was elected annually by the Aldermen and Councillors, acted as chairman of the Council, and was during his term of office, the chief burgess and magistrate of the Borough. The distinction of being the first mayor was given to William Bigg, who was already chairman of the School Board.

An even more important change was that the town became a separate Commission of the Peace. It had previously been for matters of the maintenance of law and order just a part of the county and its magistrates formed part of the Commission of the Peace for Bedfordshire and the police a county force responsible to them.

Having now a Commission of the Peace Luton had twelve Justices of the Peace in its own right and these acted jointly with the Borough Council to form a Watch Committee for the control of the Luton police. The new police force was a small one of only twelve with David Jacquest as the first Chief Constable. The county police station was already in Dunstable Place adjoining the Court House. There was now a Petty Sessions for the town under the control of the Luton magistrates but there was still a Luton Divisional Sessions presided over by county magistrates to deal with cases from villages around the town. Serious cases were, as before, sent after preliminary hearing in Luton to Bedford for trial at Quarter Sessions or the Assizes.

As a municipal borough the needs of the town were much better served. A Mechanics Institute already had a subscription library in the Town Hall which was now needed for municipal offices. In any case the library was inadequate as it depended largely on books given by kindly benefactors, the subscription being deliberately kept low. A Free Library was built in 1883 on the corner of George Street and Williamson Street and this was to serve the needs of the town for nearly thirty years. Its chief defect was that it worked on a closed-shelf system which, while it reduced to a minimum the stealing of books, gave no great encouragement to reading.

The Chamber of Commerce

Having organised our local government to their satisfaction, Luton's leaders now turned their attention to an organisation for promoting better business relations. The Luton Chamber of Commerce was founded in 1877, the result of a meeting at the Town Hall presided over by the Mayor. For many years most of its members were, inevitably, hat manufacturers. Its function, then as now, was to serve as a meeting place for leaders of industry: a forum where they could discuss and attempt to solve problems common to them all.

The major problem which concerned the Chamber of Commerce in its early days was the dependence of Luton on the hat industry. This employed more women than men and was always subject to serious seasonal unemployment and under-employment. If the industry should suffer from a recession it would cause great distress in the town. A New Industries Committee was formed consisting of representatives of the Chamber of Commerce and the Town Council.

The committee undertook a publicity campaign: it issued illustrated brochures; it advertised in newspapers and trade journals; it informed other Chambers of Commerce. The essence of the campaign was a demonstration of the many great advantages which would be enjoyed by any firm setting up business in Luton. It would be no exaggeration to assert that the committee succeeded beyond its wildest dreams.

In the meantime the Chamber of Commerce was turning its attention to other problems such as the train and postal services and, when it came, the telephone service. While these efforts were for the greater efficiency of the industrial interests of the town, the rest of the community was also to benefit from the improved services which the chamber was able to secure.

Sport Becomes More Serious

The reduction in working hours bringing with it a free Saturday afternoon allowed a greater participation and interest in organised sport. The new railway system also allowed games to be played against teams in distant towns.

This is seen in the fortunes of the Luton Town Football and Athletic Club whose supporters were a greater proportion of the population than they are today. It was formed in 1885 by an amalgamation of Luton Wanderers and Luton Excelsior and its first ground was off Dunstable Road where Brown's timber yard is now. By the turn of the century it had moved further along Dunstable Road near the site of the present Odeon Cinema. In 1890 it had the distinction of being the first professional club in the south but this is contested by some London clubs. The first professional was paid the modest wage of 5s a match! It was one of the original members of the Southern League, the Football League in those days consisting mainly of northern clubs. By 1901 it had had a spell in the Second Division of the Football League and returned to a now strengthened Southern League as it had found financial difficulties in long journeys for away games.

It was at this time that, with a team of mainly full-time professionals, it found the most famous player it has ever had on its books in R. M. (Bob) Hawkes. Bob Hawkes was a local amateur who played at left-half and most supporters went to see Bob play rather than the team. His ball control was superb and his shot deadly accurate – *he* never missed a penalty. He was a certain amateur cap for many seasons and once, while still an amateur, he gained a place in the full England team. His strangest peculiarity was that he was rarely known to head the ball but this was because he thought the game should be played with the feet and not, as many people believed, that he had once cracked his skull and that under his red curly hair was a gold plate.

LUTONIANS PROVIDE THEIR OWN ENTERTAINMENT

The bands which had heralded the opening of the railway had not been Luton bands and it is indeed uncertain when Luton did have its first brass band. It was probably the Ashton Street Mission Band, used to give more life to the services at what was later to be the Central Mission. Ashton Street has now, by the way, been renamed Gillam Street to save confusion with Ashton Road and to honour James Gillam who gave a lifetime of service to the mission. The Ashton Street Band was in demand for outside functions and here came a clash of loyalties as the mission would object to engagements if they clashed with their principles.

In 1890 some members broke away so that they could play what they chose to play where they wished to play it. So came into being the Luton Red Cross Band and it soon had the reputation of being one of the best bands in the country.

An equally famous Luton band in its own sphere of music was formed in 1896. The mandolin is not everyone's choice as a musical instrument but it was Philip Bone's and when he opened a music shop in Manchester Street he proceeded to form Bone's (later Luton) Mandolin Band and this became the best British band in what, it is true, was a very specialised field.

All churches in those days had choirs and in Nonconformist churches they could account for a considerable part of the congregation. The joy of singing so encouraged provided a nucleus for the Luton Choral and Orchestral Society formed in 1870. In time it became purely choral and thanks to a succession of devoted conductors, including Fred Gostelow, it maintained at all times a very high standard in its renderings of oratorios.

SOME LUTON WORTHIES

It is certain that Luton people at the turn of the century were not finding life by any means dull and boring and the town was in any case still small enough for most Lutonians to know each other and to take an inquisitive interest in other people's lives. In this way qualities and eccentricities became exaggerated and individuals developed reputations to which they were expected to conform. David Wootton, the librarian, was almost as well-known for the non-alcoholic horehound beer he brewed as he was for his friendly advice on books that were not worth reading.

Some looked with envy at Asher Hucklesby, a pillar of the Congregational church, who was said to have come into Luton from one of the villages without a penny in his pocket. He had built up the largest firm of merchant manufacturers in the hat trade, had a large warehouse in the middle of George Street and was to be mayor five times. In a similar line of business and with the same background was George Warren, but he was mayor only twice. He had a great interest in education and as an ardent Methodist he was in great demand as a local preacher. Warren was often accused of hypocrisy as he was supposed in the dull season to buy hats from makers at a price lower than the value of the plait from which they had been made. These it was said he sold later at a great profit. If the truth is known he probably saved many from the workhouse, or from the clutches of the pawn-brokers, whose trade flourished in the dull season.

The town was not without its men of letters, and William Austin, clerk to the Justices and Board of Guardians and steward of the manor, was Luton's most distinguished historian. Scholarship in another form came from James Saunders, a hat manufacturer and Baptist local preacher who, having little education, came to the town from Salisbury in 1859. He lost his wife while still a young man and was left with a large family that gave him constant trouble. Having forced himself to take an interest in natural history to take his mind away from personal worries he became one of the greatest botanists of the day, specialising in minute forms of plant growth.

The townsfolk knew all these well but by far the most well-known and colourful figures were Charles Irons and 'Major' Payne.

Charles Irons had in some respects a sad history as his mother had been widowed while he was yet a boy. He took it upon himself to provide for the family and in time he became town crier, keeper of the pound and the town's bill-poster. The pound was in those days on the corner of Windmill Road and Lea Road and it was astonishing to see the number of stray animals he managed to impound there and feed, pending their being claimed on payment of a mounting fine. He had a fine figure and a strong voice and donning his uniform would cry anything, notices of sales, concerts, lost property, and the sound of his bell was familiar in the streets. 'Tell Charlie Irons' is to this day with true Lutonians an accusation that someone is broadcasting information that would be better kept private. Charles Irons usually ended his crying with a Biblical quotation or an exhortation to his hearers to give up their sinful ways, for he was the most ardent of Salvationists. The hoardings of the town had always a fair assortment of texts and he would also show on them portraits of himself. The town expected the unusual from Charles but was astonished to see one day on the hoardings the announcement of his own wedding, at a somewhat advanced age, to an ex-captain of the Salvation Army.

Any encounters of Charles Irons with Major Payne must have been interesting as they were in many respects exactly opposite. Major Payne (the title was only a nickname for at most he had been a corporal in the Yeomanry) had at one time been a riding instructor and was always seen in full riding kit. Having a fine white beard he made a very distinguished figure but he was unfortunately often the worse for drink, yet, as he would have it, never drunk. He was very free with advice especially to young ladies walking with their lovers, that they should be careful to avoid all the snares of matrimony. In happier moods he would offer passers-by a prune, a large bag of which he invariably carried. The Major and Charles Irons were usually followed by a stream of abusive street urchins, who in those days took delight in others' eccentricities.

Changes in the Manor

The people of Luton have at all times had an interest in those who held the Hoo. There was a fire there in 1843, more disastrous than the one in 1771 and the second Marquess of Bute, who was actively engaged in the development of Cardiff and with the building of the Bute Docks there, was losing an interest in Luton. He consequently sold the Hoo to John Shaw Leigh in 1848. The Leigh family, one of the richest in the country, had strangely enough made its fortune from the docks at Liverpool and John Shaw Leigh himself had at one time been Mayor of Liverpool. He restored the Hoo and considerably improved and added to the large estate which had extended beyond the confines of the park itself. A new chapel was provided to replace the beautiful one built by Sir Robert Napier which had been destroyed by the fire. When he died in 1871 the Hoo passed to his son J. Gerard Leigh who the following year married Mrs Dudley Ward, already a very well-known society personality. Gerard Leigh died in 1875 and left the Hoo to his widow to hold during her life.

Mrs Leigh was a personal friend of the Prince of Wales (later Edward VII) and he with the Princess of Wales now made a number of visits to the Hoo. On the occasion of the first visit in 1878 they came also to the town where they were most enthusiastically received and conducted on a tour of hat factories and the Plait Halls. In 1883 Mrs Leigh married Christian de Falbe, the Danish minister, who died in 1896, and it is as Madame de Falbe that she is chiefly remembered in the town. She continued to take an interest in the town until her own death in 1899. In severe winters it was her custom to throw open the park and allow skating on the lake at a nominal charge, the proceeds going to the relief of poverty in Luton caused by the cold weather.

By the terms of Gerard Leigh's will the Hoo passed on the death of Madame de Falbe to his nephew, Henry Leigh, who died within a few weeks, leaving two young children. At the turn of the century the Hoo was unoccupied.

Luton Newspapers Appear

While Luton remained a small town there was no place for a local newspaper and the few who could have afforded to buy one had to be content with the London papers that arrived a day or so late in the town. For many years the *Northampton Mercury* was the only paper which claimed to cover Bedfordshire news. The *Bedford Mercury* (later *Bedfordshire Mercury*) began in 1837 and the *Bedford Times* (later *Bedfordshire Times*) eight years later. These various papers contained only occasional items of interest to people living in south Bedfordshire.

The first Luton paper is supposed to have been *The Luton Miscellany, Domestic Treasury and General Advertiser* published as a monthly by John Wiseman in 1854. When stamp duties were removed from newspapers in 1855 he published it weekly as *The Luton Times and Advertiser*, a name to be changed soon to the *Bedfordshire Advertiser and Luton Times* and it was generally known as the 'Beds. Advertiser'. In 1874 this found a competitor in *The Luton Reporter and Bedfordshire and Hertfordshire News*, also a weekly, published by R. N. Christy. This was naturally known as 'The Luton Reporter'. Both papers were Conservative and were competing with each other to gain readers who were mainly Liberal.

In 1891, Richard Gibbs, the owner of a St Albans paper, the *Hertfordshire Advertiser*, seized the opportunity to start a rival Liberal paper in Luton at $\frac{1}{2}$d, half the price of the other two. He sent two young men, Alec Gibbs, his nephew, and George Myers, to Luton to collect the news for the paper which was printed at St Albans. The success of the *Luton News*, for that was its name, was instantaneous. Newsboys were released from school early enough to pick up the papers at publishing time, 4 pm on Thursday, and ran shouting through the streets of the town. For an hour the rest of the town stood still as the paper was read in shops, hat factories and at street corners. The rest of the day was spent in discussing the latest local scandals, for all Lutonians had a great interest in each others' lives. Newspapers in those days were allowed to report all the sordid details of wife beatings, applications for affiliation orders and similar domestic cases now heard in private by the courts. The *Beds Advertiser* and *Luton Reporter* struggled on fighting a losing battle and all these papers were still in circulation in 1914.

LUTON AND NATIONAL POLITICS

Until 1885 those in the town who were fortunate enough to have the vote took part in the election of the two members of parliament who represented Bedfordshire. There was in this year a considerable extension of the franchise and every male householder in Luton had now the right to vote. At the same time a new constituency known as the South Bedfordshire or Luton Division was formed and in this Luton was the largest place. With its strong Nonconformist background and its industrial interests Luton was very solidly Liberal in its sympathies but this did not necessarily hold for Dunstable and the many villages which were also in the constituency.

The first member was Cyril Flower, not surprisingly a Liberal, who held the seat in the general election of 1886, when the Liberals were split on the Home Rule question, and again in 1892. He then went to the House of Lords, where Gladstone felt the need for more support, to become Lord Battersea. He was an exceedingly popular member, having the honour to be the first Honorary Freeman of the Borough, and even after he had gone to the Lords he continued to take a keen interest in the affairs of Luton.

In the by-election another Liberal candidate was returned in Howard Whitbread, a member of an old Bedfordshire family which had represented the county in the Whig interests for many years. The Nonconformist Liberals were not at all happy with Whitbread's candidature as, of course, he had brewing interests. He was probably equally unhappy and it is not surprising that a new candidate was found for the next election in 1895.

The 1895 election was to be the most exciting in the town's history. The Liberals lost heavily in the country and as the drink trade was the chief issue, the contest in Luton was bound to be severe. The Liberal candidate, T. G. Ashton, in the end won the seat by the narrowest of margins and the declaration of the result was followed by a serious riot. It all arose because there was a feeling that H. W. Lathom, at that time Luton's most prominent solicitor, had materially affected the result by changing sides during the election. The riot began with the breaking of the windows of his office in King Street after which there was an orgy of window breaking all over the town centre. Order was restored by the arrival of the Metropolitan Police Force which quickly cleared the town but many Lutonians had to spend the night in the fields not daring to return.

Ashton was again returned in the 'Khaki' election of 1900 when the Liberals in the rest of the country fared even worse than they had in 1895. They were very badly divided on the Boer War which was affecting Luton perhaps less than most towns as it lacked a military tradition. After the war the Town Council selected ten Luton men who had fought with the Bedfordshire Regiment in the war and made them Honorary Freemen of the Borough.

It was not surprising that Ashton was able to hold the seat in the next election of 1906 when the Liberals were swept back to power and again at the two General Elections in 1910 when Lloyd George's Budget and the Liberals' fight with the Lords were the issues to be decided. Asquith was now feeling the need for more support in the Lords and Ashton was created Lord Ashton of Hyde. He had not been a striking politician but he had won the seat in five successive elections, two of which had been especially difficult ones, and he had been the member for sixteen years.

There was some surprise at the next choice of the Liberals as it was Cecil Harmsworth, who was the brother of Alfred Harmsworth (later Lord Northcliffe), the founder and owner of the *Daily Mail*. This was considered to be the most extreme of the Conservative newspapers and not always given to a fair presentation of the news. Cecil Harmsworth convinced the local Liberals of his faith in their cause and was elected in the by-election of 1911. The war was soon to intervene and the next election was to follow it in 1918.

14 The Twentieth Century — Luton on the eve of the First World War

THE early years of the twentieth century were to witness changes that affected the whole of the future development of Luton. The most important of these was the decision of the Town Council to have its own electricity undertaking. It was mainly the result of the enthusiasm of a young town councillor. Albert Wilkinson, a member of Asher Hucklesby's firm. He attended a conference addressed by J. J. Thomson (later Lord Kelvin), the leading physicist of the day and returned convinced that cheap electricity could be the town's salvation. Most towns were having their electricity provided by non-profit-making public utilities similar in their nature to the Luton Gas Company and Luton Water Company. For Albert Wilkinson this was not good enough. The Town Council consisted mainly of successful self-made business men capable of providing the cheapest electricity in the country. He set to work to convince a somewhat cautious council but in the end he succeeded.

It was decided that the power station should be on the site of the old vicarage close to the church. James O'Neill had died in 1896 and the new vicar, E. R. Mason, lived in a new and smaller house in Crawley Green Road. As the old vicarage was the finest house remaining in the town there was some protest raised at its demolition. Holly Walk, a delightful pathway separating the churchyard from the gardens of the vicarage, was widened to become St Mary's Road thus providing access to the electricity works. Wilkinson was responsible for inviting J. J. Thomson to open the new power station. When he did so Thomson surprised those present by confessing that although he knew a great deal about electricity he did not know what it was.

The new form of power was ideal for the needs of Luton as it could be supplied in any quantity to meet the individual needs of the customer. It assisted in this way the survival of the small manufacturer in the hat industry as even homeworkers could have electric motors installed with as small as one-tenth h.p. to drive their sewing machines. More than this it was one of the factors responsible for attracting new industries to the town.

In 1901 the hat industry almost completely dominated Luton as there were only a very few firms in the town not directly or indirectly dependent on it. Brown's the flour millers and Brown's the timber merchants had been joined by a few firms in the same trades; Brown and Green's, the iron foundry, remained unchanged; J. W. Green's brewery was growing, despite the efforts of the temperance movement.

What Attracted the New Firms to Luton

The Town Council succeeded in its object in providing the cheapest electricity in the country but this was only one of a number of factors which made the town attractive to new firms. Before the new power station had been opened the Corporation, jointly with the Chamber of Commerce, had been responsible for the publication in 1900 of a booklet, *Luton as an Industrial Centre*, which it circulated widely to any who might be interested. It was the work of the secretary of the Chamber of Commerce, a very young chartered accountant, T. (later Sir Thomas) Keens. The booklet drew attention to availability of cheap land in the neighbourhood of the town for housing and for industrial development. That so much land was available was due partly to the activities of the Luton Land Company, a syndicate which by purchase and exchange of land, largely with the Crawley family, had foreseen in which directions the town would grow. As so many of the Land Company were members of either the Town Council or the Chamber of Commerce they were subject to much criticism but their foresight helped considerably the growth of the town – if indeed that was a good thing. Much of the land that was available was adjacent to the railway. Hayward Tyler's and Balmforth's factories were already by the railway, each with its own sidings and many of the new firms which came looked for this facility.

Luton was also near to London. It enjoyed low rates, much to the pride of the Town Council the members of which made their own firms pay. The Corporation could not make a profit but could make a minimum of loss to be shown in a low rate. Attention was drawn to the hat industry with its large employment of relatively well-paid female labour which could dovetail very well into other industries employing mainly male labour. It could also be a means of obtaining cheap labour for as the booklet said: 'the head of a family can afford to labour at eighteen shillings a week when he has three daughters earning fifteen to twenty shillings'. Above all Luton was a town relatively free from the restrictions of trade union organisation. All attempts to organise the hat workers had failed and while engineers were generally well organised elsewhere, Brown and Green's, Hayward Tyler's and Balmforth's were all non-union firms.

There were obviously many inducements for a firm to come to Luton.

The New Firms That Came to Luton

The first to arrive came shortly before the turn of the century. Laporte Chemicals had originally been formed at Shipley in Yorkshire in 1888, for the manufacture of hydrogen peroxide which was used considerably for bleaching. With the hat industry growing and the firms of bleachers and dyers increasing in number Laporte's soon found that much of its trade was with Luton, to which it transferred its works in 1898. It soon became concerned with other chemical processes and at all times its products met more than a local demand.

It was to meet another need of the hat industry that the British Gelatine Works was opened in 1903. In those days it was customary to stiffen straw hats with gelatine. Between the two wars it became no longer usual to do so but gelatine has, however, many uses and another new industry had come to Luton.

In an entirely different category the English and Scottish Joint CWS cocoa and chocolate factory was opened in Dallow Road in 1902.

The first of the new engineering firms which it had been hoped would come to the town came in 1905 with the arrival of the Vauxhall and West Hydraulic Engineering Company. It had originally been formed at Lambeth in 1857 and when it came to Luton in 1905 it was quite small even compared with the standards we had been accustomed to. At this time it was mainly concerned with pumping machinery, with cars very much as a side-line. In

1907 Vauxhall Motors was formed as a subsidiary company and from then more cars were manufactured.

In 1906 came a motor engineering firm, Commercial Cars, which concentrated on the manufacture of motor cars and lorries but in its early days in Luton it was small. In the meantime, in 1907 the Davis Gas Stove Company was preparing for the transfer of the greater part of its workers from Falkirk to a new foundry in Dallow Road. The arrival of these newcomers to occupy the houses in new roads off Dallow Road to form what became known as the 'Scotch Colony' created a minor social upheaval. Luton people were slow to accept these strangers being always ready to believe the worst that they heard of them. In time, however, a number of these newcomers were able to make valuable contributions to the civic life of the town.

The next firm to arrive was George Kent Ltd. This was an old-established London firm which specialised in a very highly skilled branch of engineering, the making of meters for water, gas, steam or oil. The scientists and technicians who came with the firm in 1908 were to be a great asset to the town.

In 1910 there came the Skefko Ball Bearing Company, a subsidiary of a Swedish firm. It is almost needless to relate that ball bearings have become components of most mechanically controlled devices that have increased in the modern world. The firm has grown by meeting the various requirements of its customers, for a ball bearing is of little use in itself.

It was also in this period that G. F. Farr and Sons was formed to meet the growing engineering needs of the hat industry and Charles Clay and Sons its need for ribbon. In time both firms expanded their manufactures.

By 1914 the town had a wide assortment of industries probably even greater than the most optimistic members of the Chamber of Commerce had dreamed would be possible when they formed their New Industries Committee. In the course of time a few of the new firms which came in this very important period have failed in business or left the town. Most have stayed, some to become very large concerns. On the eve of the First World War they were all still small by present-day standards, with Hayward Tyler's, having a modest pay-roll of 600, the largest firm in the town. It is, however, possible that some hat manufacturing firms, allowing for those they indirectly employed, accounted for more.

THE LUTON TRAM SERVICE

The electricity service which had meant so much to the development of the town could have other uses. Tramways were becoming popular elsewhere so Luton could well follow suit but as the providing of a municipal tram service was not one of the statutory functions of a borough an Act of Parliament was necessary. The trams themselves were not the property of the Corporation but were leased from a company which became the joint operators. The town had to provide the permanent way along which the trams ran, the power being provided by over-

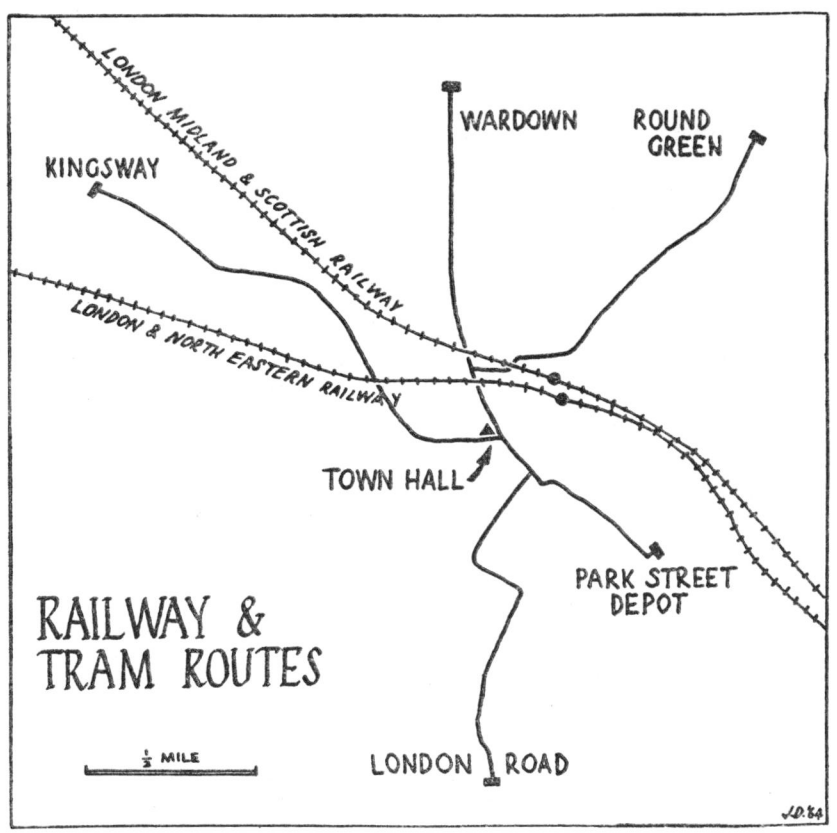

head cables. When they began in 1908 the tramways had three routes: the first was from the tram depot opposite Bailey Street, along Park Street, Market Hill, George Street, Manchester Street, Mill Street, Midland Road, High Town Road and Hitchin Road to Round Green: the second was from Park Square along Market Hill, George Street, Upper George Street and Dunstable Road to the laundry opposite the end of Kingsway. Kingsway was not there then and the laundry is no longer there now. The third ran from London Road opposite the end of Tennyson Road along London Road, Ashton Road, Hibbert Street, Chapel Street, George Street, Manchester Street and New Bedford Road to Wardown. There was subsequently a short extension from the first gate into Wardown to the gate opposite Bath Road.

It will be observed that all three routes went through George Street which meant that a strict timetable had to be adhered to for otherwise the whole of the service temporarily broke down. In addition to this it was a single track system with a few lengths of double track to allow trams to pass each other. There were the inevitable delays to frustrate would-be passengers but on the whole the service was to work to commendable efficiency. The trams had to face some very steep hills, notably Midland Road, but on very few occasions did the braking systems fail and trams run away to leave the lines. As the tops of the trams were open journeys in wet or cold weather could be uncomfortable if all the seats on the lower deck were occupied. The trams were very noisy but worst of all the lines were dangerous to cyclists many of whom became involved in nasty accidents.

Needless to say the coming of the trams caused some controversy as to whether they should run on Sundays. A poll was taken and the Nonconformists failed in a bid to keep still longer the peace of the Sabbath.

THE COUNTY COUNCIL BEGINS TO AFFECT LUTON

Following the Local Government Act of 1888 the Bedfordshire County Council came into being but with so few powers that it meant little to the people of Luton. Yet another election was necessary and they were already voting for their own Town Council, the School Board and the Board of Guardians, all of which met in Luton: the County Council had its meetings twenty miles away. The hamlets and the neighbouring villages were more affected and even more so by a further Act of 1894 which brought parish councils and rural district councils into being. Leagrave, Limbury with Biscot, Stopsley and Hyde now had some small measure of independence in having parish councils of their own but with very limited powers. They were linked with south Bedfordshire villages each having their own parish councils to form the Luton Rural District, the council of which had more services to maintain. In many senses it was badly named as almost none of its functions affected Luton.

Luton was first to be aware of the powers of the County Council when the Education Act of 1902 abolished the School Boards. This brought an unsatisfactory system of dual control, for while Luton was now, as mentioned earlier, responsible for the education of children living in the Borough up to the age of 14, it made the County Council responsible for all other education. The schools at Leagrave, Limbury, Stopsley and Hyde which had previously been under the control of the School Board were now responsible to the county. The County Council could also provide for higher education for children over the age of 14 irrespective of where they lived in the county. In short the County Council alone could maintain grammar schools, supported out of the rates, and this was the main objective of the new Act.

There was no grammar school in Luton, although a number of Luton boys were attending Dunstable Grammar School, which had been founded in 1888, and a few boys and girls were travelling each day to attend schools in Bedford and St Albans. There was an obvious need for a grammar school in Luton. H. C. Middle had hoped that the Higher Grade School would serve and there was an even stronger claim for the Pupil Teaching Centre where many young persons were already receiving a good education. The County Council in 1904 decided to open an entirely new school in temporary premises off Park Square pending the erection of a permanent building which was completed in 1908. It was to be a mixed school and to serve the needs of the whole of the south of the county. There was some doubt as to what should be its name and the governors settled finally on Luton Modern School, appointing a young mathematician, T. A. E. Sanderson, as the first headmaster, and he stayed until 1933.

The School Board had done its work so well that there was need for few new schools to be provided by the Town Council and only Beech Hill (1908) and Tennyson Road (finished in 1915) were added before the war began.

The Free Library was no longer adequate for the needs of the town and in 1910 the Corporation accepted the gift of a Public Library from Andrew Carnegie. He was present when it was opened by Whitelaw Reid, the American ambassador, who then lived at Wrest Park, Silsoe. Carnegie was added to the list of Honorary Freemen of the Borough. It was decided to dispense with the services of David Wootton as Librarian and a successor was found in T. A. Maw.

The Public Baths built by the Board of Health in 1872 were equally inadequate. A town councillor, Charles Dillingham, a self-made, very successful hat manufacturer and later Mayor, made it his special mission to persuade the Town Council to provide better baths on the same site as the old in Waller Street. These were opened in 1913 with one much larger swimming bath, but morals were so near to those of Victorian days that periods had to be set aside when women could use it alone. The large pool was boarded over in the winter months to provide the Winter Assembly Hall which was much used for concerts, dances and public meetings. This made the Plait Halls which had previously been used, a liability rather than an asset. The nearness of Luton to London would make the full list of prominent people, especially politicians, who addressed meetings in either the Plait Halls or the Winter Assembly Hall very impressive indeed. Not all very peaceful occasions!

No doubt the most important political meeting held in the town was in 1904 when Joseph Chamberlain came to a Free Trade stronghold to launch his campaign for Tariff Reform. For this occasion a temporary wooden building estimated to hold 8,000 people was erected in a meadow off Biscot Road near to the top of Studley Road. Party rivalry was probably never more intense than it was at this time.

THE TOWN ACQUIRES WARDOWN

The town acquired Wardown in 1904 and here lies an interesting story. This was originally a farmhouse and country residence known as Bramingham Shott. It was bought by Frank Scargill, at that time a prominent solicitor in the town and Clerk to the Justices, who in 1875 rebuilt the house, added lodge-houses and laid out the park. When he left Luton about 1893 he let it to B. J. H. Forder who changed its name to Wardown. This was not because of its nearness to Warden Hill but simply the fact that it had been the name of his previous house. It then passed to Halley Stewart, father of Sir Malcolm Stewart, who founded the London Brick Company, and in 1903 he decided to sell it. In all this time it had been known to Luton people as just 'Scargills'.

The price wanted for Wardown was about £17,000, and to the Town Council this seemed a lot of money, especially as it was so close to People's Park and the Moor, and they hesitated to buy. For a time it looked as if it might become a convent as it was then that the religious orders were being expelled from France. Two members of the Council, Asher Hucklesby and Edwin Oakley, purchased it privately for £16,250 and sold it back to the town at exactly the same price, the Town Council by this time having realised its mistake.

Wardown was a tremendous success. The Council proceeded to extend the lake in order to make an open air swimming pool, although it was little used for this purpose. A suspension bridge, a great curiosity at the time, was built between the old lake and the extension and boats were introduced. Bowling greens and tennis courts were laid out in the park and the cricket ground added to the many attractions. It soon became a very popular place for fêtes, band concerts and pierrot shows and the town seemed to 'go to Wardown'. This the whole of the young life of the town did, dressed in its best, after afternoon Sunday School, and so began the 'Monkey Parade' that was to continue until about 1950. The acquisition of Wardown made a great change to the future of cricket in the town. In laying out the park Scargill had included a fine cricket ground and formed his own 'Scargill's XI'. There was at the same time a Luton Town club which played on Bell's Close. When this was formed is not known but it apparently ceased for a time to be re-formed in 1904 shortly after which it began to play at Wardown.

With all the popularity of Wardown, the House, or as it was then called the Mansion, was a white elephant, and no one seemed to know what should be done with it. The best use that could be found for many years was to make it into a restaurant.

ANOTHER CHANGE IN THE MANOR

The other 'house' in Luton was in the meantime undergoing a change as the Hoo at the turn of the century was unoccupied. In 1903 it was purchased by J. C. (later Sir Julius) Wernher, a wealthy diamond merchant, who immediately began to show a great interest in the town of which he had now become the lord of the manor. Sir Julius had, however, no desire to hold on to any mediaeval rights that had lost their significance in a modern world. He was willing to sell to the town the freehold of the Corn Exchange, and to transfer to the Council the power to hold markets and fairs within the Borough. It was necessary to have an Act of Parliament to regularise this: the Act received royal assent in 1911. Sir Julius unfortunately died the following year, but Lady Wernher proceeded to give to the Corporation the right to appoint the Town Crier and the Warden of the Pound as her husband had intended to do. Charles Irons was allowed to continue these offices, but no successor was appointed when he died.

These changes did not immediately break all the links of the town with the manor as the Court Leet continued to be held each year at the Corn Exchange. It was a colourful occasion which to the end lost none of its historic dignity, but as all its powers had gone it finally lapsed in 1939.

Luton was noted for its fairs. One of these, the Fox Fair, which used to be held outside the public house with this name in Dunstable Road, had been discontinued early in the nineteenth century. The Statute Fair, held in the streets of the town in September, had been the occasion when labourers hired themselves to farmers for the coming year. By 1880, when it came to an end, it was no longer necessary and William Austin was of the opinion that the hiring only continued as an excuse to keep the fair in being. As it was associated with excessive drunkenness the Town Council, with the willingness of the lady of the manor, petitioned the Home Secretary to order the fair to cease. It was necessary to do this as it had originally been started to comply with an Act of Parliament (The Statute of Labourers).

Luton people still referred, quite erroneously, to a cattle and pleasure fair held on the third Monday in April in the streets of the town as the 'Statty Fair'. The wide verges of Park Street were occupied by pens for livestock and the whole of Park Square and the open space around the Corn Exchange were given over to the pleasure fair. It continued until 1929 when it had become impossible to pass along the streets at the height of the fair. There was a much smaller fair, for cattle only, on the third Monday in October and this was taken off the streets at the same time or possibly earlier.

The weekly cattle market continued to be held in Castle Street until 1899 when a new market was opened in Bridge Street on land previously occupied by a brewery. It remained here until 1937 when it was again moved, now to a site off Park Street near to the Baptist church. Since 1882 the market had belonged to Cumberland and Sons, probably the oldest established auctioneers and estate agents in the town. The firm closed down a few years ago and the cattle market ceased in 1959: so ended the market which had been a weekly feature of the town for a thousand years. The corn market had in the meantime been suspended in 1950 and shortly afterwards the Corn Exchange was demolished.

Entertaining the People

The town had long had its periodic visits of a circus with its spectacular preliminary procession and menagerie. There had also been visits of the like of Buffalo Bill and the shows that went with them. There was no lack of fields on the outskirts of the town where tents could be pitched for these entertainments. Touring theatrical companies had also come to find no lack of halls in which they could perform. As these had been popular there was no reason why a permanent theatre should not be successful.

This came in December 1898 with the opening by Lily Langtry, a celebrated actress, of the Grand Theatre in Waller Street. It was a pleasant, small theatre which specialised in plays requiring a limited cast. Occasionally it had a variety programme. Here could be seen Shakespeare and Shaw and even the queen of the music halls, Marie Lloyd. On Boxing Day each year began the pantomime which all, young and old, thoroughly enjoyed. An exception must be made for the Nonconformists who disliked theatres being not slow to observe that the Grand Theatre itself bore a telling notice 'To the Pit'! It was not so much the acting to which they objected, or to most of the plays, but that for every part of the theatre from the 'gods' (the gallery) to the stalls and the boxes there was a licensed bar. There were long intervals for these to be patronised. The Salvation Army no doubt shared these views but was always ready to come to terms with the Devil. Each Good Friday, when by law there could be no theatrical performances, the Army for many years booked the Grand Theatre for their great day of the year when their founder, General Booth, on occasions came down to take control. There was at least one day when the bars were closed!

The cinemas, however, baffled the Nonconformists as they had no bars and of course Bunyan and his like had never railed against them. At long last they gave in. The first moving or animated pictures were seen in Luton in tents at the fêtes in Wardown and in shows in the Town Hall, and in a hall at the back of the *Red Lion Hotel* and at the Salvation Army! The cinematograph as it was now called had become so popular that a separate building, the first cinema, the Anglo-American Electric Theatre, was opened in Gordon Street in 1909. Here one could see travel and short comedy films for 3d in the front ten rows and 6d at the back.

Then followed other cinemas, far more luxurious and charging the same prices: the Picturedrome in Park Street in 1911, the Plaza in High Town Road and the Wellington in Wellington Street both in 1912. These had an added attraction of a matinée on Saturday afternoon when the show could be seen for 1d. Gordon Street had to retaliate in 1913 with a very expensive serial and Lutonians lived breathlessly from week to week as they became immersed in the startling escapes of Pearl White.

The audience on the evening of 1 October 1910 must have marvelled to see a film showing the opening of the Luton Public Library – shot that very afternoon!

These were all moderate entertainment compared with the splendour of the Palace Theatre (now a Bingo Hall) in Mill Street. The firm which began to build it became insolvent, but it finally opened in 1912 with a mixed programme of variety and films and, the greatest attraction of all, a ladies' orchestra. Its seats were, needless to say, twice the price of its rivals.

Until about 1930 films were silent which meant that cinemas employed a pianist who accompanied the film with music appropriate to the action being depicted. It caused great amusement if the pianist's attention wandered from the film when a quick change of action could cause the playing of an unrelated tune.

The football team had in the meantime gone through a bad spell for in 1912 it was relegated to the Second Division of the Southern League, which consisted mainly of clubs in South Wales from places like Ton Pentre, Caerphilly and Pontypridd which supporters could neither pronounce nor find on a map. There was joy in 1914 when Luton was top of the division and promoted again to the Southern League, but league football was then to be suspended for five seasons. In 1905 the ground had been moved from Dunstable Road to the one now occupied by the club. This was the hey-day of Bob Hawkes, but he had a rival for popularity in the trainer W. (Billy) Lawson whose cures for sprains and all muscular ailments were so miraculous that he was more sought after than any doctor.

In the meantime Rugby football had been introduced to the town by a team formed by workers at the newly-arrived Vauxhall works who played on a pitch adjoining the factory.

On the eve of the 1914 war Luton had still most of the character-istics of a small country town and beyond the terminus points of the tramways there was open country. Between the Laundry and Church Street Station in Dunstable there was just one house on the quiet country road. This was called the Halfway House and until about 1970 stood near to where the M1 motorway crosses the road. Biscot Mill stood in solitary splendour at the end of a footpath which was the continuation of Biscot Road. Beyond Wardown was Stockingstone Lane, with a ford through the river and a footbridge and it continued as a steep and narrow lane up the hill to Round Green. New Bedford Road crossed the river twice outside the town with the first and second Mud Arches and here were truly rural surroundings. Round Green was encircled with fields on all sides save that connecting it with the town. From Park Road ran a country lane, Trapps Lane (now Cutenhoe Road), to London Road and almost opposite the bottom of this stood a delightful thatched cottage called Why-ax-ye? The steep Farley and Winsdon Hills seem to have checked development on the west side of the town and Dallow Road had been built up to about Butlin Road. Further along was Runley Wood, popularly known as Daffy Wood, where primroses and daffodils still grew wild.

In those days of restricted transport the more wealthy people of Luton lived within walking distance of the town centre and there were still a number of big houses scattered around the town such as 'Highfield', below Stockwood. This was the house of one of the Browns and later was occupied by Sir Thomas Keens. 'The Larches', off Old Bedford Road, was the home of J. W. Green. Many of the better-off families lived on Hart Hill, in Downs Road or in New Bedford Road and most of the houses still remain as a testimony to how well they were built. The middle-class lived in the mid-Victorian houses in Cardiff Road and Rothesay Road or in the then newer houses off New Bedford Road such as Studley Road.

The working-classes lived in terraced houses in the older parts of the town and many of these could quite easily be converted into small factories. Some of the newer houses had bay windows, and being built just a few feet away from the road had a small garden in the front. There were streets which were close approaching slums in the New Town and High Town areas. The worst property of all was in Adelaide Terrace off the main street and between Chapel Street and George Street West; Langley Place, otherwise known as Front Row, off New Town Street; and Bull Court, off Park Street. When these had been built they had no doubt been respectable houses but had been built around by other property.

Luton was an essentially working-class town and as in those days the skilled artisans earning £2 a week just about managed to keep respectable, the life of unskilled workers, earning half of that amount, and a submerged few, probably making only 16s a week, does not bear thinking about.

The town centre was still dominated by the hat industry and George Street had few shops, being then mainly occupied by hat warehouses. In all the streets between George Street and Guildford Street there was little other than hat factories and most evenings railway vans would be stacked house high with crates being taken to the goods yards at the station. Off the town centre were the bleachers and dyers their chimneys being a marked feature of the landscape. Luton was much less clean than it is now.

Wellington Street was the main shopping street of the town with Farmer's music shop, just arrived, on one corner and Big Deacon's on the other (Little Deacon's was on Market Hill) – they were the jewellers of Luton. In Wellington Street were Strange and Sons, the oldest established drapers, Webdale's, specialists in household furniture, and Alexander's, a women's outfitters. There were also shops in Manchester Street, Merchant and Sons for instance, whose motto was 'Keep moving', but one they did not take to heart themselves. Others were on Park Square and on the Market Hill, where Mares' shop was in those days. There was still a number of independent tailors and bootmakers as mass production had not yet fully controlled their industries. Most of the shops were privately owned but Liptons, Home and Colonial, Pearks, Boots and the London Central Meat Company were exceptions. Off Park Square there was the Penny Bazaar, owned by Hooton's. Marks and Spencer had already appeared in George Street as a very small bazaar. Shops were well known for their specialities – Rudd's for their pork pies, Schoeppler's for their sausages and Goldsmith's for their faggots, and fish and chip shops were already numerous. Most Lutonians went from time to time to look in Frederick Thurston's windows in Hastings Street, as he was a photographer in great demand when there were visitors at big houses in the neighbourhood and he had photographed more than his fair quota of famous people.

Motor cars were comparatively new and there were few firms that undertook servicing. Horses provided the normal means of transport for traders and persons such as doctors who had to travel around the town. Hackney cabs waited in Williamson Street outside the *Midland Hotel* to be hired. With so many horses there were a number of carriage works and blacksmiths.

There were many more restaurants in proportion to the size of the town than there are today and Franklin's Restaurant in George Street, near to the Library, was a favourite place for meetings of societies unattached to a church or other institution.

15 The two World Wars and Luton

THE FIRST WORLD WAR 1914–18

BRITAIN was shocked to find itself at war in 1914 especially when it was realised by the more thoughtful that it would be a long and bitter struggle. The first problem was the speed at which we could turn from an economy of peace to one of war, for ultimately a large fighting force would be required, that would need to be fed and clothed as well as armed.

Luton was first met with appeals to its young men to join the Army and many immediately enlisted in the Territorial Army, which had only recently been formed, and were drafted to the Bedfordshire Regiment to begin their training. Early in 1915 they made a brief return to the town before going abroad to take part in the Gallipoli campaign. This brought the most serious loss of lives that Luton has experienced in any war, and these were young men it could ill-afford to lose. Eventually conscription was introduced but exemption could be claimed on a number of grounds among which was owning a one-man business which would suffer. The tribunal which considered these cases had many difficult ones to decide in Luton where there were a number of small businesses.

Throughout the war there were large army camps at Biscot Mill and in the Hoo Park and from time to time smaller ones in and around the town. Church halls and vacant premises were commandeered for sleeping quarters, canteens and rest centres and the influx of soldiers was so great, it is estimated that at times there were as many as 25,000, that they were billeted in private houses. It speaks much for the good relationship between the civilian population and the troops that friendships made then are, in some cases, still continued. Soldiers were in evidence during the whole of the war, but there was to be a more painful reminder of the horrors of war when Wardown House was converted into a military hospital.

There was a great desire to help in the emergency and for men, too old for military service or otherwise exempt, there was the local Volunteer Battalion, the members of which wore a grey-green uniform, attended drills and parades and took part in exercises which, if nothing else, helped to keep up their morale. Others worked part-time in munitions works or assisted in the many clubs that were set up by the churches. This latter activity absorbed the time of the women for whom there were also sewing and knitting groups to provide comforts for the troops abroad. Charities became numerous and flag days came with increased regularity. Some enterprising daily travellers into the town from Harpenden started an exceedingly popular newspaper to raise funds for war charities. The *NTF* (nine thirty-five), so called because this was the time of the train on which they went back to Harpenden each night, was taken over by the proprietors of the *Luton News* and later became the *Tuesday Telegraph* and finally ended its days as the *Beds and Herts Pictorial*.

The war brought its domestic trials with the black-out, and shortages of one commodity after another. Queues, quite unknown before the war, soon became commonplace. Rationing, when it came, was badly organised and towards the end of the war the system of food distribution in the town was so poor that the workers in the Luton factories staged a one-day strike. This resulted in a re-organisation of the local Food Council, after which there was some improvement.

Industrial Changes During the War

The greatest effect of the war on the town was the adaptation and expansion of the newly-arrived engineering works to deal with war contracts. Some new firms arrived and an aircraft factory (Hewlett and Blondeau) was opened at Leagrave. A large shell-filling factory was built at Chaul End and a temporary station opened on the railway there. The women who worked at this place could be recognised easily by their orange-yellow faces. The rapid expansion of the munitions factories brought a large influx of labour with the result that trade unionism, almost unknown in Luton before the war, increased as the trade unions seemed in the war conditions to exercise a great power. National labour problems now affected the town for the first time as diluted (i.e., unskilled) labour had to be allowed to do work which had previously been restricted to skilled workers. When it was proposed to allow diluted labour on other than war work there followed the Munition Strike of 1917 which was the first big industrial dispute to affect the town. As there was no hall large enough to accommodate the strikers' meetings they were held on the Town football ground every morning during the ten days that the strike lasted.

The hat industry continued and there was no attempt to curtail it, but it was often short of materials and always short of labour as the higher wages in the engineering works attracted away the women workers and those men who had not joined the armed forces. It is not known on what grounds the sewing machine agents were allowed to have a special licence to trade with the enemy, but without it the industry could not have survived as most of the sewing machines were made in Germany and it was essential to have replacement parts. The war brought permanent changes to Luton as the hat industry, having lost most of its export trade as a result of the war; never regained its previous position, while the engineering and chemical industries, although they declined from their war-time output, were at no time reduced to their pre-war level. Luton had become an engineering centre.

The Burning of the Town Hall

The war ended on 11 November 1918 but the peace was not signed until 28 June 1919, after which plans were made throughout the country as a whole for peace celebrations to take place on Saturday 19 July 1919. The Town Council prepared in an all too familiar manner to decorate the streets, to have a long procession with floats provided by firms and organisations, five bands in the procession, the entertainment of 9,000 children in Wardown Park where the procession would end, a firework display and at the end of it all a Mayor's banquet during the following week. They did not take into their reckoning two ex-service men's organisations – the Comrades of the Great War and the Discharged Soldiers' and Sailors' Federation. These had little in common as the Comrades were sponsored by generals and admirals wanting some of the better aspects of life in the forces retained while the Federation existed mainly to press for adequate pensions and secure employment for those who had served in the war. Both were indignant that they had not been consulted and put forward a rival plan which would allow for the culmination of the peace celebration to be a mass thanksgiving service on the following day. The Free Church Council, a body representing the Nonconformist churches of the town, agreed with this and asked the Mayor, Henry Impey, to consider it. They probably had cause later to regret this. The plan was turned down by the Town Council which said that it hoped all would join in their own celebrations. Both the Comrades and the Federation resolved to boycott the whole affair.

As the celebration day drew near a general indignation in the town grew especially after the Thursday when the *Luton News* published the list of those invited to the banquet, which included no one who had served in the armed forces, and printed the reasons given by those who declined their invitation.

The procession was marshalled in the Park Street Recreation Ground when those in charge of it were faced with a dilemma. At the last minute the Comrades had changed their mind and sent in a hastily prepared float depicting 'Jackie Cornwell, v.c.'. It was, unfortunately, as subsequent events showed, put at the end of the procession. The route was along Park Street by the Ivy Leaf Club, the headquarters of the Federation, which stood at the corner of Lea Road. The Federation was at full strength here, lining both sides of the road with every maimed man they could muster to the fore. Across the road hung a large streamer saying: 'Don't pity us, give us work'. Their fury knew no bounds when the Comrade's float arrived and they fell in behind to follow the procession to the Town Hall.

At the Town Hall the Mayor, in accordance with the printed programme, had already stopped the procession twice to read the proclamation of the peace. He now foolishly halted it yet a third time to read the proclamation once more, adding thanks to the Comrades for changing their minds. This acted as a signal to the already furious crowd to rush forward, at which the Mayor and his party quickly disappeared inside. The mob followed and failing to find the Mayor proceeded to smash the tables and chairs laid ready for the banquet and break all the windows. All this was easily achieved as the chief constable, with most of his police, was at the head of the procession by now approaching Wardown.

It was a strange afternoon with the Mayor conspicuously absent. The uneasy crowd thought he must still be at the Town Hall but if the truth had been known he was hiding in a cell at the police station. Night came with a large crowd assembled at the Town Hall, the thought in many people's minds that it would be burned. The chief of the fire brigade was already on the top of the building with a fire hose keeping the crowd at a safe distance. Some more daring than the rest faced the force of water to break the windows of a garage opposite to steal petrol which they took across to the Town Hall. The fire took hold quickly and at midnight the clock, which had been installed to celebrate the peace of the Crimean War, struck for the last time.

Disgraceful scenes followed as the police came on to the streets again to assist the fire brigade. Fire hoses were slashed as police and firemen were thrown off the fire engines. No one was killed but some were badly injured. Farmer's music shop at the corner of Wellington Street was broken into and a grand piano dragged out to accompany the singing of *Keep the Home Fires Burning*. Shops were looted and so it continued until troops from a camp at Biscot Mill arrived and formed a cordon around the smouldering building. Oddly enough they do not seem to have been resented by the crowd.

On the following day a contingent of the Metropolitan Police came down to clear the streets. They repelled yet another attack quite easily, this time on the police station. By that time the Mayor, a completely broken man, had left the town – never to return. When law and order was restored a number of arrests were made but those who were sent for trial were given astonishingly light sentences at the Assizes by the judge who said that there had been some provocation.

A stigma was left on the town which Lady Wernher did much to remove by inviting all the ex-service men with their womenfolk to the Hoo for their own peace celebration. She also gave the town the Memorial Park, off London Road, in memory of her younger son who had been killed during the war. The Discharged Soldiers' and Sailors' Federation went into an eclipse but it was only slightly responsible for all that had taken place. In any case its days were numbered for it was soon to be amalgamated with the Comrades of the Great War to form the British Legion.

About the same time that Lady Wernher gave the Memorial Park to the town, Miss Joan Crawley (later Mrs Crawley-Ross-Skinner) made a gift of the fine stretch of hills, known as the Downs, off Dallow Road.

Politics in the Inter-War Years

Before the First World War Luton had clearly stamped on it the apparently indelible imprint of Liberalism and all the Parliamentary elections we have described were straight fights between the Liberals and the Conservatives. The Labour Party in Luton may be considered to have begun in 1904 with the formation of the Luton and District Trades and Labour Council which contested a few seats for the Town Council before the war. The distinction of being the first Labour councillor went in 1919 to W. J. Mair, a foundry worker. He, by the way, appealed to the mob after it had shown its first indignation during the unfortunate riot to proceed no further.

There were more trade unionists in the town following the arrival of the new firms in the engineering industry, and a big increase in trade union membership when these firms expanded during the war. It was then no great surprise that Labour should present its first candidate in the so-called Coupon Election which followed immediately after the war. Its choice was a local man, Willet Ball, a trade union journalist who was a born fighter but in those days usually spoke with more bitterness than persuasion. He was afterwards to give a life of service to the town as a magistrate and a member of the Education Committee. Cecil Harmsworth held the coupon and was easily elected as a Coalition Liberal – there was no Conservative opponent – and from that time the Labour Party contested every election.

In 1922 the Coalition ended and the Liberals, having been split for six years, were again united. Cecil Harmsworth retired from the Commons and later went to the Lords, and it was the Liberals this time who found a local candidate in Harry Arnold, a timber merchant who had been mayor. The seat was won for the first time by a Conservative, Sir John Hewett, but there was another election in 1923 when it was won back for the Liberals by

Geoffrey Howard. He held the seat for one year only and the Conservatives won it again with Terence O'Connor. Neither Sir John Hewett nor Geoffrey Howard was member long enough to leave any deep impression, but O'Connor in his five years was generally popular.

It was in 1929 that Leslie Burgin was returned as a Liberal, being opposed by both of the other parties, and this was the last time that the Liberal Party won Luton without the support of another party. The economic crisis came in 1931 and the Liberal Party split again and it was as a National Liberal with Conservative support that Dr Burgin held the seat in the General Elections of 1931 and 1935. He was not able to defend the seat in 1945 as he was taken ill and died. Like T. G. Ashton he had represented Luton for sixteen years, but had only to fight three elections to do so. He was a good member who was ever ready to deal with the needs of the constituency, but he will be remembered chiefly as the first member for Luton to achieve Cabinet rank.

The Labour Party, which had in these inter-war years failed to win the constituency, had managed to build up a small but effective group on the Town Council. It was in this period that elections for the Council were fought for the first time on a party basis.

LUTON IN THE GREAT DEPRESSION

The trials in the field of politics are but a reflection of the uncertainties of life in the period which was one when most people felt that their life was in jeopardy and the future held little hope. If there had been any novelty in the Munition Strike there was none in the railway strikes and the engineers' strikes and lock-outs that followed the war and affected the town. The biggest strike of all was, of course, the General Strike of 1926 in which Luton was to play a strange part. The TUC had called out the printers and in doing so had made a big mistake as, wireless then being new, it starved the country of news. To remedy this both sides produced news sheets. While the TUC issued the *British Worker*, the Government replied with the *British Gazette*, edited by Winston Churchill. An edition of the latter and two other national newspapers were printed in Luton where there was sufficient non-union labour.

The great depression which was later to grip the country affected at times most of the firms in the town, but Luton was, on the whole, less affected than most places.

There was comparatively little unemployment in the town. It is probably true to say that Luton was the most prosperous – or least depressed – town in Britain between the wars. There were two reasons for our good fortune. First, Luton enjoyed the diversity of industry described in the last chapter; it was improbable that all our industries would be hit at the same time by unemployment. Second, and more important in the circumstances, the depression in Britain was mainly experienced by heavy industries like ship-building, coal, and steel. There was, in spite of the depression, an increasing demand for the goods which Luton made – for example, cars and the ball bearings essential to them. After all, even during the worst of the depression, most people were still in work. They were encouraged to buy through the relatively new system of hire-purchase.

Thus the depression left Luton comparatively unscarred. Yet it led to a wave of immigration from the distressed areas of Tyneside, Clydeside and South Wales. Thousands of people left their homes in these areas to seek work in Luton. The successful ones settled here.

In this period Vauxhall Motors increased its payroll from 1,000 in 1920, to nearly 7,000 in 1935, thanks in part to becoming incorporated into General Motors in 1925. It had its temporary setbacks as did most other Luton firms in the inter-war period. Some new firms actually came to the town, including Electrolux, later famous for its vacuum cleaners and refrigerators. Like Skefko it was of Swedish origin and when it came in 1927 it first took over the site of the old aeroplane works at Leagrave. In 1936, before the Airport itself was opened, Percival Aircraft (later Hunting Aircraft) began production on an adjoining site.

The fortunes of the hat industry in this period are especially interesting. It lost much of its export trade as a result of the war, and its supplies of plait were seriously affected by the war between Japan and China which began in 1931, but the remarkable adaptability of the industry, which has at all times been its most striking feature, was its salvation. Braids and sisal hoods were used instead of straw for light summer hats and felt-hat making, which had up to 1914 been only a subsidiary production, now began to increase gradually until it accounted for the greater part of the trade. At the same time the manufacturers, who had been content before the war to send hats away packed in hundreds in crates to be trimmed in the milliners' shops, now began the trimming of the hats themselves, and what is known, perhaps erroneously, as the millinery trade, began to develop. In this way the manufacturers were able to take away the greater part of the manufacture of women's felt hats from the felt hat industry at Stockport and Denton. Attempts by Luton manufacturers to make men's felt hats all failed!

These changes brought another new industry, cardboard box making, to Luton, but they sounded the death knell of the merchant manufacturers who had seemed so important in the industry in 1914 but had virtually disappeared by 1939. The merchant manufacturers had made no hats but bought them from the small makers to sell to the wholesalers.

The revolutionary change from straws to felts was assisted greatly by the astonishing development of the firm of Stewart Hubbard. In 1914 Hubbard was but one of a number of small bleachers and dyers serving the trade but he was always given to an inventive turn of mind. The war over and anticipating the change to felts he decided to master the production of hoods, visiting Italy to do so and employing skilled labour from the north. By 1939 he could claim that the firm was the largest in the hat industry in the world. Simultaneously, other firms including Lyes, Barford Brothers and Blundells (a subsidiary of the drapery firm) were becoming engaged in the same manufacture. The men's felt hat industry suffered badly from this competition, especially as it coincided with a tendency for men to cease wearing hats, and it, too, had lost an export trade.

The Luton hat industry was in 1939 very much smaller than it had been in 1914, but it is useful to note that the firms which had closed were usually the largest and that it was still often the smaller units which were weathering the storm.

It is not perhaps surprising that with so much distress in some other parts of the country, and the comparative prosperity here, the population of the town continued to increase in the inter-war years. Still more houses needed to be built and, with a determination now to deal with the problem of slums, there was a beginning of subsidies for housing and council house estates. This gave a new scope for builders and while, before the war, local builders had been content to erect individual houses, leaving it to outside firms to take the bigger contracts, there was now a chance to expand. Prominent among the builders who took this opportunity was H. C. (now Sir Herbert) Janes who developed a flourishing business by 1939.

A NEW TOWN HALL

One of the first problems facing the Town Council was the provision of a new Town Hall, for the Council offices were now scattered in buildings around the town. There was some doubt as to the best site, as the town was now becoming off centre, and while George Street had been in the middle of the township in 1850 it was certainly not so now. Other sites were considered as a possibility with the development of a Civic Centre that could do Luton justice. George Street was, however, changing and shops were replacing the warehouses that had so recently been one of its features. It had already been decided to have the War Memorial in front of the old site and this was unveiled in 1922. In short, notwithstanding the fact that the town was expanding northwards, George Street was becoming even more a centre.

The Town Hall was finally completed in 1936, the clock being a gift to the town by Albert Wilkinson who had been elected mayor for the sixth time in 1928 but had died shortly afterwards. There was some disappointment that the building did not in fact have a hall, especially as the Plait Halls, which could be used for big meetings, had been converted into a covered market in 1925. A hall to seat 1,500 people for public meetings, concerts, exhibitions and dances became one of the greatest needs of Luton. Most Lutonians were not a little amused to learn that the new Town Hall was constructed with fireproof materials!

Another problem to be solved was the use of Wardown House. It was finally decided to use this as a museum in 1931. The founding of the Luton Museum and Art Gallery was largely the work of T. W. Bagshawe, who had already started a small museum at Dunstable. The Luton Library Committee had been persuaded to house a small collection in part of one room at the Library with

Mr Bagshawe as honorary director. Charles E. Freeman had already begun his distinguished curatorship during which time the collection was transferred to Wardown and the one in Dunstable amalgamated with it. It was a small beginning for what is now an excellent museum. In the meantime Freeman became in 1947 the first editor of the *Bedfordshire Magazine* which he continued to edit until his death in 1965.

THE TRAM CONTROVERSY

The biggest controversy of the inter-war years arose over the trams. In 1931 the Council decided to sell them, with the transport rights which had been obtained earlier, to the Eastern National (now United Counties) Omnibus Company. The town became sharply divided, the more socialistically minded being reluctant to see the transport rights go, and the rest anxious to take the cash, £64,000, that the town had been offered. It was a very involved question as many people thought that the trams were very cumbersome and by this time they were holding up traffic in the narrow streets. The vital question was not, however, the trams but the transport rights. At the height of the controversy the *Luton News* was advocating selling and the *Saturday Telegraph* was opposed to it. When the Council finally agreed to the contract for sale the *Telegraph* had the most effective poster the town ever saw, as it just said 'SOLD'. The fight was not, however, over as the transaction needed the consent of the Minister of Transport and we had then a Labour Government. The Minister ruled that the Corporation had taken over transport rights for all time and could not sell them. His decision did not mean that the trams were saved as the Council proceeded to scrap them and replace them with its own bus service. The last trams ran in Luton on 16 April 1932.

Shortly afterwards the Home Counties Newspapers had to seek permission from the Council to put a clock on its building in Manchester Street and Charles Osborne, a forthright member of the Council, observed that it was fitting that the clock had two faces, one looking towards the Town Hall reflecting the support of the *Luton News* of sound and sensible local government, and the other turning its face from it as the *Telegraph* had done.

H

This may be a suitable opportunity to note that the *Luton News* had bought the *Bedfordshire Advertiser* in 1915 and that the *Luton Reporter*, which had held on bravely, finally succumbed in 1926. The *Saturday Telegraph* had in the meantime begun its career in 1914 and it has already been observed how the *Tuesday Pictorial* had come into being. For a brief period from 1936 until 1940 there was a regular evening paper in the *Evening Telegraph* but it was not continued. Although all our local newspapers were published by one company, the local press made an honest attempt to be impartial.

THE HAMLETS COME BACK TO LUTON

With the growth of Luton northwards the fields which had in 1914 separated the township from the hamlets were developed into streets of houses. The Eastern National was already running a frequent bus service to the villages around the town and the question of an extension of the Borough boundary now arose. The town could give the hamlets services they badly needed and so with two incorporations in 1928 and 1933, Leagrave, Limbury and Stopsley, with small parts of other parishes, were taken into the Borough. It was not without some resistance as a number of the people concerned felt that they were being 'taken in', in more senses than one. With these additions Luton was now, with the exception of the parish of Hyde which included the Hoo, approximately the size that she had been in the days of the large royal manor of the Domesday Book.

The first motor buses had operated from Luton as early as 1910 and within a few years the Road Motors Company, formed in 1912, was operating services to Letchworth and St Albans. In 1925 the Road Motors and some other small services were bought by the National (later Eastern National) Omnibus Company and by this time there were regular services on a number of routes. Shortly after the war excursions and coach trips became a regular and popular feature.

It was in 1934 that London Transport was given the monopoly of all country routes south of the town. The spheres of influence of the various bus undertakings operating locally became very complicated but it will be seen that they had their origin in matters of historic interest.

Some new schools (Denbigh Road, Maidenhall Road, Hart Lane and Beechwood Road) were built by Luton in the inter-war years to meet the needs of the growing town, although by incorporating Leagrave and Stopsley it acquired two schools which had been built comparatively recently by the County Council. There were, however, big changes at the Modern School which had by 1919 grown so large that it was thought necessary to separate the boys from the girls. A school was started for the latter in Alexandra Avenue and under the firm but understanding control of Helen K. Sheldon the High School developed. The Park Square premises continued to be used by the boys and increasingly more in the evenings as a Technical Institute. It was partly to give more scope for technical education that in 1938 a new school was built in Bradgers Hill Road for the Modern School for Boys (it changed its name to Grammar School in 1944). Park Square was then used for a new Technical Day School and an evening Technical College. These developments of higher education were still at this stage the responsibility of the County Council.

Other developments in this period included the provision of a new Court House in 1937 to replace the one which had served the town since 1856 but it was in looking forward rather than to the past that the Town Council decided to build an airport. The plans were some time in their development and already Percival Aircraft had begun production in 1936 on the site adjoining which had been reserved for factories. The airport was finally opened in 1938. In the meantime an open air swimming pool was opened in 1935. Adjoining this a larger swimming bath was provided in 1965 and as this had also slipper and shower baths as well it made the Waller Street baths finally redundant.

The achievements of Luton in the years between the two wars were by no means trivial, but they were mainly those of meeting the needs of an expanding population. Compared with what the town had done in the twenty years prior to the war, its progress had now gone forward piecemeal and, apart from providing the Airport, what it had done had lacked imagination. The period, was, however, one of crisis and tension so it is perhaps to the credit of the town that it did at least achieve something.

The strangest aspect of life in these uncertain years was that apart from the new Town Hall, the finest buildings erected in the town were cinemas, and these seemed to come with increasing rapidity as the silent films gave way to sound. First came a small and intimate cinema, the Empire, in Bury Park Road in 1921 – it is now a Jewish synagogue. Then in 1929 came the Alma at the bottom of Alma Street. This building was near Luton's very first cinema which was gutted by fire in peculiarly suspicious circumstances – one of the fire bugs was caught! The Alma later had a chequered career as a cinema, theatre, cinema, theatre, and finally a dance hall, when it changed its name to the Cresta. It was eventually pulled down to make way for a block of shops and offices. Just before the Second World War came the Union (later the Ritz) in Gordon Street also near to the first cinema, the Savoy (now the ABC) in George Street and the Odeon in Dunstable Road. In 1939 Luton had no fewer than eight cinemas as well as the theatre and even this was at one period showing films.

The football team was due for promotion to the Southern League in 1920 but as in that year the Football League was reconstructed it found itself instead in the Third Division (Southern Section). There followed some very successful seasons and among the prominent players on the books were Ernest Simms, a temperamental but prolific goal-scoring centre-forward, and Sidney Hoar, a local wing player, who could score goals from a corner kick. A new grandstand was opened in 1922 to replace one which had been destroyed by fire. A great day came in 1936 when 'Joe' Payne scored ten goals in one match; which is still a record. Then followed a wonderful season, 1936–37, which ended with promotion to the Second Division.

In the meantime the Red Cross Band, a popular attraction at the football matches, had in 1923 won the national 'Crystal Palace' championship for brass bands and was winning annually the south of England brass band contest. Then in 1930 came a crisis as it had to find a new name, there being an international agreement that 'Red Cross' must be reserved for relief work. As the Luton Band, the name it assumed, its success was just as well assured. It was at this period that the band had as conductors Fred Mortimer and his son, Harry, who was one of the greatest cornet players of all time.

A New Hospital and More Churches

Hospitals had still to be provided by voluntary means and notwithstanding extensions to the Bute Hospital it was still inadequate for the needs of the area. With the assistance of fund-raising the Luton and Dunstable Hospital was finally completed in 1939 on a site adjoining a Maternity Hospital that the Luton Corporation had already built. As its name suggests the new hospital, which was adequately provided with the most recent medical and surgical equipment, was intended to serve the needs of a wider area than the town.

The churches were similarly meeting the needs of an increasing population, although in the inter-war years the Nonconformists, who by this time were being more generally known as the Free Churches, were losing a great deal of their earlier influence. The Congregationalists had already built a new church in Bury Park and the Baptists in 1938 founded a new church in Blenheim Crescent. Both of these denominations, like the Methodists, were now rebuilding some of their smaller churches on the outskirts of the town. The Methodists before 1914 had been extending their work with many new churches such as those in North Street and Castle Street (Mount Tabor), and between the two wars built a new church in Dunstable Road. It was some years prior to 1914 that the Salvation Army had its Citadel as well as the Temple. It would be wearisome to account for the foundation of each of these new churches but no doubt each had a history of patient effort with, at times, some anxiety.

Between the two wars new Anglican churches were opened: St Andrew's off Biscot Road, and All Saints' off Dunstable Road, while St Christopher's at Round Green was built mainly from money raised by the children of the diocese. The corrugated iron Roman Catholic Church in Castle Street had in 1910 been replaced by a permanent one and before the outbreak of the second war, work had been begun with temporary buildings in Gardenia Avenue at Leagrave to pave the way for St Joseph's Church.

The uncertainties of those days are also seen in the increase of new religious forces in the town of Jehovah Witnesses, Christadelphians, Mormons, Seventh Day Adventists and Christian Scientists.

LUTON IN THE SECOND WORLD WAR (1939–1945)

The world war of 1939 was not the shock and surprise that the earlier war had been, as Luton, in common with the rest of the country, had been the scene of some of the grim events that prepared us for war. Blackshirt Fascists were in evidence and a man had died in Bute Street during the demonstrations of an angry mob against them. Communists had held their rival meetings, the police striving hard to keep the peace. A strong and active local branch of the League of Nations Union supported by the churches gave its further support to the general hope that in the end sanity might triumph and war be averted. The hopes of the most optimistic were diminished when Air Raid Precautions (ARP) were begun in 1938 and when in the same year, at the time of the Munich Crisis, gas masks were distributed to school children.

The broad pattern of the war when it at last came was, so far as it affected Luton, much as the other war had been, but the differences are worthy of note. During the two days before the actual declaration of war 5,000 London children were evacuated to the town and then followed a number of blind people and expectant mothers. These were all found homes, much as the soldiers in the previous war had been found billets, but when the bombing of London did not come as early as it had been expected, many of the evacuees returned. Of those who remained some still live in the town. The Women's Voluntary Service had already been formed and this was able to organise much of the local relief work that now became again so necessary.

The Air Raid Precautions which so many had treated lightly before the war now became a serious reality. Deep tunnels were constructed at various places in the town and underground shelters in school playgrounds. Children were trained to do their lessons in the shelters during the periods of the air raid warnings which in 1940 were frequent. During the war no fewer than 900 such warnings were sounded in Luton. Shelters were also built in the streets, and many people had small ones in their gardens before the war had actually begun. Others were built hurriedly and still remain to be used as tool sheds and outhouses. Many Luton families grew accustomed to sleeping in shelters but most preferred to take the risk of being bombed while still sleeping comfortably in bed. Every adult male person had to take his turn as a fire-watcher either at his place of work or in the street in which he lived. There were some exempt from this who had joined a now increased Special Constabulary or were active in ARP service.

From the beginning of the war there was again the black-out and prominent buildings and factories were camouflaged to obscure them from the air. Luton was, however, still visible and smoke screens were then made on clear nights which hid the town in a thick smoky mist. The first air raid, and the worst, was in broad daylight on a Friday afternoon, 30 August 1940. The first bombs dropped on the Vauxhall works and then a stream followed across the town. In this raid 194 bombs fell, 59 people were killed and 140 were wounded. During the remainder of 1940 and in the early part of 1941 there were to be many more air raids on the town and then a lull until 1944 when flying bombs made Luton one of their objectives. A rocket bomb fell in Biscot Road on 6 November 1944 and killed 19 people, injured 196 and damaged 1,524 houses. During the whole of the war 107 persons were killed and over 500 injured in air raids on Luton, but this was slight compared with the damage done to some other towns of comparable size, such as Coventry. For nights in succession the fires in London resulting from raids could be seen clearly from the higher parts of the town.

That Luton was a military objective, there can be no denying, for once again the various factories were geared to a war production, each factory specialising in some product more or less related to its peace-time trade – but what of the hat industry?

The Hat Industry faces another 'War'

This again suffered badly as the various firms were allowed only a quota, that is a specified limited production compared with their previous output. Some found this too small to allow them to stay in business and transferred their quota to another firm for the war period. Many of these did not return to the trade. The factories thus vacated were taken over for some war-time production but in the meantime some of the hat manufacturers had managed to obtain government contracts. A crisis came for the industry when the Board of Trade, in a desire to make Luton a purely munition area, made an order to transfer the whole of the hat industry to Gateshead-on-Tyne. Luton rose as one man to save the industry for the town with which it had been so long associated. Ultimately the President of the Board of Trade announced to a deputation representing varied interests in Luton that it had not been his intention to move the industry at all and there was a feeling of general relief.

It is difficult now to realise the full extent to which Luton was involved in the war effort. Estimates show that 12,000 men and women joined the armed forces and these were to be on active service in Europe, Africa and the Far East. Towards the end of the war about 20,000 women, some of them directed to do so, were engaged in various kinds of work, in many instances previously done by men. Nor was this all as the Home Guard, formed of men not available for various reasons for the services, was always ready, as were youth organisations, such as the Sea Cadet Corps, Air Training Corps, Boy Scouts, Girl Guides and Boys' Brigade, never stronger than they were in the war years, to deal with an emergency should it arise.

In the attempts to discourage travelling, people were asked 'Is your journey really necessary?' and urged to spend 'Holidays at Home'. They were encouraged to provide their own entertainment and it is interesting to note that it was during the war that the Luton Girls' Choir earned for itself its national reputation.

The story of the choir is reminiscent of that of the Luton Band. It began as a choir for girls formed in 1936 by Arthur Davies, then choirmaster of Wellington Street Baptist Church. Its excellence brought it great popularity, with so many outside engagements that its independence was the only logical course. Mr Davies maintained a strict discipline with *his* choir and set standards from which there was no deviation for girls had to leave the choir when they married or reached the age of 23. They have travelled widely – even to Australia – and appeared in a Royal Command Variety Performance. They have raised over £100,000 for charities.

The war probably affected the civilian population more than the previous one had done, but its trials were less irksome as many of the mistakes were not repeated. There was in the Second World War no thought of food strikes. An enormous burden was thrown on the social services and many Lutonians will remember the long mayoralty of John (later Sir John) Burgoyne.

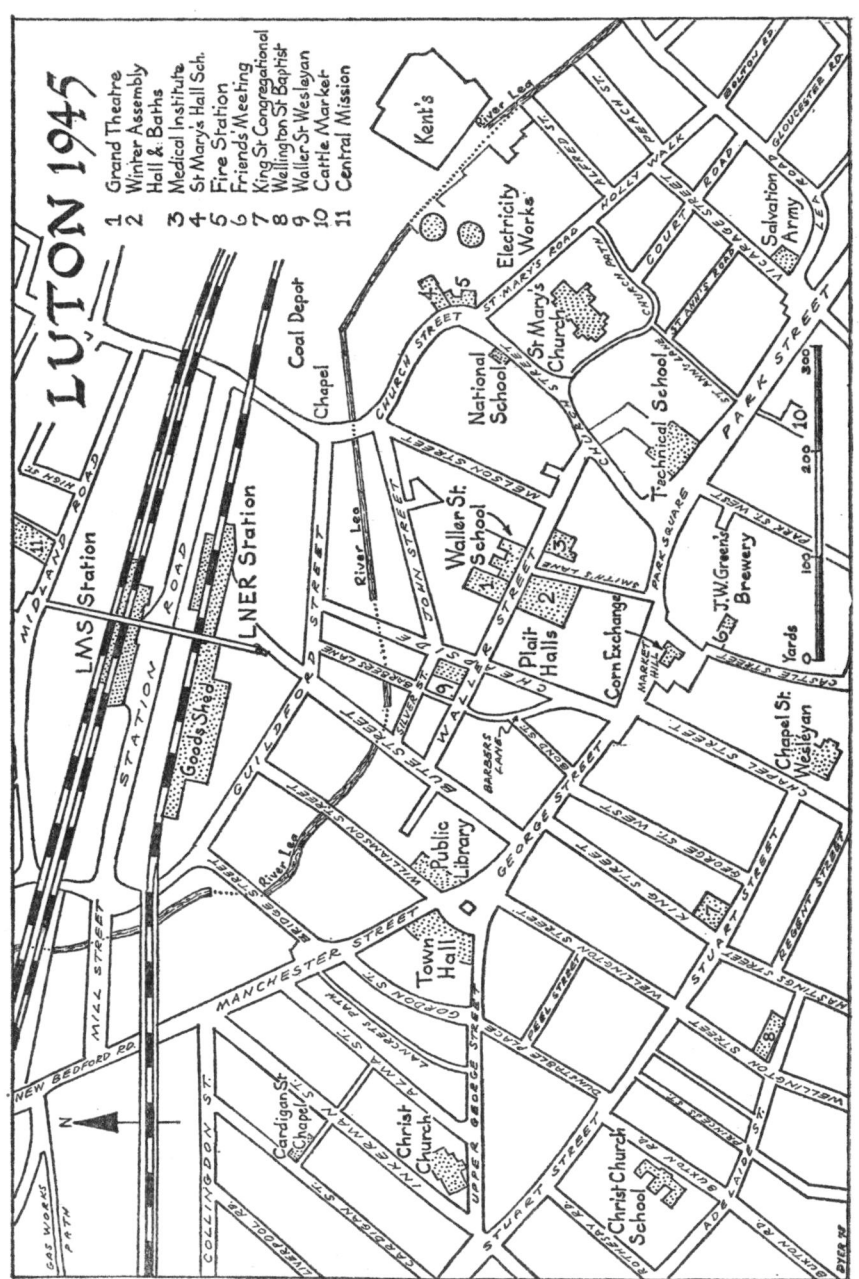

J

16 Luton since the wars

THE return to peace brought many changes. Dr Burgin was unable to defend his seat in the House of Commons, which he had held for so long, and for the election which followed immediately the united Liberal and Conservative Party had to find a candidate somewhat hastily. There was a swing in the country to the Left that was reflected in Luton which for the first time returned a Labour member in William Warbey. He was a very capable politician and made an exceedingly good member in the five years he was to hold the seat.

There had been no elections for the Town Council for seven years and the Labour Party had no difficulty at all in gaining a majority of the elected councillors, but were faced with the dilemma that there were then four aldermen to be elected by the councillors. If they had, as was customary, chosen these from among themselves, they would have temporarily lost the control of the Council which they felt, quite correctly, it was the will of the electorate should be theirs. They found a solution by electing as aldermen four persons who had not previously been members of the Town Council. This aroused much criticism from their opponents and the 'alderman question' became a talking point in the town for many more years to come. The Labour majority on the Town Council meant that Luton at long last had a Labour mayor the distinction of being so coming to W. G. (Jack) Roberts in 1945.

At the time of the next General Election in 1950 the now large South Bedfordshire constituency was split into two. One, the Luton constituency, included the whole of Luton except Leagrave and Limbury. These were combined with Dunstable and some of the neighbouring villages to form a new South Bedfordshire division. Mr Warbey fought the Luton constituency but was defeated by Dr Charles Hill (now Lord Hill of Luton), but the other was held by Edward Moeran for Labour. In the following year this was won by Norman Cole fighting as a Liberal-Conservative and he held it in elections again in 1955 and 1959. Dr Hill in the meantime retained Luton in the 1951, 1955 and 1959 elections and in 1963 went to the House of Lords to become Lord Hill of Luton. He had been a very popular member and he was a well-known national figure as the 'Radio Doctor' before he had taken to politics. Like Dr Burgin he too had achieved Cabinet rank. In the by-election which followed in 1963 Labour again won Luton with Will Howie as the new member.

In the more recent elections a revived independent Liberal Party has contested the seats and in the 1963 by-election the Communist Party appeared for the first time. In the 1964 election Howie and Cole held their seats but in 1966 both went Labour with Howie returned again and G. E. Roberts for South Bedfordshire. In 1970 there was a complete reversal with C. F. C. Simeons winning the Luton seat and W. D. Madel, South Bedfordshire. Before the 1974 elections there was a redistribution of seats with Luton, in view of its size, being given two seats. Both went to Labour with B. C. J. Sedgemore returned for Luton West and I. M. Clemitson for Luton East.

In recent years Luton has tended to follow national trends in its political allegiance but it has not always been so. In the seventy-nine years since Luton first returned a member, four have held the seat between them for fifty-six years: Ashton, Harmsworth, Burgin and Hill. Cole held his seat for fifteen years.

RECONSTRUCTION PLANS
After the war there was a serious housing shortage in Luton. It was estimated that due to a large expansion of the building industry in the inter-war years there had been 1,200 unoccupied houses in the town in 1939, but with the continued growth in the population and the number of houses which had been destroyed by enemy action the situation had become reversed. There were also a large number of houses built in the period of expansion between 1840 and 1860 which needed to be condemned. New schools were also badly needed, firstly to accommodate the increased number of children and secondly to replace schools that had long since ceased to be able to function as they were intended to do.

In the first few years following the war a number of prefabricated houses were erected as a temporary measure to ease the worst of the problem. In the meantime large council housing estates were planned for Farley Hill, Leagrave, Limbury and Stopsley. There were still restrictions on the building of private houses, so the Housing Committee of the Town Council had a long list of would-be tenants for council houses who were given points according to their need for a house. When the immediate needs were met, and of course they were never done so fully, steps were then taken to clear the older parts of the town. At this point there came the rival claims of building houses on the sites now made vacant, or developing them for light industry areas. A solution was found in allowing a number of them to become, at least for the time being, car parks, for as Luton's prosperity increased the number of cars rose more than proportionately.

It was obvious as soon as the war was over that the pressure on land around Luton would be very great indeed and the Bedfordshire County Council produced in 1947 its *Development Plan*, the object of which was to show how the whole of the county should be allowed to grow in the following years. It proposed that a 'green wedge' should be maintained between Luton and Dunstable and that Luton's growth should be severely restricted. The Luton Town Council in the meantime produced its *Report on Luton* which made the case for a considerable extension of the town so that it could plan the future development of population and industry. The plans, excellent as they may have been, came to nothing and both Luton and Dunstable were allowed to expand into the green wedge until they joined, and Luton spread over into the area which the county had hoped to keep rural. Further development in some areas has been effectively checked by the opening of the M1 motorway in 1959.

Recent Industrial Developments

The already established engineering works still grew and there was a fear for a time that the large Vauxhall works would have to move if it were not allowed to expand. Such an event would have brought great distress, as by 1955 it employed nearly 17,000 workers. In that year it began the making of Bedford trucks at Dunstable and in 1963 took a part of its production to Ellesmere Port in Cheshire.

At that time its payroll was 25,000. Commer Cars also opened a new factory at Dunstable in 1954. The firm was by this time part of the Rootes Group which itself in 1970 became absorbed by Chrysler United Kingdom Ltd. It is little wonder that Luton has become more famous for its cars than its hats.

Also in the post-war years Skefko (its name was changed to SKF (UK) Ltd in 1973), opened a larger factory at Sundon Park (1942) and Kent's and Electrolux have also grown considerably. The British Aircraft Corporation ceased to operate at the Airport in 1966 and so made way for yet another extension of Vauxhall. In 1962, the old Davis Gas Stove Company (then Jackson Industries) closed its works in Dallow Road.

This loss was compensated for to some extent by the development of a clothing industry with the arrival of Ellis and Goldstein's, Skirtex and the Ballito Hosiery Mills. Another new industry came with Westly's, a subsidiary of Lye and Sons, and the manufacture of ribbons and elastic. For a time we also had a cigarette factory.

With these expanding businesses and new arrivals the oldest firms remained small and were in most cases incorporated into bigger concerns, e.g. Hayward Tyler's, Balmforth Boilers and Brown and Green's. In 1939 Balmforth's manufacture was undertaken by an associate firm in the Midlands. It returned in 1958. Brown and Green's, Luton's oldest engineering works, closed down in 1973. J. W. Green's brewery, which had grown by taking over other concerns, was itself merged first with Flowers and finally in 1961 with Whitbreads. A new brewery was opened at Leagrave in 1969 after which the long familiar brewery off Park Square ceased as such but continues for administrative purposes pending its final closure.

Luton's oldest industry weathered the storm of a second war far better than it was feared that it would. The war-time bombing of London and the increasing difficulties of continuing production there brought a number of the London firms to Luton after the war and checked to some extent a decline which was setting in due to fashion changes and the tendency for even fewer women to wear hats. The most striking feature of the industry in the post-war years has been a dramatic collapse of the hood-making industry which is comparable only with its sudden rise. S.

Hubbard Ltd having first of all concentrated their production in their large Luton factory, then transferred it to Dundee before passing out of the industry completely. The other hood manufacturers either ceased production or cut their output considerably with the result that little felt-hood making is now done in the town.

At some critical stages in the town's rising prosperity, its great variety of industries has been its greatest asset.

SOCIAL SERVICES SINCE THE WARS

The greatest developments in the social services in the post-war years have been in the fields of education. Of the older schools New Town Street was closed in the period of the First World War and St Mary's Hall shortly afterwards. Waller Street closed at the time of the Second World War to become a Youth Headquarters. With the population moving from the town centre many new schools had to be provided on the fringe and these were all built with spacious surroundings with adequate playing fields in sharp contrast with the asphalt playgrounds of the old schools and the only football pitch on the nearest recreation ground. In 1965 two of the old church schools, Queen Square and Christ Church, were closed and a new church school opened in Beaconsfield, off Crawley Green Road. St Matthew's alone remains of the church schools but is no longer under church control. It is interesting to note that five of the new schools are Roman Catholic. The fight for the School Board seems very strange in retrospect. No doubt the greatest change has come in the provision of technical education. The Technical School, which had been housed in temporary premises adjoining the Technical College, was given a new building in New Bedford Road to become a technical grammar school and this made way for a greater extension of the Technical College and the occupation temporarily of disused factories close by. A new College of Technology was in the meantime being built in stages, as the work it was doing could not cease. It was finally completed and officially opened in 1960. It had at one period over 10,000 students, including a number full-time or working on degree courses. It was to relieve some of the pressure thus created that Barnfield College (Luton) was begun in 1971. This new college has 6,500 students of whom 500 are full-time. This is a great advance on the Technical Institute of 1908 which catered for but a handful of evening students. In the meantime there have been opened a number of Evening Institutes in schools in the town and in which a large number of courses are offered.

A similar development has been seen in the Library Service. The Carnegie Library had indeed served a useful purpose but, even with branch libraries, was eventually to be inadequate. A new Central Library built in a modern and refreshing style with a gramophone record and music library, as well as a theatre and lecture room, was completed in 1962 and later visited by the Queen.

Progress at the Airport was slow until Customs facilities were obtained in 1962. Its grass runways were inadequate for modern traffic and in 1960 a concrete runway of 5,000 feet was constructed to which further extensions have since been made. The main use of the Airport now is for independent airline operators providing charter inclusive holiday tours but there are numerous scheduled services. There is some freight traffic and a number of executive aircraft belonging to private firms are based at Luton. It is also used for diversions from London and Gatwick Airports. The Airport will undoubtedly play an increasing part in Luton's future development. The increase in the number of passengers using it has risen from under 5,000 in 1960 to 213,000 in 1965 and 3,200,000 in the year 1973–74.

The expansion of the Airport brought much opposition from those who had to suffer from the noise of the aircraft. An effective pressure group, Ladacan (Luton and District Association for the Control of Aircraft Noise) was formed to gain most of its support from people living outside the town but beneath flight paths. Comparatively few people living in the town itself were badly affected.

The town's sewage disposal also gave cause for much anxiety especially as a very efficient and up-to-date plant was installed at East Hyde in 1942. The effluent flows into the river Lea which, apart from it, would be a mere stream, for Luton's waste water adds nearly ten million gallons a day. This has been purified and is chemically as pure as water can be in the circumstances. For many years the Corporation had to fight what appeared to be a losing legal battle with Lord Brocket who owned a beautiful park, with a lake formed by the river, about eight miles below East Hyde. The Metropolitan Water Board was also affected as the river forms part of the water supply of the London area. In the end a settlement was made but Luton's sewage disposal is still a difficult problem which it is hoped can be solved by a new installation at Chalton which sends its effluent into a tributary of the river Ouse.

In 1945 the Town Council bought Stockwood from Mrs Crawley-Ross-Skinner which broke the long direct connection of the Crawley family with the town. It had been used as a hospital during the war and although it belonged to the town it was used for some years as a children's hospital. As it proved difficult to find a useful purpose for it, this once stately home was unfortunately demolished in 1964. The grounds are now a public park.

The affairs of the Luton Water Company which had served the needs of the town well since 1865 have undergone great change. Their local sources of supply reached their limit in 1966 when they were augmented by supplies from the Ouse made possible by the Grafham Water Scheme. In the meantime Whitehall was planning larger water authorities to deal with sewage disposal as well as the supply of water and in 1974 the Luton company was absorbed into the Lee Valley Water Company. Some local industrial concerns, notably Whitbreads, Laportes and Vauxhall, have, however, their own independent boreholes. When Whitbreads opened their new brewery in 1969 with yet another borehole the supply from their old one became part of that of the water undertaking.

The General Cemetery Company, which had been set up in 1854, was taken over by the Corporation in 1946. An additional cemetery was provided at Stopsley in 1951 and a crematorium opened in 1960. The Church Cemetery is still owned privately.

The present Head Post Office in Dunstable Road was opened in 1957 to replace one in Upper George Street which was built in 1923, but as this is nearer the town centre it continues to be used as a sub-Post Office. In its turn this had replaced a much smaller one which was at the corner of Barber's Lane and Cheapside. This was apparently built in 1881 to replace earlier ones in Park Street and George Street. The telephone service which had much increased in recent years was, after long preparation, put finally on Subscriber Trunk Dialling.

It was in 1937 that Luton was provided with a new railway station but there was much regret that it had still only three platforms as this sometimes caused a great delay in trains especially when the main lines were blocked. The fourth platform was provided in 1960 when a diesel service was introduced and since then there has been a much improved service to Bedford and London. In 1962 the passenger service between Dunstable and Leighton Buzzard was suspended and on 24 April 1965 the last passenger train ran on the line from Welwyn to Dunstable. Goods trains still operate between Luton and Dunstable but south of Luton the line is completely closed.

The Life of the People

The post-war years have seen many changes in the everyday life and habits of the Luton people. The cinemas which seemed all-absorbing in their attractions before the war soon lost their appeal and six of the eight we had in the town had to close their doors. After striving hard to survive, the Grand Theatre also closed and was then rebuilt for a supermarket. The 'Grand' had become very uncomfortable and shabby compared with the luxurious cinemas, but it was a pity that it had to go.

The fortunes of the football club were variable. In 1955 after some very successful seasons in the Second Division it gained pro-motion to the First Division. Then followed four glorious seasons during which it was unquestionably one of the best clubs in the country. Given popular opponents it was difficult to force one's way into the ground. The most memorable season in the club's history came in 1958–59 when it reached the FA Cup Final only to be defeated by two goals to one. In the days of this excitement plans were made for a new ground that would hold the 40,000 spectators who would be anxious to see football of this vintage. Then followed disaster with falling gates and only one more season in the First Division. The club then dropped through the intervening divisions to the Fourth Division from which it rose as quickly as it had fallen. There was some consolation that these vary-ing fortunes were shared by some even more well-known clubs.

In a period when more social services were being provided by the State it is refreshing to find no lack of voluntary social welfare work, LUDUN, inspired mainly by Mr L. W. Plewes, originated in Luton and Dunstable Hospital and is an experiment in the rehabilitation of injured persons through useful industrial production. Some of the problems of an ageing population have been met by the provision by Sir Herbert Janes of Janes Village. This is a self-contained community for older folk in which each has his own separate house but may benefit from some services provided for the whole. Another problem of age was met by Dr Snellgrove who organised VESPER, the main object of which is to find useful employment and occupation for the elderly.

The charities of the town were much benefited by the wills of Sydney C. Aylott, a hat manufacturer who introduced the bandeau to give a better fit for ladies' hats, and Frederick C. W. Janes, the founder of a sewing-machine firm who patented the 'Lutonia' machine which was much used in the hat industry. As both provided for almshouses it seemed wise to merge them with the trust already existing for the control of the Chobham Street almshouses. These were in any case now becoming old. They were demolished and rebuilt in 1963 to become the Aylott-Janes Almshouses. In this way there has been a continuity of various charities dating back nearly four centuries.

The educational charities, all very small, have by no means lapsed but since education is now free are not easy to administer. From time to time, however, it is still possible to find means whereby the objects of these charities are still satisfied.

The churches have met the needs of a growing population in new ways. The Methodists have closed some of their churches in the town centre to build others – their magnificent church in Chapel Street was renamed the Luton Industrial Mission. The Church of England has built new churches to create more parishes but the most marked increase has come from the Roman Catholics who now have six churches. In 1963 the Quakers moved from the Meeting House in Castle Street which had been theirs so long to a new one in Crawley Green Road. A very old sect, previously without a church in the town, is the Presbyterians who now have one in Villa Road. They have recently combined with the Congregationalists to form the United Reformed Church. Perhaps the most refreshing aspect of church activity in the post-war years has been the opening of churches on the new building estates simultaneously with the erection of the houses.

The long monopoly of Home Counties Newspapers Ltd of the local press was broken in September 1967, with the arrival of the *Evening Post*, a daily newspaper which chose Luton as the main centre for its news. Local editions covered a wide area of north Hertfordshire and further north as far as Milton Keynes. In the face of this competition the *Tuesday Pictorial* ceased publication in May 1970, and the *Saturday Telegraph* in November 1971, leaving the *Luton News* as the only local weekly newspaper.

THE COUNTY BOROUGH QUESTION

At the time of the setting up of the county councils about eighty large towns were made county boroughs. These were to have the combined powers of an administrative county and a municipal borough, but as so little had been found for the counties to do they had not much more power than a large municipal borough or urban district. Apart from a few created for purposes of local prestige, such as Canterbury, they had a population of over 50,000 and they included all the large towns of the country such as Birmingham, Manchester, Liverpool, Leeds and Sheffield. For London there was a separate and very complicated system. It was understood that a population of 50,000 would be the population necessary to become a county borough.

Luton had a population in 1881 of only 23,960 so it was obviously not considered in the first instance to be large enough to become one of the new county boroughs. By 1961 the population of Luton had risen to 131,505 while that of some of the towns, which may have had 50,000 in 1888, had now only a population of 60,000. In 1961 there were 84 county boroughs and over a half of these had a population less than that of Luton. Also Luton had been for many years the largest place in the country which was not a county borough, except for one or two towns on the fringe of London whose future was obviously bound up with a reconstruction of the local government of the London area. If it had been a matter of size alone Luton ought to have been made a county borough long before she indeed was, but there were many difficulties in the way.

Luton's population had grown to 49,978 by 1911. In 1914 a Provisional Order, which would have given county borough status to the town, was approved by the Local Government

Board. The confirming Bill was, however, rejected by Parliament. There was little dismay as the town at this time controlled all the essential services that its people needed and the county directed little more than its higher education. Between the wars the situation did not change greatly as most of the additional powers given to the county councils were concerned with some aspects of the health services, of no great moment, and agriculture, which scarcely affected Luton at all. An exception must be made for the Public Assistance Act (1929) which to no one's great regret at long last brought to an end the old Poor Law and the Boards of Guardians. Public Assistance, as it was now called, was administered by the county councils and while the new system brought much unpopularity with 'the dole' and means test, it did not affect Luton much.

After the end of the Second World War in 1945 there came great changes in Government policy which resulted in Luton losing many of the services which she had striven hard to develop and of which she was so justly proud. There were good reasons for the changes for it must be realised that there were small municipal boroughs with a population as low as 2,000 which were obviously not large enough to control some services effectively. There was an obvious need for larger education authorities, police forces and fire services. It was the policy of the Government to put these and other services in the control of administrative counties and county boroughs to make sure that the units were large enough. Good as this was as a broad principle Luton's population was now 100,000 and it was obvious that she was well able to continue to control these services. It was, however, also true that Luton's population was a third of the whole of the county and a further extension of her boundaries would make it more. If Luton retained the services it would make two education authorities, police forces and fire services in the county and it was possible that each might be less efficient than a large one would be. For a time it appeared that the Government was thinking in terms of having two kinds of county boroughs, some all-purpose and controlling all services, others sharing their services with other authorities. These were anxious days for Luton. Let us, however, account for the services that the town lost.

The fire services had during the war been incorporated into a

National Fire Service as a co-ordinated part of the national defence system and it was of course a very necessary thing to do. Luton firemen, including those in the Auxiliary Fire Service, which had been created on the eve of the war, were called to great distances, including London, at the height of the bombing. After the emergency Luton's Fire Service was, in 1947, put under the control of the Bedfordshire County Council. This may be a suitable opportunity to deal with the local fire service which was taken over by the old Board of Health in 1864. At this time the main Fire Station was in Stuart Street but shortly after the incorporation in 1876 a new fire station was built in Church Street next to St Mary's Hall. Until 1914 the firemen were part-time and voluntary and were called from their homes or places of work when there was a fire. It was then that a nucleus of full-time firemen was recruited and the first motor engines replaced the old popular horses. In 1930 the town had the most serious fire in its recent history when Vyse's factory in Bute Street was gutted and eight people were killed. The Church Street Fire Station was replaced by one in Park Street in 1940 and it was in 1956 that the County Council provided the very modern station in Studley Road, off New Bedford Road.

It was also in 1947 that the Borough Police Force was incorporated in the County Constabulary and this brought much protest for at the same time over a hundred other towns lost control of their police.

The story with education was very different as the Butler Education Act (1944) put the whole of education, primary and higher, under the control of administrative counties and county boroughs. Luton, in view of its size, was made an 'excepted district' with delegated powers from the County Council which allowed it considerable authority as it was subject only to the approval of its estimates by the county. The Luton Committee for Education, which reported to the Luton Town Council, consisted of sixteen Luton borough councillors, four members appointed by the County Council and four co-opted members. In some respects this new arrangement gave Luton a greater control over education than it had before, as the Committee was to be responsible for both primary and higher education. There was, however, a sense of inferiority as the County Council had to approve the estimates, and matters of disagreement had to be referred to Whitehall.

Luton also lost control of another service in electricity, not to the County Council, but by nationalisation. It is little wonder that Luton town councillors complained that their powers were being reduced almost to that of a parish council.

The Struggle for County Borough Status

Each successive loss of powers to Luton was raised in the House of Commons by Mr Warbey, who was then the member, but with no avail and the only solution was the promotion of another Private Bill. This was done in 1950 but the Minister of Health asked the House of Commons to reject the Bill which it dutifully did. In 1951, when Dr Hill was now the member, a third Bill was introduced and it was again defeated on a free vote, but with a smaller majority. The Minister (it was the period of the second post-war Labour Government) in advising the Commons to reject the Bill said that problems such as Luton had could not be solved by piecemeal legislation and that the only solution was a complete overhaul of the whole system of local government.

Luton prepared a fourth Bill for 1952 but did not proceed with it as at this time it was engaged in the long High Court action with Lord Brocket, and the Judge had inferred that a town which could not cope with its sewage disposal problem could not expect to get greater powers in other directions. The fourth Bill was nevertheless introduced in 1954 but was again, on the advice this time of the Minister of Housing and Local Government (for the functions of the various ministries had been changed), rejected by a small majority. A promise once again was made that the Government would introduce legislation that would deal adequately with Luton's position and that of similar towns. It was by now a Conservative Government and all Luton was getting from either party was sympathy and hopeful promises and both Socialist and Tory backbenchers were demanding a better deal. Dr Hill's hands were tied to some extent as he was by this time a member of the Government but he lost no opportunity to state Luton's case.

The town had not given up hope and promoted yet a fifth Bill which the House would consider in 1955 with similar ones from Ilford and Poole. The Minister on this occasion asked the sponsors to withdraw their Bills as he had had discussions with the various organisations most concerned with local government which could only result in some general legislation. Luton withdrew its Bill and later in 1955 the Government announced that it proposed to set up a Commission to consider the cases of application for county borough status.

These various post-war Bills had obviously brought Luton into conflict with the Bedfordshire County Council and the earlier Bills of 1950 and 1951 had been directly opposed by the county, but the later ones were not met with the same amount of opposition. We may now ask what was the relationship between Luton and the County Council during this period. Any thought that the latter consisted of country gentlemen and farmers unaware of the needs of an industrial community is far from the truth of the position. During this period Luton had virtual control of its education, and with highways, for which the County Council had nominal control so far as main roads in the town were concerned, there had been no attempt to interfere. With planning, a new responsibility of the county, Luton was given the power of day to day control of development within the borough subject to strict limitations. The preparation of the Development Plan was retained by the county. By virtue of its size Luton had a large representation on the County Council and from 1935 to 1952 its chairman was Sir Thomas Keens, a Luton member whose love for his native town no one could doubt. Indeed at one stage of the height of the struggle the Mayor of Luton was none other than Lady Keens. When Sir Thomas retired he was succeeded by Sir Frederick Mander, another distinguished Lutonian, who held office until 1962. During this period also the chairmen of a number of the more important committees of the County Council were Luton members.

Between 1950 and 1955 Luton had promoted four Private Bills in Parliament and had withdrawn the last on what appeared to be a promise that a Commission would be formed. This had not been done by 1957 and when a sixth Bill was being contemplated it was announced that the Commission had been set up with the instructions that 100,000 was the population that a town should have to be assumed big enough to take the responsibilities of county borough government. Luton's case was considered in 1958 and in

March 1960 the Commission recommended that Luton's case was one which demanded the full status. The long struggle appeared to have ended in victory, but time dragged on and fears arose that this was yet another promise which would not be fulfilled. In August 1962 it was announced that the Government had accepted the Commission's recommendation but no date was given for its implementation and it was not until November 1962 this was decided – it was to be 1 April 1964. The Minister's Order was not, however, finally approved by Parliament until 5 February 1964. The struggle was at long last over!

COUNTY BOROUGH STATUS AT LAST

What difference did county borough status make to Luton? It meant in the first instance that the town regained control of its police force and fire service and that its education, planning and highways were no longer subject to any nominal supervision by the county. In 1966 the town lost complete control of its police service when a joint Bedfordshire and Luton Constabulary was established. In addition it took from the county some other services including welfare work, which had been delegated to Luton since 1961, and certain health services, concerning maternity and child welfare, and matters of licensing, such as motor car registration. It also meant that all the rates raised by Luton were at the complete disposal of the town whereas previously about two-thirds of this either went to the county or was in some way controlled by it.

On 1 April 1964 all the employees of the County Council working in Luton in the transferred services became employees of the Corporation and on the same day property such as schools, clinics, police and fire stations previously belonging to the county were similarly transferred to the town.

Although Luton became a borough with all the additional powers of an administrative county it did not follow that it was a geographical county. Neither was what remained to form the new administrative county. Together they made Bedfordshire. Sportsmen from Luton were still eligible to represent the county and the county cricket XI still played some of its games in Luton with Luton players in the team. Cultural societies continued their work as before, completely regardless of any change in local government organisation. The Bedfordshire Historical Record Society was still concerned with the history of the county as a whole and the Bedfordshire Natural History Society with the full content of its fauna and flora. They, with many other voluntary bodies, were able to please themselves.

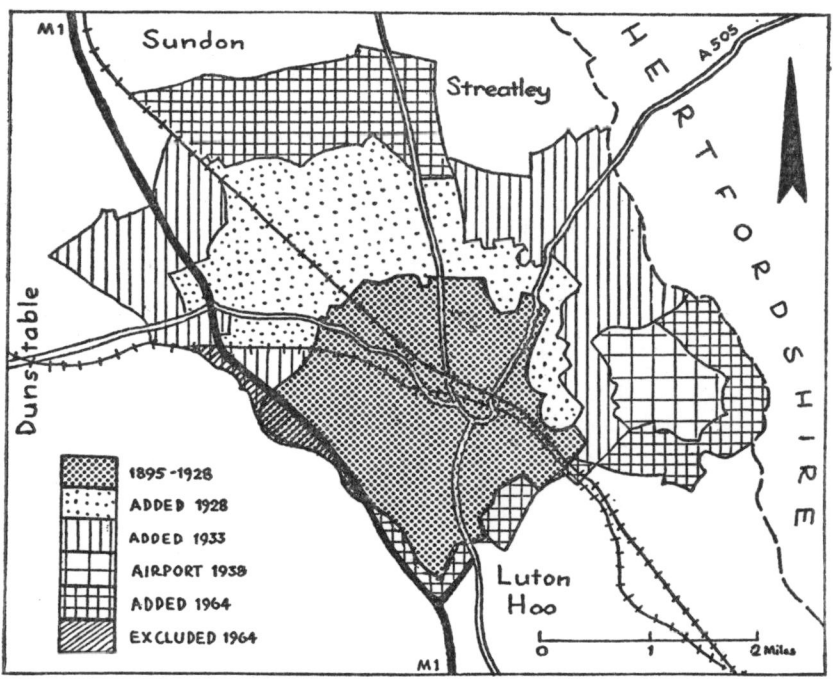

THE COUNTY BOROUGH AT WORK

The town enjoyed county borough status for a brief period of only ten years in which some considerable changes were seen. Education was a major problem as the eleven-plus examination for the selection of those presumed to be fitted for a grammar school education was, in the opinion of many, unsatisfactory. A comprehensive system of education seemed to be a solution but there were many forms which this could take. Although subject to much protest it was decided to have a Sixth Form College to which young persons would be eligible to go. The Grammar School seemed to be the school best fitted although it meant the end of the High School for Girls. The retirement of Mr K. B.

Webb in 1965 at the end of a distinguished headship of twenty-seven years at the Grammar School eased the way for the change which took four years to implement fully. Other schools were made co-educational High Schools although one was retained for boys and another for girls to meet any objections of parents to co-education. In 1965 the town took a further step in opening a day College of Education at Putteridge Bury for those wishing to train to be teachers.

A long struggle by the town to maintain its own system of public transport came to an end in January 1970 when the town's bus service was taken over by the United Counties Omnibus Company.

A re-development of the town centre was, however, the Town Council's greatest concern. The town had grown quickly in the middle of the nineteenth century with the result that much of the property in the town centre was built in this period. A great deal of it was long overdue for demolition. Some people had sentimental attachments to buildings here and there but few of these had any architectural merit. The streets laid out in the same period were too narrow to allow traffic to run freely and systems of one-way streets brought only temporary relief. There was much to commend a wholesale clearance and a planned re-development.

The Arndale Centre, undertaken by a development company, is already (1974) well advanced and will in the course of time occupy the whole of the area between George Street and the railway, from Bridge Street to Church Street. This means the disappearance of whole streets familiar to Lutonians for more than a century – Cheapside, Waller Street, Guildford Street, Bute Street and Williamson Street and with them Smith's Lane and Barber's Lane, both probably as old as the town itself. All the shops of this area will eventually be in the Arndale Centre but with no traffic except the loading bays reserved for them. Multi-storey car parks will house the cars of those shopping. Some familiar buildings have already gone but most had outlived the purpose for which they had been intended. After the Quakers no longer needed the old and first National school for an Adult school it had become a Trade Union club. The Grand Theatre became a supermarket and Waller Street School – once the Higher Grade School – became a youth club, and never a suitable building for such, in a part of the town with few young people. The Plait Halls had become a covered market, the stall holders in which could be just as satisfied in a similar one in the Arndale Centre. The National Health Service had made the Medical Institute no longer necessary and it had been wound up. A similar story could be told of the old Public Baths and Waller Street Methodist Church as well as many a factory and shop. Older people have regretted their going but would have been happier if what is superseding had been just a little more attractive.

With the demolition of older property outside the Arndale Centre, mainly to make new and better roads, other long familiar buildings have gone. Like those within the Centre some had ceased to serve their original purpose. Such are the Queen Square schools and the old British school in Langley Street. But it was because it was unsafe and with a congregation too small to maintain it that the King Street Congregational Church was demolished. It was a noble building and for many years the most prominent landmark in the town.

Among some of the older buildings spared in this mass demolition are isolated houses and shops as well as the Union Church dating back to 1836, part of the workhouse (now St Mary's Hospital) which was built in the same year, Wellington Street Baptist Church, the old Primitive Methodist Church in High Town, and above all the parish church itself. This had long been dwarfed by taller erections including for some time the cooling towers of the electricity works, now unfortunately gone. Some controversy was caused when an extension was made to the church to provide for social activities in connection with it. Some held that there should be no extension, others that the proposed extension was not in keeping with the rest of the church. Future generations will no doubt accept it for it is by no means the first time in its long history that an addition has been made to the church.

Luton Ceases to be a County Borough

Local government in England developed in a piecemeal manner failing to keep pace with a shifting population. In the nineteenth century when few services were under the control of local authorities it was a matter of less consequence but during the present century a change has long been overdue.

In April 1974 a new system became operative. Apart from London, which ten years previously had become subject to its own change, there are now six metropolitan counties which are, like London, large entirely built-up areas and a number of non-metropolitan counties consisting of both urban and rural areas. A few of these new non-metropolitan counties including Bedfordshire, coincide approximately with the old geographical counties. They are divided into districts of which there are only four in Bedfordshire. By this means a few large towns in the country, e.g., Bristol, Plymouth, Southampton and Portsmouth have become districts and Luton is also one. Generally speaking towns smaller than Luton have been combined with adjacent rural areas to form districts and in consequence have lost some of their separate entity.

The county authorities deal with most major services leaving the district authorities to control those affecting their immediate neighbourhood. In the course of time the county authorities will delegate the operation of some services to some of the district authorities. It is consequently too early to know how Luton will ultimately be affected by the change. One important feature of the new system is that urban areas have equal representation with the rural areas on the council of the new county authorities. This means that twenty-nine of the eighty-three county councillors represent Luton, so large a proportion of the population of the county live in the town.

As Luton itself is a district there are few changes of great consequence as the new District Council is responsible for the same area as the old Luton County Borough Council although of course the services it controls are fewer. The Luton District Council will be elected as a whole every four years, there being no aldermen, thus eliminating one aspect of local government which was not entirely satisfactory. Luton, although a district, will also continue to be a borough with the chairman of the District Council acting as Mayor and the vice-chairman as the Deputy Mayor. The coat of arms, granted in 1876 when the town first became a borough, has been transferred to the new council. Time alone will tell how much of the ceremony and dignity for so long attached to the old system will continue with the new.

It is unfortunate in some respects that these changes, some of them no doubt long overdue, have come two years before the centenary of the incorporation of Luton as a borough.

LUTON IN 1974

Since 1914 new population and industrial structures have arisen in Luton. During this period the population of England and Wales has increased by 35 per cent but that of Luton by over 300 per cent, the result mainly of a migration from elsewhere into the town. This is nothing new as in the period of growth of the hat industry many came into Luton, mainly from the neighbouring villages – some came from further afield and not surprisingly, from Italy. Each new firm in various other industries which came had brought its nucleus of skilled labour. In the inter-war depression, when the town enjoyed a comparative prosperity, there was a further influx. It was estimated in 1936 that 13 per cent of the working population had arrived recently from Wales, Scotland and the north of England, the then depressed areas.

Since the Second World War there has been a further immigration with the 1971 Census returns showing that nearly 6 per cent of the population had been born in Ireland and over 5 per cent in the New Commonwealth, principally the West Indies, India and Pakistan.

Those who have come into the town have at all times been young and in building up new homes and families have added to the proportion of children whose parents were not born in the town. In all this time the population has been mixed so it is not surprising that it has gained a good reputation of happy relations with newcomers. It was among the first to appoint a Race Relations Officer to ease any problems which might arise from its most recent influx.

The census return for 1971 and statistics of employment for the Luton Employment Exchange make it possible to estimate the structure of the population of the town:

Those in employment	70,500
Too young to go to school ..	15,500
At school	34,000
Retired, housewives, etc ..	41,400
	161,400

There are 74,500 registered at the Luton Employment Exchange which includes a number of villages near the town Returns also show 26,000 more men in employment than women The Census returns in addition show 15,500 persons in the town over the age of 65.

The industrial structure is no less interesting, showing how much the broadly engineering industries have overtaken the hat industry. The figures and percentages given below relate to the total number registered at the Luton Exchange:

	Male	Female	Total	%
Vehicles (mainly car manufacture)	19,697	1,810	21,507	28.7
Engineering (Mechanical, Electrical, Instrument and Metal trades)	10,892	3,677	14,569	19.4
Professional and Scientific Services	1,768	5,033	6,801	9.0
Distributive Trades	2,647	3,029	5,493	7.3
Clothing (including hat industry)	906	2,648	3,592	4.8
Transport (including Airport)	2,250	1,114	3,364	4.5
Building	3,041	343	3,384	4.5
Public Administration	1,524	1,031	2,555	3.4
Food, Drink etc (including brewing)	1,183	417	1,600	2.1
Printing and Publishing	845	396	1,241	1.6
Gas, Water and Electricity	831	184	1,015	1.4
Chemicals	461	354	815	1.1

The remaining 12.2 per cent are engaged in various other industries and services.

Luton now adjoins Dunstable (population 31,790) and Houghton Regis (population 10,300) with many of the workers employed in factories in other parts from which they live in this now large conurbation. Of the 25,469 registered at the Dunstable Exchange 30 per cent are engaged in vehicle manufacture and 19.3 per cent in other engineering and metal trades, 10.1 per cent are engaged in printing and publishing and only 0.4 per cent in the clothing trades but otherwise there appears to be little difference in the population and industrial structure of Luton and Dunstable.

The largest firm in Luton in 1914 (Hayward Tyler's) employed 600 persons but this is small compared with some firms today and it is indeed surprising how very few employ a large proportion of the labour:

Vauxhall Motors	23,400	(including 5,000 at Dunstable works)
SKF (UK)	5,000	
Chrysler	4,100	(including 3,200 at Dunstable works)
Electrolux	2,200	
George Kent	2,200	
Ellis and Goldstein	800	
Whitbread	700	
Hayward Tyler	650	
Laporte	600	

The concentration of production into fewer and larger firms has increased the output per worker employed but notwithstanding this small firms continue to appear, especially to provide ancillary services for the larger ones. How rapidly firms may grow is seen with Vauxhall Motors, the town's largest firm:

Year	Total output	Exports	Employees	
1903	43	—	150	Factory at Vauxhall, London.
1906	15	—	180	Factory moved to Luton, 1905.
1907	69	—	200	Vauxhall Motors Ltd formed.
1920	689	97	1,023	
1925	1,388	95	1,820	Vauxhall join General Motors.
1935	48,671	15,314	6,726	
1950	87,454	61,471	12,659	
1955	143,567	76,071	16,487	Dunstable works opened.
1962	220,805	111,930	24,879	Ellesmere Port plant opened.
1971	331,186	116,448	37,256	

Almost a hundred years ago the newly formed Chamber of Commerce was deeply concerned that the town depended too much on its hat industry. There could be a fear now that it depends equally as much on the car industry. The future of the town is much involved with the problems of a continued demand for home produced cars and with their export. Fears are also expressed that so many of the important firms on which the town depends are under international rather than British control.

We have tried to trace the history of Luton from the earliest times and as we come to the end, recall it as the large Domesday manor with the menacing castles of Waudari and Falkes de Breauté; we conjure memories of the excitement of Colonel Gilpin cutting the first sod for the railway and of Lord Kelvin opening the electricity works. The town never stood still and what the future holds for it will be largely its own making.

Index

Ackworth, George, 84; John, 65, 70, 82.
Adam, Robert, 97.
Air raids, 182–83.
Airport, 174, 179, 189, 191.
Alfred, King, 22–24
Almshouses, 87, 111–12, 194.
Ames family, 111, 118.
Ampthill Flyer, 108.
Anglo-Saxon Chronicle, v, 19, 25, 39.
Argyll Avenue (Saxon cemetery), 17–18, 20.
Arndale Centre, 45, 202–03.
Arnold, Harry, 172.
Ashton Street (Central) Mission, 144.
Ashton, T. G., 150, 173.
Assheby, David de, 60.
Athelstan, King, 26.
Augnel, John, 60.
Austin, Charles Addington, 120–21; Samuel, 91; Thomas Erskine, 121–22; William, 17, 38, 83, 112, 121, 133, 146, 160.
Aylott, S. C., 194.
Aylott-Janes almshouses, 194.

Bagshawe, Thomas W., 17, 176.
Bailey, George, 142.
Ball, John, 63–64; Willet, 172.
Ballito Hosiery Mills, 189.
Balmforths Boilers, 131, 152–53, 189.
Bands of Hope, 133.
Baneburgh, Hugh de, 55.
Banking, 120–21.
Baptists, 93–95, 117, 137, 181.
Barber's Lane, 101–03, 192.
Barford Brothers, 175.
Barnard, Richard, 69.
Barnard Chantry, 69.
Barnfield College, 15, 190.
Barton, Thomas of, 57.
Barton Cutting, 107.
  Hill Farm, 7, 10.
Baths, Public, 112, 158, 179; Swimming, 112, 158–59, 179.
Battersea, Lord, 149.
Beauchamp, William de, 47.
Beckett, Thomas, 44.
Bedford, 41, 47–49.
Bedfordshire Magazine, 177.
Bedfordshire Regiment, 150, 167.
Beech Hill School, 158.
Belgae, 12.
Bell's Close, 125, 159.
Bequests, 87, 114, 194.

Bereford family, 60, 65.
Bethune, Earl Baldwin de, 44, 46.
Bible Five, 137.
Bigg, William, 138, 142.
Bigland, Cornelius, 114.
Birde, John, 91.
Biscot, 21, 24, 31, 33, 38, 50, 54, 63, 83, 119, 157.
  Adam de, 51.
  Early church at, 20.
  Mill, 17, 20, 102, 164, 167, 171.
  School, 138.
  Vicar of, 137.
Bishopscote, 21.
Black Death, 60–62.
Blows Downs, 1, 10.
Blundell family, 122; Henry, 53, 137.
Blundell's Stores, 175.
Boer War, 150.
Bone, Philip, 145.
Boundaries, Borough, 201.
Brache Mill, 36.
Bradgers Hill, 16, 179.
Braibroc, Henry de, 49.
Bramingham, 15, 54, 84.
  Shott, 159.
Breauté, Falkes de, 46–49.
Brewing, 119, 152, 189.
Brickmaking, 2, 79, 84, 128.
Bridge Street, 90, 100, 107.
British Aircraft Corporation, 189.
  Gelatine Works, 153.
Brocket, Lord, 191, 198.
Brothersed House, 82.
Brown family, 99, 119, 152, 164; Daniel, 99, 116; L. (Capability), 97.
Brown and Green, 119, 122, 131, 152–53, 189.
Building industry, 175–76.
Bunyan, John, 93–94.
Burgin, Leslie, 173.
Burgoyne, Sir John, 185.
Bus companies, 177–78, 202.
Bute, Third Earl of, 96–98; Marquess of, 99, 115–16, 118, 140, 147.
  Hospital, 140, 181.
  Street, 124, 182.

Caesar, Julius, 13.
Camden, William, 86.
Canals, 108.
Carnegie, Andrew, 158.
Carruthers family, 130.
Cassivellaunus, 13.

James I, 81, 87.
Janes, F. C. W., 194; Sir H. C., 176, 194.
Janes village, 194.
Jessop, John, 91, 93.
Jewish synagogue, 180.
John, King, 46–47.
Johnson, Samuel, 98.
Justices of the Peace, 109, 142.

Keens, Sir T., 152, 164, 199; Lady, 199.
Kensworth, Baptist Church at, 93.
Kent, George, Ltd, 154, 189, 207.
Knight, Daniel, 70–71.

Ladacan, 191.
Lammer, John, 82.
Lammers Manor, 83.
Land Company, 152.
Langley Street School, 116, 139.
Laporte Chemicals, 153, 192, 207.
Larches, The, 164.
Latchmore family, 121.
Lathom, H. W., 150.
Lawson, W., 163.
Lea, River, 1, 35–36, 45, 47, 83, 191.
Lea Road, 88, 100–01, 111.
Leagrave, 7, 12, 14, 24, 83, 107, 157, 178, 186; Common, 124; High Street, 15; Primary School, 35, 54; School, 138, 179.
League of Nations Union, 182.
Lee Valley Water Company, 192.
Leigh family, 147.
Lepers' hospital, 57.
Lewsey Farm, 24.
Library, 114, 142, 158, 163, 191.
Limbury, 19, 50, 54, 65, 83, 157, 178, 186; Mead, 36.
Literary Institution, 114.
Lockhart, George, 141.
Loring, Roger de, 60.
LUDUN, 193.
Luton, John de, 62; Band, 180, Manor of, 32, 55–56; System, 134.
Luton Hoo, 15, 36, 83, 87, 90, 97–98, 147–48, 160, 167, 171; Chapel, 92, 147.
Luton News, 40, 148–49, 168, 170, 177, 195.
Lyes, 126, 175, 189.
Lygeanburgh, 19–20.
Lymbury, Philip de, 62.
Lynchets, 16.

MI motorway, 16, 35, 164, 188.
Madel, W. D., 187.
Magna Carta, 46–47.
Maiden Bower, 7, 9.
Maidenhall Road School, 179.

Mair, W. J., 172.
Manchester Street, 88, 90, 101.
Mander, Sir F., 199.
Mandolin Band, 145.
Manning, W. H., 14.
Manor Court, 57.
Mare, Abbot de la, 62–65.
Market Hill, 101, 111.
Markets, 34, 44, 111–12, 160–61, 176; Plait, 104–05.
Marks and Spencer, 165.
Marshall, Alice and William, 46, 49, 53.
Marsh Farm Estate, 9.
Marsom, Samuel, 71, 94; Thomas, 94.
Martin, Master, 51.
Mason, Rev E. R., 151, George, 86.
Matilda, Empress, 39, 41.
Mayors of Luton, *xiii*.
Maw, T. A., 158.
Mechanics Institute, 142.
Medical Institute, 132, 203.
Medicine and medical profession, 120, 132, 163.
Mees, Charles, 129.
Mesolithic man, 6.
Methodists, 99, 116–18, 135, 137, 181, 194.
Middle, H. C., 135, 157.
Middle Row, 111.
Mill Street, 36, 45, 163.
Mixes Hill, 2–4, 84.
Moat House, Limbury, 65.
Modern School, 157, 179.
Moeran, E., 187.
Monkey Parade, 159.
Montague, Mary Wortley, 96.
Montfort, Simon de, 52–53.
Moor, The, 102, 107, 123–24, 139, 159.
Morcar (priest), 29.
Mortimer, Fred and Harry, 180.
Motor-car manufacture, 152–53.
Municipal Borough status, 140–42.
Museum and Art Gallery, 176.
Myers, George, 148.

Napier, Sir John, 78, 96; Sir Robert, 87, 89, 92, 103, 147.
Neolithic period, 6–10; burial, 6, 16.
Nether Crawley, 83.
New Bedford Road, 12, 107, 164.
New Industries Committee, 143, 154.
New Mill (End), 36.
New Stone Age, 6–7.
New Town, 165; Street School, 137, 150.
Newspapers, 148, 168, 177–78, 195: see also *Luton News*.
Nonconformists, 156, 161–62, 170: see also Baptists, Congregationalists, Methodists, Presbyterians, Quakers.

Northwood, 83.
Norton Road, 57.

Oakley, Edwin, 159.
O'Connor, Terence, 173.
Offa, King, 21.
Old Bedford Road, 125, 134; School, 138.
'Old Bell Inn', 108.
Old Stone Age, 2–5.
O'Neill, Rev James, 70, 118–19, 134–35, 137–38, 151.
Osborne, Charles, 177.
Road, 36, 111.
Overseers, 109.

Palaeolithic period, 2–5.
Paris, Matthew, 41, 54.
Parish Church (St Mary's), 15, 26, 36, 38–39, 67–72, 203.
Registers, 85.
Park Square, 26, 36, 88, 109, 157, 161, 189.
Street, 94, 101, 161, 163; Baptist Church, 94, 113, 117, 119, 161.
Street West, 109.
Parks, 125, 171–72: see also Luton Hoo.
Wardown.
Parliament, Members of, 124, 172–73, 186–87.
Passive Resisters, 139.
Payne, Joe, 180; Major, 146–47.
Peasants' Revolt, 64–65.
Peile, Thomas, 118.
Penthelyn, John, 73.
People's Park, 16, 125, 159.
Pepper Box, 111.
Percival Aircraft, 174.
Plait Halls, 112, 141, 158, 176, 203.
Plewes, L. W., 193.
Police, 114, 142, 150, 170–71, 183, 197, 200.
Pomfret, John and Thomas, 92.
Ponds, 102, 111.
Poor Law, 109–10, 140, 196.
Pope's Meadow, 125.
Population, xii, 34, 86, 101, 109, 195.
Postal service, 95, 143, 192.
Pound, The, 146, 160.
Power, Andrew, 62.
Prayer Book Five, 137.
Presbyterians, 194.
Prices of commodities, 58, 86.
Pride, Samuel, 132.
Primitive Methodists, 116–18, 137.
'Prince's Head', 90.
Prior, Dr, 99.
PSA, 135.
Public houses, 133–34: see also names of individual public houses.
Pupil Teaching Centre, 157.

Putteridge Bury, 202.

Quakers, 92–93, 99, 113, 116, 119, 121, 131, 133, 135, 137, 194, 202.
Queen Square School, 116, 190.

Rabbit', 'The, 102, 134.
Race Relations Officer, 205.
Railways, 109, 122–25, 152, 193.
Ramridge, 83; End, 63; Abbot Thomas, 83.
Ravensburgh Castle, 11, 13, 26.
Rectory, 73.
Red Cross Band, 145, 180.
Red Lion', 'The, 83, 111, 162.
Richards, John, 114.
Richmond Hill, 16.
Riots, 150, 170–71.
Roads, 6–7, 10–15, 20, 24, 107–08; Roman, 13–15.
Roberts, G. E., 187; W. G., 186.
Rochele, Richard de, 62.
Roman Catholics, 136, 181, 194; schools, 190.
Roman occupation, 14–17.
Roman roads, 13–15.
Rootes Group, 189.
Rose, Thomas, 86.
Roses, Wars of the, 76–78.
Rosslyn Crescent, 12.
Rotherham family, 69–70, 88; Sir John, 81–82, Thomas Attwood, 91; Thomas, 82, 84.
Round Green, 2, 45, 84, 181.
Meeting, 117.
Rugby football, 163.
Runfold Avenue and Estate, 14, 17, 50.
Runley Wood, 164.
Rutland Crescent, 42.

St Albans Abbey and Abbots of, 38, 41–44, 47, 50, 54, 62, 64, 74, 83, 85.
St Anne's Hill, 42; Lane, 101, 114.
St Mary's Hall, 138, 190, 197; Hospital, 110, 203; Road, 45, 151.
St Matthew's School, 137, 190.
Salisbury Arms', 'The, 134.
Salvation Army, 135–36, 146, 162, 181.
Sandby, Robert, 87.
Sanderson, T. A. E., 157.
Santingfield, 43.
Saunders, James, 146.
Saxons, 16–21.
Scargill, Frank, 159.
School Board, 137–39.
Schools, Adult, 116, 133–35; plaiting, 104; Sunday, 115, 136: see also Education and names of individual schools.

213

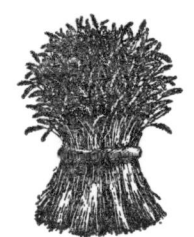